ISBN 978-1-333-67774-9
PIBN 10534614

AMERICAN LUMBERMEN

THE PERSONAL HISTORY
AND PUBLIC AND BUSINESS ACHIEVEMENTS
OF
ONE HUNDRED EMINENT LUMBERMEN
OF THE UNITED STATES

CHICAGO:
THE AMERICAN LUMBERMAN
1905

OR more than a century the manufacture of lumber was the foremost industry of America. Until the last decade it employed more men and capital and produced more wealth than any other pursuit. The development of this industry, and the achievement of this distinction required the energy of men of brain and brawn and the direction of men of exceptional ability and courage.

The life histories of some of the men, living and dead, whose initiative and executive ability, whose prophetic vision and practical wisdom, made them and their calling great, are assembled in this volume. These are the biographies either of pioneers or of the associates or successors of pioneers, of men of yesterday or men of today. Many won additional distinction as statesmen, soldiers, bankers or merchants. Thus they contributed not only to the history of the lumber industry but also to the history of the nation.

They were men who recognized and utilized opportunity. Some were themselves pioneers in settlement and development; many were the sons of fathers who helped to clear the land for settlement. They breathed the breath of the forest and learned its secrets and its possibilities.

The face of history is ever turned toward the west, and so the lumber industry of the United States and Canada has followed the pathway of the sun. One time the sash saw tugged slowly at the eastern fringe of a forest that seemed impenetrable and inexhaustible; now the mammoth mill mingles its song with the music of the surf rolling in from the Pacific.

In this westward march each progressive step has brought forth the pioneer; and, as the industry has moved onward, there have sprung up mighty men to receive and preserve to the nation the gushing stream of wealth set flowing by the ax of the first woodsman.

It was inherent ability and not wealth that made these lumbermen. As one reads the history of their lives he finds they were often men of little means and sometimes men of limited education; but while mints make money and books make learning, God makes men.

This volume will be found a record of man making rather than money making or scholar making. Herein will be found men of strong constitution, of mental and physical endurance, of steadiness under adversity, of energy, ambition and determination. What men are, rather than what they do, is vital. Theirs was and is a great industry; but greater than the forests they conquered and better than the wealth they earned is the good they contributed to our national life.

CONTENTS

CONTENTS

An old Persian philosopher gave much praise to the man [illegible] had

grown before [illegible] the busy turmoil of the [illegible]tury we have [illegible] to commemorate the ways by which the brainy business[illegible] the sum of commercial activity [illegible] comparatively new [illegible] or [illegible] its utility [illegible] adds something to the existence of living.

Albert T. Stearns, of Boston, Massachusetts, has done more to bring cypress into general modern use than any other man in America. Mr. Stearns was born at Billerica, Massachusetts, in 1821. His brother was the late E. H. Stearns, of the Stearns Manufacturing Company, of Erie, Pennsylvania [illegible] of saw mill machinery invention [illegible] Albert Stearns, the father, was a Massachusetts farmer, among whose possessions was a saw [illegible] mill. The latter was of the frame-saw type. The [illegible] gathered their first knowledge of machinery at this mill.

In 1843 Albert T. Stearns made his bow to the lumber world by establishing a retail yard at Waltham, Massachusetts. This was the first lumber yard in that city and is still continued, as the property of the Buttrick Lumber Company, to whom he sold it in 1849 and immediately established a yard at Neponset, now a Boston suburb. From this modest start has grown up the mammoth yard and manufacturing plant of the A. T. Stearns Lumber Company, of which Albert T. Stearns is president and still active in management.

For many years the specialty of the Stearns company has been the production of wooden gutters, extensively used in nearly all New England house construction. Pine was the

ALBERT T. STEARNS

Albert T. Stearns

An old Persian philosopher gave much praise to the man who made two blades of grass grow where only one had grown before. In the busy turmoil of the twentieth century we have little time to commemorate the ways by which the brainy businessman adds to the sum of commercial activity. However, the man who brings a beautiful and comparatively new wood into daily commercial use, or rediscovers its utility, surely adds something to the substance of living.

Albert T. Stearns, of Boston, Massachusetts, has done more to bring cypress into general modern use than any other man in America. Mr. Stearns was born at Billerica, Massachusetts, in 1821. His brother was the late E. H. Stearns, of the Stearns Manufacturing Company, of Erie, Pennsylvania, distinguished in the annals of saw mill machinery invention and production. Abner Stearns, the father, was a Massachusetts farmer, among whose possessions was a saw and grist mill. The latter was of the frame-saw type. The Stearns boys gathered their first knowledge of machinery and lumber at this mill.

In 1843 Albert T. Stearns made his bow to the lumber world by establishing a retail yard at Waltham, Massachusetts. This was the first lumber yard in that city and is still continued, as the property of the Buttrick Lumber Company, to whom he sold it in 1849 and immediately established a yard at Neponset, now a Boston suburb. From this modest start has grown up the mammoth yard and manufacturing plant of the A. T. Stearns Lumber Company, of which Albert T. Stearns is president and still active in management.

For many years the specialty of the Stearns company has been the production of wooden gutters, extensively used in nearly all New England house construction. Pine was the material originally employed for this purpose, but now cypress solely is used. For the making of this product Mr. Stearns invented and constructed a marvel in woodworking machinery. It is a machine that removes the core of a gutter in one piece, by means of a cylinder saw, leaving it available for reduction into moldings and other valuable products. As the material used for this purpose requires clear stock, the saving made by this machine has proved a handsome profit in itself.

In 1871 a little cargo of hard pine arrived from Pensacola, Florida, in which were four or five thousand feet of cypress. This was the first of that wood Mr. Stearns had ever seen. The material was evidently sent as a sample but scarcely attracted his attention. In fact it laid around the yard for three or four years almost forgotten and absolutely unsalable.

About this time Mr. Stearns began the erection of an office building at the Neponset plant and his inability to dispose of the little lot of cypress induced him to utilize it for the doors and trim of this building. When the job was completed the idea was suddenly presented that he had discovered just the material he had been seeking for some years—a cheap substitute for white pine in the manufacture of wooden gutters.

The finishing was crude and the lumber not of the best quality and the importance of the fact that he had found one of the most desirable finishing woods in the world did not occur to him at that time. His interest in the wood, however, was great enough to induce him to start an investigation of the subject. He could learn little save the fact that there were large quantities of cypress in the almost inaccessible swamps of the gulf country but there was no way of getting out the timber, that it would sink like lead when green and that there was very little of the lumber produced. He made up his mind, however, that he wanted cypress and in 1881 went South with the intention of making a personal hunt for it. He succeeded in contracting for a quantity of it at Stockton, near Mobile, Alabama, and bought all that was obtainable. During the next two years he had 5,000,000 feet of the lumber afloat at one time on its way to Boston. From the moment he saw the finished product in his office, cypress won Mr. Stearns' confidence completely, and this faith never flinched nor wavered. In New England it was another matter. The dealer, the contractor, the builder and the house owner would have none of it. The New Englander is notoriously conservative. He had always had white pine gutters in the past and white pine gutters he would have in the future or none at all. But Albert T. Stearns is of the same stock and his ire was up—his "Yankee" aroused. His reputation and his fortune were at stake. He pleaded for the use of cypress gutters, he coaxed, threatened and cajoled, all to little purpose, and finally reached the extremity where he furnished cypress gutters free, with the guarantee that he would replace them with white pine if they did not prove satisfactory. His faith and persistence eventually won out, but how near the venture brought him to bankruptcy will probably never be known to anyone but himself, for A. T. Stearns is not given to talking of his own affairs.

In 1883 Mr. Stearns acquired large cypress holdings on the Apalachicola river, organized the Cypress Lumber Company and erected the big saw mill at Apalachicola, Florida, which today is said to be one of the model cypress plants of the country. It consists of a double band saw mill, equipped with special and extra heavy machinery. The plant produces upwards of 20,000,000 feet a year, largely cypress, with some hard pine and cane ash. Frederick M. Stearns, Mr. Stearns' eldest son, is manager, with principal office at Boston.

Perhaps the largest, and certainly the most interesting, product of the Stearns plant is its cypress doors.

When Albert T. Stearns entered the lumber field, his business was conducted in his own name. Later, when he associated with himself his other sons, Albert H. and Waldo H., it became known as A. T. Stearns & Sons and has since been changed to and incorporated as the A. T. Stearns Lumber Company.

Mr. Stearns has always "blazed the trail" that others might follow. He was the first ready made house builder of the United States, shipping portable houses to California via Cape Horn in 1851. He was the pioneer of the world in the production of machine stuck moldings and for many years shipped large quantities abroad. He was the original exponent of yellow pine rift flooring, now a standard flooring product of the country. He was the discoverer of cypress as a commercial product.

His persistent and successful fight in the Woodbury pressure bar case saved hundreds of thousands of dollars to the planing mill fraternity of the country.

Each one of these business improvements has an ethical value away beyond the monetary significance it may have meant to its originator. A great business venture carried through to successful completion means an inch or two added to that stride of civilization by which America's sturdy sons outstrip the world.

LIBRARY
OF THE
UNIVERSITY
OF
CALIFORNIA

GEORGE D. EMERY

George D. Emery

The foremost factor in the mahogany lumber trade of America is George D. Emery, president of the George D. Emery Company, whose mahogany manufacturing plant at Chelsea, Massachusetts, just across the Mystic river from Boston, is the largest of its kind in the world. Mr. Emery gained his lumber experience in our native woods and more especially in that one which in quality and value nearest approaches mahogany—the black walnut—in Indiana and sections of the Mississippi river valley. His first connection with the lumber trade was in 1849-50, when, at the age of fifteen, he began work as a tally boy in the white pine yard of Oliver Bugbee, at Buffalo, New York. A little later Mr. Bugbee entered the hardwood trade and Mr. Emery became his buyer in Michigan, Ohio and Indiana, gathering together stocks of lumber which were concentrated at Toledo for shipment by vessel to Buffalo, whence they were taken by canal to Albany, then the great distributing market for New England.

After nine years of this sort of experience Mr. Emery made his first incursion into the manufacturing field, with the assistance of the then familiar mulay saw mill. This was in Noble county, Indiana. Seven years later he relinquished the hardships and hazards of primitive hardwood manufacture and became again a buyer and shipper, this time for Skillings, Whitneys & Barnes. Two years later he went back into manufacturing again and this time was successful, principally because of the possession of a larger capital than he had controlled during his previous venture. He built and owned a number of mills and for several years made his headquarters at Indianapolis, where he ran an extensive plant. His operations were in the black walnut and oak of Indiana, Illinois,

Iowa, Kentucky and Missouri, a line of manufacture which was at its maximum in the early '70's. With the increasing scarcity of walnut he obtained supplies along the Mississippi and Missouri rivers and later as far south as the Yazoo delta and along the Red river and lower Mississippi.

Thirty-one years after his first embarkation in the lumber business, in 1881, Mr. Emery found that the walnut field, in which he had been the largest producer in the country, no longer afforded opportunity for operations upon the great scale on which he had conducted them. At this time he turned his attention to mahogany. Mahogany manufacture as ordinarily conducted in America is based upon the purchase of the logs, and the actual operations originate with their arrival at the American mill. Mr. Emery, however, started his mahogany operations with the tree in the forest, following out the plan which he had successfully pursued in his walnut enterprise.

It is an open secret that, at one time in the history of the venture, if it had been closed the capital of over one-third of a million dollars which Mr. Emery put into it when he turned his attention from walnut to foreign woods would have been entirely a minus quantity. But the business was not closed. Mr. Emery once, in a reminiscence on this incident of his career, remarked: "I never could understand why, when a man gets knocked down he shouldn't get up again." The "get up" quality is very prominent in Mr. Emery's makeup, as might be suggested by the square lines of his mouth and jaw and by the massive proportions of his entire physique. Many a man would have been entirely satisfied with such an experience as Mr. Emery first had in the saw mill business with his mulay saw. But to his dogged persistency, however, the fact that in some venture he had not been so successful as might have been wished was a most excellent reason for making the attempt again with a marshaling of new forces.

The mahogany lumbering portion of this great business has grown to a magnitude where it employs over 1,000 men, only about 150 of whom are Americans. Two steel steamers, each with a capacity for carrying 1,100,000 feet of round logs, built especially for the mahogany carrying trade, together with thirty miles of standard gage railroad and a commissary department equal to the maintenance of a standing army, are adjuncts to the enterprise.

The location of Mr. Emery's woods operations are in Nicaragua, where his company owns the entire mahogany concessions of the country. In Honduras it has the principal mahogany holdings, and in the Gulf of Darien district of Colombia, South America, it has other immense grants. Mr. Emery's great woods interests in the tropics were directed for years by his son, Herbert C. Emery, who, at the age of twenty, assumed their charge but was obliged to relinquish the work in 1903 because of failing health. Herbert C. Emery is now vice president of the George D. Emery Company, and is his father's first assistant in the conduct of the great enterprise. His successor in the woods work is Sam D. Spellman, second vice president of the company, who has headquarters at Bluefields, Nicaragua. Mr. Emery's personal relations to mahogany begin with its arrival at the magnificent quay upon one side of his Chelsea manufacturing plant.

There is manifest about the sawing department of the mill very little of the rush and bustle of a pine manufacturing plant operated with a view to a big sawing record. Still it has a capacity of about 15,000,000 feet annually in lumber, while in the superficial feet of veneers manufactured its capacity runs into stupendous figures.

In January, 1904, in connection with Samuel Segar, Mr. Emery's house established a foreign branch at East Greenwich, London, where it has a mahogany saw mill plant, six acres of yard room and a fine dock on the bank of the Thames. This branch is known as the Segar-Emery Company and distributes its products to the English and continental trade.

A man who has contributed materially to the success of Mr. Emery is George L. Cade, treasurer and financial man of the George D. Emery Company, who has been associated with the Emery interests for many years.

Mr. Emery in 1859 married Miss Sarah Gowen. She died in 1889. In 1892 he married Mrs. Helen L. Bliss, a lifelong friend of his first wife. The family consists of two sons and one daughter. The elder son, Herbert, is identified with him in his mahogany business. The younger son, Daniel G., was, until recently, connected with the United States Gypsum Company, of Chicago, in which George D. Emery has a large interest, but since that time he has been purchasing agent for the George D. Emery Company.

The daughter recently graduated from Bryn Mawr College. An elder daughter died ten years ago. Mr. Emery's affiliations are domestic. He inclines rather to simple home living than to club or public life. He is an active member of the Congregational Church at Allston, a suburb of Boston. In politics he has for many years been a Republican. Such time as is not devoted to his many business interests is spent very largely in his home at Allston, among his books and plants and flowers.

No man loves his family with greater devotion than George D. Emery and, in this connection, an anecdote is related of him which perhaps aptly illustrates the dogged determination of a man willing to fight the inevitable—a man whose courage never falters amidst calamity.

Cable advices had warned him that his son Herbert was ill with fever many miles back in the tropical forest. The next cablegram laid on his desk early one morning by Mr. Cade read: "Bearers bringing Herbert out of woods, dangerously ill, recovery extremely doubtful, probably dead before this reaches you." Mr. Emery read the message. He made no comment. The square jaws came together with a snap. He sat at his desk the entire day and transacted business in the methodical manner which was his wont, and by no sign or gesture was it manifest to his associates that his very heart strings were being torn asunder.

Charles Hebard

It is something in this life to have achieved a great commercial success; to have attained a high position in the business world for one's self and financial independence for one's family. Yet these accomplishments are many as compared with the successes of those who have won commercial distinction and at the same time have lived the lives of Christian gentlemen and won the good will of other men.

Christian integrity and commercial integrity are not always synonymous. Charles Hebard, of Philadelphia, Pennsylvania, gave to both the same definition. He was born at Lebanon, Connecticut, January 9, 1831, and died at his home in Philadelphia, June 11, 1902. He was a descendant of Governor Bradford, and was reared on the farm of his father, Judge Learned Hebard. His first venture in life on his own account was in school teaching near his native town during 1849. In 1850 he made the laborious overland trip to the then remote state of Iowa and paid a brief visit to an uncle. The following year he repaired to Scranton, Pennsylvania, where he engaged with the Lackawanna Iron & Coal Company as a clerk in its general merchandising establishment. In 1853 Mr. Hebard removed to Tobyhanna (then called Naglesville), near Scranton, erected a saw mill for a syndicate of his former employers and began the manufacture of lumber from a 40,000 acre tract. He continued with the successors of this house, Dodge, Meigs & Dodge. The mill there erected was one of the first three steam saw mills built in Pennsylvania and the product was spruce and hemlock. Mr. Hebard went with Dodge, Meigs & Dodge originally as an employee, but before the conclusion of the operation became a partner.

In 1867 Mr. Hebard moved to Williamsport, Pennsylvania, and with Anson G. P. Dodge leased the Dodge mills and began the manufacture of pine lumber. The firm originally was Dodge & Co. and afterward Dodge & Hebard. This operation was continued for several years and produced large quantities of lumber. The Dodge mills in their day were among the most celebrated in Pennsylvania.

In 1870 Mr. Hebard moved to Detroit, Michigan, and, in connection with the late R. K. Hawley, established the Hebard & Hawley Lumber Company at Cleveland, Ohio. The company built a saw mill at Cleveland and supplied it with logs towed from Lake Huron ports. Mr. Hebard was the inventor of the bag boom and this method of holding logs in tows was first employed by him in connection with the Cleveland operation. He sold his interest in the Hebard & Hawley Lumber Company to Mr. Hawley in 1872. He returned to Williamsport and in connection with R. M. Foresman and Dexter Smith, under the firm name of Hebard, Foresman & Smith, leased the Krause & Herdic mill and again became a Williamsport lumber producer, so continuing up to 1877. In that year he became interested in the white pine timber of the upper peninsula of Michigan, and consummated the purchase of a large tract of splendid white pine on Keweenaw Point. The Hebard & Thurber Lumber Company was organized and a mill was built at Pequaming, which was a pioneer operation on Keweenaw bay. This was a circular and gang mill and was completed in 1878. In 1882 H. C. Thurber, of the company, parted with his interest to Mr. Hebard and Charles Hebard & Son succeeded, the new member of the firm being Charles S. Hebard. The saw mill erected at Pequaming has been gradually transformed and rebuilt but has been in continuous operation, most of the time with double shifts, for twenty-seven years.

Charles Hebard & Son in 1897 established the H. M. Tyler Lumber Company, of North Tonawanda, New York, as an assorting and distributing operation. Charles Hebard was the largest stockholder, Charles S. Hebard was the president of the company and Daniel L. Hebard was a director.

Mr. Hebard, in association with his sons, Charles S. and Daniel L., purchased the immense Okefenokee swamp in southeastern Georgia and almost up to the time of his death he was full of plans to forward a gigantic lumber enterprise in that section of the country. The Okefenokee swamp consists of approximately 350,000 acres of cypress, yellow pine and gum timber and occupies a conspicuous place on every map of Georgia. The tract lies less than fifty miles from Jacksonville, Florida. Mr. Hebard's plans, which will be consummated by his sons, contemplated the erection of large saw mills on the property and the building of a railroad to tidewater on the Satilla river, just south of Brunswick, Georgia. This arrangement for railroads and saw mills gives the operation outlets by the way of the Plant System, Seaboard Air Line, Southern railway and by sea.

For many years Mr. Hebard spent his summers in the saw mill town of Pequaming, where he was the owner of practically every structure in the village. Here he surrounded himself with competent assistants and to all employees were accorded free dwelling houses, free schools, free churches, free water and free fuel. The village is picturesquely situated and in every respect is an ideal saw mill community. Mr. Hebard's idea of the retention of ownership of the land and houses surrounding his saw mill was not to make his laborers more dependent but to guarantee that they should be independent of saloons and other corrupting influences. His plans in this respect worked most admirably. In 1889 Mr. Hebard purchased Sugar Loaf, a beautiful home at Chestnut Hill, Philadelphia, which he occupied a portion of each year. Latterly he constructed another fine home at Thomasville, Georgia, which had been his winter resort for several seasons.

Mr. Hebard was much interested in educational and charitable work, and was a regent of the University of Michigan from 1888 to 1896; he was a member of the Loyal Legion; a trustee of the Jefferson Medical College of Philadelphia and on the hospital committee, and a member of the famous Union League Club of Philadelphia.

Mr. Hebard's life was a very happy one. A widow and the two sons before mentioned and two daughters survived him. He was one whose faith in mankind was great, and whose charity was as wide as want. He was ever fond of quoting these lines from Bryant's immortal Thanatopsis:

So live that when thy summons comes to join
The innumerable caravan which moves
To that mysterious realm where each shall take
His chamber in the silent halls of death,
Thou go not, like the quarry-slave at night,
Scourged to his dungeon, but, sustained and soothed
By an unfaltering trust, approach thy grave
Like one who wraps the drapery of his couch
About him and lies down to pleasant dreams.

And one who thus lived passed into the great beyond when this man died.

LIBRARY
OF THE
UNIVERSITY
OF
CALIFORNIA

WILLIAM M. McCORMICK

William M. McCormick

A man prominent in Pennsylvania hemlock history during the height of the development of that branch of the lumber industry, covering the past twenty years, is William M. McCormick, of Philadelphia.

Mr. McCormick was born in Lycoming county, Pennsylvania, on a farm near Williamsport, in 1846. He is a Scotch-Irishman, five generations removed. His father, Seth T. McCormick, was a farmer, pioneer lumberman in a small way, and eventually a lawyer. The boy William was brought up on the farm. As the family was in very moderate circumstances his opportunity for the training obtained in schools was limited. Mr. McCormick, however, gained his education in the great college of experience, and his Irish perception and Scotch reasoning power helped to graduate him with high honors.

At the age of fourteen he went to Williamsport and secured employment in a planing mill at sixty-two cents a day. Here he worked for two years. He gradually drifted into the vocation of a lumber inspector, and between inspecting lumber during the summer season, scaling logs in the woods in the winter and shipping lumber he spent the succeeding eighteen years of his life.

Mr. McCormick was one of the first traveling lumber salesmen out of the Williamsport country and in that calling he was eminently successful. Eventually he became manager in turn of several lumber manufacturing concerns.

His first real start in commercial pursuits on his own account was in 1886, when he removed to Philadelphia, which city has ever since been his home, leased an office which is described as being only of sufficient size to accommodate a desk and two chairs, and entered into the wholesale lumber trade as a buyer and seller of hemlock lumber. His years of training as an employee in every detail of the production, sorting and sale of the Pennsylvania product stood him in good stead and his success was assured from the start. Very speedily his transactions in hemlock grew to such an extent that he was soon buying and marketing approximately 75,000,000 feet annually, and he is still continuing on about the same scale.

A few years ago Mr. McCormick became interested in the possibilities of North Carolina pine and was made president of the Peart, Neilds & McCormick Company, which became the owner of a large area of loblolly pine in southern Virginia, and which has since conducted a large plant there for the manufacture of lumber and box shooks.

More recently, with associates, Mr. McCormick has purchased 100,000 acres of poplar, oak, chestnut and hemlock timber lands in Blount and Monroe counties, Tennessee, and has constructed a railroad into the property in connection with the Marysville division of the Southern railway and has built a large saw mill, with planing mill adjuncts, at Townsend, Tennessee. This is the Little River Lumber Company, of which also Mr. McCormick is president. He is, besides, interested in other timber properties and in sundry other real estate and business enterprises.

William McCormick's personal history is unique in the respect that his commercial success has been achieved within the past eighteen years. As boy and man he was a student and a worker, satisfied to exchange the best that was in him for the knowledge of lumber affairs that it brought him. Then he entered business on his own account and his mistakes have been few. To those who know Mr. McCormick well it is an axiom that what he does commercially is right; his "lumber sense" is proverbial and his judgment on a lumber proposition unquestioned.

Personally, Mr. McCormick is a square-shouldered, blockily-built man with a hand that, although almost effeminate, has always a hearty grasp; a smile invariably lurks about his lips and a merry twinkle in his eye. He is the personification of cordiality to both friend and stranger. His friendship he gives but rarely, but once a man's friend he has the reputation of sticking to him for all time. In the modern acceptance of the term he is not a polished man. Many times he is blunt to the point of offending people unacquainted with his manner. He is a man who invariably refers to a spade as a spade. He dislikes sham and affectation. He abhors double dealing and insincerity. His sympathies are as catholic as his public spirit is broad, but perhaps his dominant characteristic is a sense of humor, which is kindly. He laughs with you but never at you. To illustrate: A friend of many years is the eminent Philadelphian, Robert B. Wheeler. Some years ago there was a financial transaction between them in which a matter of interest was involved. Mr. Wheeler figured the interest at a certain sum and Mr. McCormick computed it at another. Eventually, Mr. Wheeler's accounting was accepted. Meeting him a few days later with a party of mutual friends, in a manner of utmost gravity as though it were a commercial deal of vast importance, Mr. McCormick explained to the gentlemen his version of the accounting and insisted that Mr. Wheeler had defrauded him of one dollar. "Now," continued Mr. McCormick, "Bob Wheeler makes a pretense of being a devout Baptist. Last Sunday I watched him. He put a silver dollar on the contribution plate. That was my dollar."

Mr. McCormick is a strict believer in honest and upright business methods, and a man who will not treat commercial affairs in the same way can do business with him but once. He is a man who wins friendship from most people and respect from every man. His love for his fellow man is as generous as was Abou Ben Adhem's and his charity like the sky of Heaven which o'erhangs a suffering world.

Seth T. Foresman

Seth T. Foresman, of Williamsport, Pennsylvania, was born in Washington township, February 26, 1838. Like many other American boys he obtained his education entirely through his own efforts. When his duties on his father's farm permitted he attended the township school and then took a course at Dickinson Seminary. In the interval he taught the country school in order to procure funds for the advance of his own education.

Soon after Mr. Foresman had attained his majority his father disposed of his farm and moved to Williamsport, where in 1863 Seth T. Foresman took the initial step in his business career. His first venture was as a contractor. He assisted in the construction of five of the largest saw mills in Williamsport and built what is known as the Lumber Branch railroad, a spur from the Pennsylvania line, which affords shipping facilities for all the mills in the city. He also superintended the construction of a number of the log basins as well as various other improvements for the benefit of lumber operators.

In 1869 Seth T. Foresman erected a large planing mill at the foot of Grier street, Williamsport, and, forming a partnership with Thomas J. Frow, entered into business under the firm name of Frow, Foresman & Co. This was his first lumber venture and it did not prove successful. In the face of this reverse Fletcher Coleman, one of the most prosperous of the manufacturers, tendered young Foresman a position on a salary which he lost no time in accepting. This was in 1872.

In 1873 Mr. Foresman entered into partnership with Samuel N. Williams for the manufacture of lumber. Their first season proved exceedingly profitable, but in 1874 the firm's entire possessions were wiped out by fire. With scarcely a backward glance at the smoking ruins of his fortune he, figuratively speaking, took off his coat and again went to work on a salary, this time with A. C. Finney & Co., with whom he remained one year as an employee. Then he sought his former partner, S. N. Williams, and in 1876 they bought an interest in the firm, which was reorganized as Finney, Williams & Co., and began operations at the Star mill.

A. C. Finney disposed of his interest to his partners in 1877 and they organized the firm of Williams & Foresman, which continued prosperously until 1898. The firm was then incorporated, forming what is known as the Bowman-Foresman Company, with Mr. Foresman as president, J. W. Bowman, vice president and J. Roman Way, treasurer. This association of capital, energy and pluck, in 1877, has endured for a quarter of a century as one of Williamsport's greatest and most successful lumber concerns. During the intervening years the mill has sawed on an average 20,000,000 feet of lumber annually, the logs being from the concern's own extensive timber lands in Clearfield and Indiana counties, acquired from time to time as the business extended.

Mr. Foresman is also largely interested in West Virginia with the Bowman Lumber Company, of which concern he is vice president. It has extensive operations on the Coal river in Kanawha and Raleigh counties. This company has been very successful, and it owns in that region over 200,000,000 feet of standing timber and 60,000 acres underlaid with valuable coal deposits.

He is one of the originators of the Lycoming Rubber Company, at present one of the most important of the industries of Williamsport, an establishment that employs over 500 persons in the production of boots and shoes. This great and valuable plant has been merged with the United States Rubber Company and is operated at its full capacity. Mr. Foresman is a stockholder in the West Branch National Bank and a director and stockholder in the Lycoming National Bank, two of the leading financial institutions of Williamsport. In addition he is interested in numerous minor manufacturing establishments in Williamsport and the county. He is one of the foremost figures in the Williamsport Board of Trade and has been vice president of that body as well as chairman of several of its important committees. Mr. Foresman has long been a member of the Lumbermen's Exchange of Williamsport, in which for several years he has served as a member of the stray log committee, and has aided in the recovery of many million feet of logs carried away by floods. His own firm suffered heavily in the loss of logs and lumber in the great floods of 1889 and 1894.

As an evidence of the esteem in which he is held by the community, of which he has been an honored member for nearly a half century, may be mentioned a banquet tendered to him by the businessmen of Williamsport on February 26, 1898, on the sixtieth anniversary of his birth.

With his family, consisting of his wife and four children, Mr. Foresman resides in a beautiful home on West Fourth street, Williamsport, where he is a communicant of the Third Presbyterian Church and his interest in and support of church affairs have been notable for many years. He is a Free Mason and a Knight Templar, Masonry being the only secret society with which he has ever been affiliated.

Few men in Williamsport have been more deeply concerned in charitable organizations than has Mr. Foresman. He is president of the Boys' Training School and a member of the advisory committee of the Home for the Friendless. He is also president of the Williamsport Young Men's Christian Association.

Mr. Foresman has always taken a keen interest in politics. He was the unanimous choice of his party for the congressional nomination in the fifteenth congressional district of Pennsylvania in 1902, but withdrew his name. The only office he has ever accepted was that of councilman from his ward, and this was held for many years, he serving in the select branch of the municipal legislature. He was for years president of the body and served as chairman of some of th important committees. He has frequently been menti a candidate for mayor but could never be induced to the nomination.

Seth T. Foresman's progressive course through life, by the wonderful and untiring energy that has charac his every venture, is worthy the emulation of the a young man who desires to succeed in his life's calling.

bought a large tract
afterward to Brown,
ganized their busin...
In 1872 he built
1873 Andrew Kaul,
Kronenwetter and Ko
ker & Co., and purch
ling Run mills. Fi
interests of his partr
until 1884, when the l

Andrew Kaul

In the achievement of success opportunity is essential; but a man who will make the most of the opportunity is also necessary. A man to whom the opportunity came and who, by inheritance and preparedness, was ready for its coming was Andrew Kaul. He was born at St. Marys, Pennsylvania, July 15, 1845, and was educated in its common schools. During his school days he assisted in the work on the homestead and was thus engaged until 1862 when he entered the employ of John Brooks as a woodsman. The following year he worked for Joseph Lanzel and Peter Kleiner.

Mr. Kaul became an individual and successful contractor in large mill stocks in 1865 and in 1868 he returned to St. Marys, purchased a quantity of pine lands and built his first mill on the head of Iron Run, which he operated for eight years.

In 1871 he entered into partnership with J. K. P. Hall and bought a large tract of pine in Wisconsin, which was sold afterward to Brown, Early & Co. The partners then reorganized their business under the firm style of Hall, Kaul & Co.

In 1872 he built the Summit mills, near St. Marys. In 1873 Andrew Kaul, George Walker, Joseph Lanzel, Charles Kronenwetter and Konley Bros. formed the firm of Kaul, Walker & Co., and purchased a large tract of timber and the Stirling Run mills. Five years later, Mr. Kaul purchased the interests of his partners and continued to operate the mill until 1884, when the historical bush fire wiped away the industry.

The original firm of Kaul & Hall, in 1879, opened up the Cascade and Hazel Dell bituminous coal mine at St. Marys and continued to operate the Cascade mine at St. Marys until 1893. In later years it has increased its coal territory by 8,000 acres of land on which are the Shawmut and Toby Valley mines and are operating the Paine mines near Centreville, in Elk county.

At about the same period was constructed the St. Marys & Southwestern railroad, twenty-five miles in length, which connects with the Pennsylvania system at St. Marys, and with the Erie road at Hydes and Dagus' Crossing. In 1894 the firm built the Buffalo & St. Marys railroad, fifty miles long running from St. Marys to Clermont, and connecting with the Western New York & Pennsylvania railway. These properties were sold in 1899.

In 1880, in partnership with J. W. Gaskill, Mr. Kaul purchased 7,500 acres of timber land on West creek and the West Creek Manufacturing & Mining Company's mills at Beechwood. A year later J. K. P. Hall purchased Mr. Gaskill's interest, C. R. Kline coming in at a later date.

Mr. Kaul was one of the founders of the St. Marys Carbon Company, and was its vice president at the time of his death. He was also a director of the St. Marys Sewer Pipe Company, the Pennsylvania Fire Proofing Company and the St. Marys Brewing Company, and it was through his instrumentality that these industries were located in his native town.

The prosperous lumber enterprises of which Mr. Kaul was the head were only a part of his great commercial activity. Mr. Hall and he associated themselves with Kistler, Lesh & Co. and formed the St. Marys Tanning Company. This is now one of the largest tanning concerns in the country. In 1882 The Portland Lumber Company was organized by Andrew Kaul, J. K. P. Hall, J. S. Hyde and W. H. Hyde, and it was incorporated in 1889 with Mr. Kaul as president. It operated large saw mills at Vineyard Run, Carman, Croyland and Portland Mills, all in Elk county. Two of these mills are still in operation. This single industry has manufactured more than 100,000,000 feet of white pine and 600,000,000 feet of hemlock and other woods. It owns approximately 30,000 acres of uncut timber land.

Kaul & Hall began the manufacture of lumber at Rathbun, in eastern Elk county, in 1885. In 1896 operations were moved to St. Marys and one of the largest mills in the state erected. This mill produces between 40,000,000 and 50,000,000 feet of lumber a year and has a supply of 150,000 acres of timber land in eastern and northern Elk county. In 1899 this concern was incorporated as the Kaul & Hall Lumber Company, with Mr. Kaul as president.

In 1887 the Penn Lumber Company with Andrew Kaul as president was organized to market the large production in which he was interested, and it handles approximately 100,000,000 feet of lumber annually.

In 1888 Mr. Kaul organized the St. Marys Gas Company, which purchased gas lands in McKean and Elk counties, constructed sixty miles of pipe line, and now supplies a large district including St. Marys and Emporium with natural gas. He later organized the St. Marys Water Company, which supplies the city with water. Mr. Kaul was practically manager of both of these concerns up to the time of his death.

In 1890 Mr. Kaul and Mr. Hall became interested in the St. Marys Bank. They conducted it as a private institution until 1903 when it was reorganized as the St. Marys National Bank, with capital stock of $125,000. It now has $1,000,000 in deposits and a surplus of $25,000. In 1903 Messrs. Kaul and Hall organized the St. Marys Trust Company. Mr. Kaul was vice president of both of these institutions.

In 1899 Mr. Kaul and his son William established an extensive stock farm for the breeding of trotting horses. It has modern stables, a miniature race track an eighth of a mile long under cover, and an out-door track half a mile long. It has maintained at times two hundred horses and has produced many high-class trotters and pacers.

In the same year Mr. Kaul and his partner erected a modern bank and office building at St. Marys, and a year later a magnificent department store building, which they operated. It handles over $500,000 worth of merchandise annually.

In that year in connection with his son, John L. Kaul, and L. Truman, of Brookville, Pennsylvania, he purchased a half interest in the Sample Lumber Company. Eventually father and son became sole owners. The mills are located at Hollins, Clay county, Alabama, and the timber holdings now amount to more than 1,000,000,000 feet of standing timber, of which the cut is 40,000,000 feet a year.

November 14, 1865, Mr. Kaul married Miss Walburga Lanzel, a daughter of Michael and Catherine Lanzel, of St. Marys. Their family is a large one.

Mr. Kaul was the virtual founder and the progressive spirit of Jimanandy park, euphoniously named in honor of himself and partner by grateful and admiring friends who have enjoyed its hospitality. It is stocked with game and fish and has a spacious club house. Throughout the pages of the local history of Elk and Cameron counties the name of Andrew Kaul appears as a supporter of every project contributing to the wealth and happiness of the people.

Andrew Kaul was a man of the people. Though he had gained large wealth, he built about himself no wall of pride or ostentation. Simple in manner, plain of speech, warm of heart, direct in his aims and methods, he commanded an unservile respect and liking that is a better tribute to character than any fawning to riches or station. So, when he died, he was sincerely mourned by the entire great community of which he was a part. His death occurred January 24, 1905, in Philadelphia, and he was buried in that hill town of Pennsylvania where he was born and in which he had lived all his strong and useful life.

LIBRARY
OF THE
UNIVERSITY
OF
CALIFORNIA

later he went to [illegible] [illegible] mill and [illegible]

In 1883 [illegible] White married Miss Virginia Kent, daughter of Alexander G. [illegible] lumberman who is credited with having [illegible] raft of lumber into Tonawanda. That year he was sent to Louisiana by the firm and spent two years there in its interests. In 1885 he engaged in business for himself in New York City, establishing the partnership of White & Rider. This firm was succeeded in 1890 by White, Rider & Frost with offices at Tonawanda and New York, who for a time carried on a buying and selling business, but in 189[illegible] they put in a stock of lumber at Tonawanda and have since conducted a yard business. The members of the firm were Pendennis White, Laurens P. Rider, William C. Frost and Herbert L. and Guy White, [illegible] latter being brothers of Pendennis White.

PENDENNIS WHITE

Pendennis White

Pendennis White, of North Tonawanda, New York, is a wholesale lumberman who has not only achieved success in his private business, but has performed and is continuing to perform notable public service in the improvement of relations between wholesaler and retailer to the great advantage of both branches of the trade. Mr. White was born at Albany in 1860. His father was Alfred White, a prominent railroad man connected, at an early date, with the Detroit & Milwaukee railroad, now a part of the Grand Trunk system. Pendennis White spent his early boyhood in Detroit attending the city schools. His business life, he frankly affirms began at fourteen in a hardware store at two dollars a week.

Mr. White's first connection with the lumber business was in 1879, when he went to Otsego Lake, Michigan, in the employ of Gratwick, Smith & Fryer. Here he scaled logs in the winter and measured lumber in the summer. Two years later he went to Tonawanda for the same firm and there acted as mill and yard superintendent for two years.

In 1883 Mr. White married Miss Virginia Kent, daughter of Alexander G. Kent, an old time lumberman who is credited with having brought the first raft of lumber into Tonawanda. That year he was sent to Louisiana by the firm and spent two years there in its interests. In 1885 he engaged in business for himself in New York City, establishing the partnership of White & Rider. This firm was succeeded in 1890 by White, Rider & Frost with offices at Tonawanda and New York, who for a time carried on a buying and selling business, but in 1893 they put in a stock of lumber at Tonawanda and have since conducted a yard business. The members of the firm were Pendennis White, Laurens P. Rider, William C. Frost and Herbert L. and Guy White, the two latter being brothers of Pendennis White.

Early in 1901 Pendennis White retired from the company of White, Rider & Frost and organized the house of White, Gratwick & Co. in connection with W. H. Gratwick and G. A. Mitchell, W. H. Gratwick (formerly W. H. Gratwick, junior) being a son of Mr. White's first employer in the lumber business. The firm name of White, Gratwick & Co. was shortly changed to White, Gratwick & Mitchell. Since that time this concern has operated a large white pine distributing yard at Gratwick, a suburb of Tonawanda on the Niagara river, opposite Tonawanda island. It maintains its chief office at the yard, with general offices at Buffalo.

Messrs. White and Gratwick had been business associates previous to the establishment of the new concern as they, with Merrill, Ring & Co., of Duluth, Minnesota, make up the Split Rock (Minnesota) Lumber Company. This house has had a white pine output for several years of from 40,000,000 to 50,000,000 feet of lumber. The same interests are also to a large extent engaged in lake shipping and have a large fleet of ore carriers.

In 1904 Mr. White, associated with George A. Mitchell, George N. Stevens, jr., and William A. Eaton, organized a jobbing house at New York City, under the firm name of The Stevens-Eaton Company. Mr. White is president of this company.

Mr. White is interested in the Wood Products Company, of Buffalo, which controls nearly all the crude wood alcohol produced in the United States and owns refineries where the alcohol is redistilled and purified, forming the wood alcohol of commerce. He is also identified with several lumber insurance companies and is president of the Lumber Insurance Company of New York.

This in brief is the chronological record of a man who has obtained an enviable distinction in the lumber history of this country, and has become particularly eminent in furthering the idea of commercial reciprocity in his line of endeavor. He is a thorough believer in the idea that any measure that is good for the community of the lumber trade is good for him as an individual. With this idea paramount he has been foremost in the work, which he has conducted through the National Wholesale Lumber Dealers' Association, of just trade relationship between manufacturer, jobber and retailer. Also, with this idea in view, has he become interested in lumber insurance affairs and is the real head of the insurance movement growing out of the association.

While White, Rider & Frost were charter members of the National Wholesale Lumber Dealers' Association, Mr. White was not prominently identified with the movement until 1897 when, at the Cleveland meeting, he was made chairman of the committee on trade relations. This happy choice brought to light remarkable talents that otherwise would have been hidden. The man and the place found each other and have been in company ever since. Mr. White never does anything superficially. He felt honored by his selection for the chairmanship of a committee of whose duties he knew very little. His character was such, however, that he immediately began to make a study of the possibilities of trade relationship in the lumber business. His work has been most successful and immensely valuable to the trade. The results of Mr. White's persistent and unflagging endeavor soon caused him to be the foremost individual in the association and in 1902, at the annual meeting of the National Association, held at Chicago, although Mr. White was unable to be present, owing to illness, he was unanimously chosen president of that organization, which position he held two successive terms. The same remarkable talent that he evinced in his work on trade relationships and as president of the national organization he is now exercising in the insurance end of the lumber business, to the manifest advantage of the lumber trade.

Personally, Mr. White is a tall, alert, dignified gentleman, whose very appearance bespeaks the thorough-going man of business. While, doubtless, as selfish as the average business man he has learned the value of commercial fairness and

reciprocity. This lesson he has urged trade to their manifest advantage for all

In his mingling with his fellows Mr. ification of dignity intermingled with co To be numbered among his friends is a associated with him is an honor.

John C. Turner

This is the story of the business career of one of the youngest of the distinguished lumbermen in the United States—John Charles Turner, president of the J. C. Turner Cypress Lumber Company, of the city of New York. He was born of German parentage at Troy, New York, in 1860. When nine years old he moved with his parents to Toledo, Ohio, and as a boy of tender years was impressed with the responsibilities of life by employment in the Norcross chair factory. About three years afterward this factory was moved to Hillsdale, Michigan. Thither young Turner followed and there he completed his apprenticeship as a chairmaker. Not only did he work daily at the making of chairs, but his evenings and Sundays were devoted to study and he eventually fitted himself for admission to the Hillsdale College. He was graduated from this institution in 1879 as president of his class and its youngest member. During his college career he sold law books to defray his expenses. Three years later the faculty of the college bestowed upon him the degree of Doctor of Philosophy. From 1879 to 1881 Mr. Turner taught school at Put-in-Bay, Ohio.

Mr. Turner's career as a lumberman began in 1882, when he engaged with Cook & Wilson, then a leading firm of white pine wholesalers at Michigan City, Indiana, as traveling salesman. His field of work was in Indiana, Illinois and Missouri, and from the start he was a successful road salesman.

In 1885 he joined the Chicago house of Street, Chatfield & Keep in a like capacity. There he remained for a year, and then was admitted to partnership with that leader of the white pine lumber trade, Joseph Rathborne, of Chicago, under the firm name of Joseph Rathborne & Co. This was in 1886. About this time Mr. Turner became impressed with the intrinsic merit of gulf cypress as a wood and of its possibilities as a legitimate substitute for white pine, in both lumber and shingles. He made an extended trip to the Louisiana cypress producing fields, then in their infancy as a lumber section. His interest in cypress became an enthusiasm, which resulted in his becoming the purchaser of cypress shingles and lumber at wholesale. He put on a line of barges from the cypress country to East St. Louis, Illinois, from which point he distributed his purchases by car throughout a half dozen states. Mr. Turner was an indefatigable worker and his trade grew and prospered. A single day's purchase of cypress by him as far back as 1888 aggregated 15,000,000 feet.

The cypress output of the Gulf country did not commensurately increase with the expanding demands of the trade that had been built up by Mr. Turner, and so in 1889 the Louisiana Cypress Lumber Company was organized by Joseph Rathborne, himself and others, with J. C. Turner as secretary and manager. The company bought timber properties and erected a double band mill at Harvey, across the Mississippi from New Orleans. This operation has been continued ever since and is one of the most prosperous institutions in the South, thus fully demonstrating the acumen of Mr. Turner's judgment.

In 1895 Mr. Turner concluded that he could enlarge his opportunities and commercial possibilities in the cypress field by once more entering the jobbing trade. His foresight has been amply demonstrated. He left New Orleans and went to New York, and, with a capital of only $25,000, organized the J. C. Turner Cypress Lumber Company. On his retirement from the South the Southern Cypress Lumber & Shingle Association passed a resolution that recited the history of the invaluable work Mr. Turner had already performed in connection with the exploitation and sale of cypress throughout the United States, indorsed his plan for the installation of a wholesale distributing yard at New York and concluded with an encomium on his character and ability.

Better than all this, however, the individual cypress manufacturers of the South had come to know J. C. Turner intimately and well. They knew that his integrity, his ability and his judgment were no chimerical qualities, and, although the cash capital of his company was small, his standing with the cypress manufacturers was such that he commanded unlimited credit at once. This confidence of the cypress producers, possessed then by Mr. Turner, he possesses today in an increased ratio. It has been his largest and most valuable asset and has resulted in his becoming the most extensive handler of cypress lumber in the world. In addition to that, the Turner Cypress Lumber Company has become one of the largest owners of cypress timber lands in the United States. It is estimated that the company's holdings aggregate fully 1,000,000,000 feet.

Opening a distributing yard at Irvington, New York, in 1895, Mr. Turner has compassed a commercial growth from an annual sale of 6,000,000 feet to one of between 40,000,000 and 50,000,000 feet. When it is considered that the cypress handlings of this house are entirely of the good end of the stock it will be seen that the business is one of the largest jobbing lumber enterprises in the country. The Turner cypress plant at Irvington has a dock and yard storage capacity of upwards of 20,000,000 feet. This plant has but recently been completed and has planing mill facilities.

The Turner plant is splendidly equipped for distribution by both water and railroad, which assures prompt service to the trade of New York and throughout the East.

In April, 1903, the Turner Cypress Lumber Company was reorganized under the laws of the state of New York with a paid up capital of $500,000. The company carries, either at points of production or at its yard at Irvington, an average stock of 35,000,000 feet of cypress.

Mr. Turner is largely interested in the Ocmulgee River Lumber Company, a large cypress and yellow pine producing concern, which has a paid up capital of $300,000. This company's seat of operation is at Lumber City, Georgia. Mr. Turner is also heavily interested in the Taylor-Cook Cypress Lumber Company, of Brunswick, Georgia, at which point its saw mill is located. This company has cypress and yellow pine holdings aggregating 150,000,000 feet.

December 29, 1887, Mr. Turner married Miss Louise E. Andrews, the daughter of B. P. Andrews, of Lincoln, Illinois.

Mr. Turner's general offices are located in New York City, from which point he personally directs every detail of purchase, transportation, sale, distribution and finance of his corporation, with the same untiring energy and persistency with which, as a boy, he attained his education and later his supremacy in the commercial world.

John N. Scatcherd

Of blended English and Irish ancestry is the subject of this sketch. The paternal grandfather of John N. Scatcherd emigrated to America from Yorkshire, England, early in the last century, while his mother's family was of Irish origin and came from Dublin. John Scatcherd, the paternal grandfather, located on a homestead near Toronto, Canada, on which property he built a saw mill, carding mill and tannery. He brought with him some inherited means, and was a man of recognized standing in the community, becoming a member of Parliament and representing the "West Riding" of Middlesex until his death.

His son, James N. Scatcherd, father of John N. Scatcherd, was born at Wyton, north of London, Canada, and emulated the career of his father, carrying on lumber operations as his chief occupation in Canada until 1855, when he went to Buffalo, entering into the lumber business there in 1857. He handled pine and black walnut chiefly. In 1878 he abandoned the white pine business and confined his interests thereafter entirely to hardwoods.

It was on September 12, 1857, in Buffalo, that John N. Scatcherd was born. His mother was Ann Belton Scatcherd. His primary education he received in Buffalo and graduated at the age of fifteen from Hellmuth College, London, Ontario, in 1872. For two years thereafter he traveled largely in this country, and at seventeen entered the employment of his father as tally boy in the Buffalo yard. He was required to learn all the departments of the business by practical experience. He piled lumber, drove teams, inspected lumber, and finally became yard foreman. In September, 1879, he was admitted to partnership with his father and the firm became Scatcherd & Son, which title it has ever since retained.

James N. Scatcherd, the father, died in February, 1885, by which date the firm had secured recognition as one of the foremost hardwood concerns in the United States. The Scatcherds bought lumber through the middle West and originally all their receipts were by water, but as they enlarged their buying territory this changed, until the rail business predominated and the lakes were used merely for the transfer of bulk lots from upper lake mills.

For a number of years the firm had buying headquarters at Indianapolis, from which office it purchased large quantities of hardwood, principally oak and poplar, in Indiana, Kentucky and Tennessee. In 1892 this buying office was moved from Indianapolis to Memphis, where Scatcherd & Son have large yards and two saw mills. The Memphis mills are stocked with logs purchased in the timber territory tributary to Memphis, and especially in Arkansas, Mississippi and Louisiana. The firm's specialty for many years has been oak, both white and red, and it is also a considerable factor in ash. From the Memphis mills and yards the product is shipped to all parts of the United States, and a large export trade is carried on also. The principal office and a large yard are still maintained in Buffalo, which is the home of Mr. Scatcherd. He was married in 1879 to Mary E. Woods, of Buffalo, and the result of the union is a daughter, now aged twenty-three, and a son of nineteen.

Mr. Scatcherd's business interests are extensive and varied. He is president and the principal stockholder in the Batavia-New York Wood Working Company. This plant is at Batavia, New York, with an office in New York City. This is one of the most prominent manufactories of high class interior finish and cabinet work in the United States. From 1892 to 1896 Mr. Scatcherd was president of the Bank of Buffalo, of which he is still a director. He is a director in the Third National Bank of Buffalo and also in the Buffalo Loan, Trust & Safe Deposit Company. All of the foregoing are strong financial institutions Mr. Scatcherd is also president of the

Ellicott Square Company, which owns the finest office building in Buffalo. It is ten stories in height, covers an entire square, and is one of the handsomest office buildings in America.

Mr. Scatcherd has been honored both within and without the business of which he is a worthy representative. For three years he was president of the Buffalo Lumber Exchange; for two terms he was president of the National Wholesale Lumber Dealers' Association, and last year was continued as one of the trustees of the association; he was chairman of the Finance Committee of the Pan-American Exposition; he is a member of the Buffalo Club, of the Ellicott Club, the Country Club and the Park Club, all of Buffalo; of the New York Club and the Republican Club of New York City. For three years he was president of the Buffalo Republican League, and is an ex-member of the Republican State Committee. He takes an active interest in politics and in 1897 was named for mayor of Buffalo on the Republican ticket, but, as he says, "was defeated by a very handsome majority."

Physically Mr. Scatcherd is strongly built and has a pleasant face, in whose features the Irish strain of his ancestry is distinctly visible. Mentally, also, he has the nimble Irish wit and the persuasive tongue that goes with it. He is an easy talker and one of the cleverest and wittiest speakers that ever participated in a lumbermen's banquet. But his mental make-up is not all of the light order. He has the capacity of hard and clear thinking, and the combination of solidity and brilliancy makes him a dangerous antagonist in a debate as well as a businessman whom it is difficult in any way to get the better of. He is of social disposition, and seems to prefer the sobriquet of "Jack," by which he is known in the hardwood trade, to the more dignified name by which he was christened. He has kept himself in good physical and mental condition by judicious recreation. He is an enthusiastic automobilist and has somewhat of a reputation as a golfer. With all his hard-headed common sense, he is of a buoyant temper-

ament, and wherever his interest is ar
social or business affair, he is certain
enterprise. And so the impress of his
only in the lumber business, but in the
prises with which he is identified.

Frank H. Goodyear

Among prominent names in the lumber industry that of Goodyear stands among the first. Indeed, the Goodyear lumber business has assumed such gigantic proportions that whoever considers Pennsylvania hemlock must also consider the activities of the Goodyear brothers, for hemlock and Goodyear are almost synonymous terms.

Frank Henry Goodyear, of Buffalo, New York, the senior partner in the firm of F. H. & C. W. Goodyear and founder of the business, was born at Groton, New York, March 17, 1849. He was the son of Dr. Bradley Goodyear and is of Scottish and English descent. He received a good education in the East Aurora Academy and through private tutors, after which he spent some time in teaching the district school. He then went to Looneyville, New York, where he became bookkeeper for Robert Looney, who operated a number of saw mills and a store at that place.

It was in 1872 that his residence in Buffalo began and the business which he established there has grown to mammoth proportions. He began in a small way but extended his operations by degrees until he became possessed of extensive timber, coal, railroad and iron properties and their development occupied all his energies. For the manufacture of raw material saw mills had to be built and in a few years he had six of these in operation. For the conveyance of the product to market railroads became an imperative necessity and the Sinnemahoning Valley and the Buffalo & Susquehanna roads came into existence. He is the principal owner and controlling factor in these enterprises. The Sinnemahoning Valley railroad which was built entirely with his capital is now merged into the Buffalo & Susquehanna system.

In 1887 Mr. Goodyear's brother, Charles W., a prominent

attorney in Buffalo, joined fortunes with him, forming the firm of F. H. & C. W. Goodyear, which was reorganized into the Goodyear Lumber Company, January 1, 1902. F. H. Goodyear was made president. The annual output of hemlock of this concern is over 200,000,000 feet. On the Buffalo & Susquehanna railway, of the managing board of which F. H. Goodyear is chairman, there are now manufactured annually approximately 300,000,000 feet of hardwood, pine and hemlock. The mill of the Goodyear Lumber Company at Galeton, Pennsylvania, is equipped with three large bands and one large resaw and cuts 300,000 feet a day. This is believed to be the largest saw mill in the East. All of the mills of the Goodyear Lumber Company run night and day the year around.

The Goodyear Lumber Company operates 102 miles of logging railroads. The logs are loaded with the Barnhart log loader, and the idea of loading logs by steam, in the manner in which the Barnhart loader handles them, was first put into effect by Frank H. Goodyear. This concern conducts one of the largest logging and manufacturing businesses under one management in the United States, and it is the pride of the company that, notwithstanding the magnitude of its operations, it has been able to concentrate them under its own control. The Goodyears own their timber, operate logging railroads and mills, and a main line of railroad which delivers its product, together with the traffic of a considerable community, to the trunk lines. The logging operations are conducted in a rough country, and it is this fact, in part, which led to the invention and development of the Barnhart steam log loader. The Goodyears were cutting 100,000,000 to 120,000,000 feet a year. The logging expense was heavy, particularly so because of the difficulty of concentrating logs at skidways. It was evident to Frank H. Goodyear, the managing partner, that if these logs could be scattered along the track wherever they would most easily come out of the woods a great expense would be saved. And then there was the further consideration that a machine which would pick up these logs from anywhere along the track, would load them on the cars cheaper than they could be loaded from skidways. Such proved to be the case. Then it naturally occurred to quick witted and practical Frank H. Goodyear, that the ordinary steam derrick or a modification of the steam portable shovel might be adapted to this work. Taking into consultation the Marion Steam Shovel Company, of Marion, Ohio, the result was the Barnhart, or Goodyear, steam log loader. The Goodyear Lumber Company is now using steel log cars, equipped with automatic couplers and air brakes.

Mr. Goodyear has become interested in bituminous coal mining to a large extent and is president of the Buffalo & Susquehanna Coal & Coke Company. He is president of the Buffalo & Susquehanna Railway Company, which is completing a railroad from the Reynoldsville district in the soft coal fields in Pennsylvania to Buffalo, New York. Mr. Goodyear is vice president of the Buffalo & Susquehanna Iron Company, which has two large furnaces at Buffalo, the most modern in the United States, with a capacity of 225,000 tons of iron a year. This plant is located at South Buffalo and, with iron, coal and coke plants, cost $5,000,000. This company owns large tracts of ore lands in the Lake Superior region. Mr. Goodyear is also a director in the United States Leather Company.

Mr. Goodyear is interested in southern timber and in 1902 he and those associated with him made an initial purchase of 90,000 acres in Louisiana and Mississippi. These holdings since that time have been largely augmented. This venture is known as the Great Southern Lumber Company. F. H. Goodyear is president. The timber is mostly longleaf pine and consists of 300,000 acres. This company also owns the East Louisiana railroad.

September 13, 1872, Mr. Goodyear married Miss Josephine Looney, of Looneyville, New York, and of this marriage four children were born: Mrs. Grace Depew, Mrs.

Josephine Goodyear Sicard (deceased), Mrs. Florence year Wagner and Frank Henry Goodyear, junior. H. Goodyear is first and last a businessman, one of thos feels that when he has discharged his commercial oblig with credit to himself and his fellow man he is adding prosperity of the greatest nation on earth.

He has never held public office, except that in 18 was appointed by President Cleveland as a commissio examine government lands on the line of the Northern P railroad.

Mr. Goodyear is fully entitled to all the success h won, for it has been due entirely to his peculiar and st abilities, backed by perseverence and hard work.

CHARLES W. GOODYEAR

Charles W. Goodyear

The lumberman who can bring to his business a special training in some other line that has relation to the industry is additionally equipped to achieve distinction in his chosen life work. Much of the success of the Goodyear brothers in Pennsylvania may be attributed to the legal learning and analytical mind of Charles W. Goodyear, one of the brothers. He has had the unusual honor of winning a high place for himself in a profession and then in a business; first as a lawyer and subsequently as a lumberman.

Charles W. Goodyear, of Buffalo, New York, was born at Cortland, Cortland county, New York, October 15, 1846, his ancestors transmitting to him a blending of English and Scotch blood. He received his schooling in the academies of Cortland, Wyoming and East Aurora. Adopting law as his profession, he studied in the office of Laning & Miller in Buffalo, was admitted to the bar in 1871 and practiced law in Buffalo until January 1, 1887, when he entered into partnership with his brother, F. H. Goodyear, under the firm style of F. H. & C. W. Goodyear, to engage in lumbering and railroading. This was the inauguration of the present business of the Goodyear Lumber Company, the Buffalo & Susquehanna Railway Company, the Buffalo & Susquehanna Coal & Coke Company and the Great Southern Lumber Company.

Although Mr. Goodyear is now best known as a lumberman, he won distinguished success as an attorney before entering the lumber business. His legal training has also been of value to him and to the lumber trade of the entire country since he transferred his activities from the law to lumber. While engaged in the active practice of law he was a prominent member of the bar of Erie county for a number of years. He was district attorney of Erie county for a time and was a law partner of former President Grover Cleveland.

His varied abilities made him prominent in the movement by lumbermen to prevent the removal or reduction of the import duty on lumber, whether by direct legislation or by means of reciprocity treaties, at a time when the industry felt that such change would result to its serious detriment. His legal, oratorical and parliamentary talents, as well as his high standing as a lumberman, were recognized by the convention of lumbermen that met to consider this problem, and he was made president of the body.

The operations of no single company engaged in the lumber business in the United States make a story more fascinating than those of the Goodyear brothers. Their enterprises have been almost dramatic at times, for they have quietly stolen a march on business rivals and made many bold strikes which have been actually sensational. "Find a way or make one" has been a rule with them. By the building of important railroads they have divorced themselves from dependence on fickle logging streams, and challenged the respect of the railroads of the country. They have shown that their abilities lie not only in the selection of timber and the manufacture of lumber, by engaging in coal, iron and other enterprises with equal success.

The operations of this concern in Potter county, Pennsylvania, have been enormous. They have hauled away millions of dollars' worth of lumber from the splendid forests of that county. More recently they have gone into Elk, Lycoming and Sullivan counties and acquired 600,000,000 feet of hemlock, pine and hardwood, meaning a cut of ten years in duration, which should yield them a fortune in profits. The Buffalo & Susquehanna railway, which they own, makes access to the new timber easily possible, and the timber will enhance the value of a railroad which is already one of the best paying short lines in the state.

It was shortly after Charles W. Goodyear became identified with his brother that the Goodyears began their remarkable campaign in Pennsylvania. They went into the Austin-Galeton region and purchased many miles of hemlock and hardwood which were then practically inaccessible. This timber stretched along Pine, Kettle, Sinnemahoning and Young Woman's creeks, and was cut off from ordinary lumber centers by high mountains. Much of it was indeed miles from a stream that would float logs. The presence of this timber was not unknown to lumbermen of Williamsport and other West Branch lumber towns, but the apparent expense of bringing the logs to a town for manufacture seemed to make prohibitory any investment. It would have been such had the Goodyears been content to follow an ordinary scheme of operations.

Their plan, however, did not contemplate bringing these logs to some point of manufacture lower down. Having acquired thousands of acres of highly valuable timber difficult of access, they built saw mills at the edge of the forest at which to turn the timber into lumber. They also built a steam railroad of standard gage which was designed not only to get this lumber to market but to make a railroad property of permanent value. Thus, while the lumber mills were being built at Austin and Galeton, the Buffalo & Susquehanna road was laid from Ansonia, on the Fall Brook road, to connect with the Philadelphia & Erie railroad at Keating Summit, near Emporium. The road was fifty miles long and between Corbett and Wharton traversed a range of mountains surmounted by the switchback plan. Another wise move was in making all the connecting feeders of standard gage, so that the cog gear engines and the log cars could run on either the main road or its branches.

The Goodyears were thus made independent of uncertain mountain streams and their engines and cars were moving logs twelve hours a day all the year around. The log ponds were kept free of ice with steam. The mills were equipped with electric lights to permit of night operation. All these preparations required years of time and immense sums of borrowed capital; but the saws had scarcely begun to eat their way into the Pennsylvania hemlock when the Goodyears began to pay back and today they are multimillionaires.

They have since pushed on to wider fields. They built their railroad northward to Buffalo. They bought the railroad from Gaines Junction to Wellsville, New York, giving them another market connection with the Erie. The Buffalo & Susquehanna was advertised as the scenic road of northern Pennsylvania and well equipped passenger trains did a big business, showing the wisdom of constructing the original road in a substantial manner. Huge tanneries were erected at Galeton, Manhattan and Costello and the bark from the Goodyear hemlock was thus utilized. The brothers have interested themselves in another great Pennsylvania product, for they have bought coal lands which their road makes accessible.

Since Charles W. Goodyear and his brother, Frank H., joined interests their operations have been little short of colossal, but Charles W. Goodyear has other interests. His greatest good fortune, however, is the result of a partnership into which he entered March 23, 1876, when he married Miss Ella Conger. They have four children—Anson Conger, Miss Esther, Charles W., junior, and Bradley Goodyear.

Mr. Goodyear is a member of the First Presbyterian Church of Buffalo and of the Buffalo Club, Saturn Club, Country Club, Ellicott Club and Falconewood Club and also the Lawyers' Club of New York. He was formerly a Democrat but, like many another, was forced to become an independent in politics.

Theodore S. Fassett

Theodore Stewart Fassett, of Buffalo, New York, has helped to make much of the lumber history of Tonawanda, New York. In everything that has tended toward the development of Tonawanda Mr. Fassett has been a potential factor. He was born at Albany, New York, February 19, 1848, the son of Asa Fassett, a native of western Massachusetts. The boy received his primary education in the excellent public schools of Albany, and before he was twelve years of age won in competition a scholarship in the Albany Academy, which annually awarded one scholarship to the best pupil in each of the public schools, there being at that time no high school in the city. Theodore spent two years at the academy and then, securing his father's consent, began his business career as bookkeeper in a large factory. A year later, at the age of sixteen, he became bookkeeper for W. H. Gratwick & Co., at that time an Albany lumber concern, with which he remained for seven years.

Major Asa Fassett, his father, died in 1872 and soon afterward the son, giving up his employment in Albany and refusing the offer of a partnership in one of the well established Albany lumber firms, went westward. Studying the situation on the Niagara river, he quickly appreciated the advantages of Tonawanda as a point for the reshipping of lumber from the lake to the canal, a business which at that time was in the first stages of its development. Mr. Fassett found that most of the docks then in existence were in control of the forwarding firm of Hollister, Lane & Co., and found also an opportunity ready to his hand in the disposition of Mr. Hollister to sell his interest for a reasonable sum. He purchased this interest with borrowed capital, and with his brother, James A. Fassett, and Mr. Lane, of the former concern, formed the firm of Lane, Fassett & Co., which entered into business in 1873. Many of the old friends of Mr. Fassett and his father in the Albany lumber trade diverted as much as possible of their business to the new firm, which during its first season shipped about 60,000,000 feet of lumber. The panic which occurred in the latter part of its first year in business involved Mr. Lane personally in financial difficulties and led in turn to the failure of the new concern just as it was getting on the road to success. Mr. Fassett, however, had already demonstrated his commercial ability and was offered another opportunity by James R. Smith, then of the firm of Mixer & Smith, of Buffalo, and in 1874 the newly organized firm of Smith, Fassett & Co. began the business in North Tonawanda in which it has continued until the present time.

Until 1881 the shore of the Niagara river furnished to the lumbermen doing business at North Tonawanda their piling ground and storage docks. About that time an island lying in the river, with nearly two miles of water front, appealed to Smith, Fassett & Co. as offering exceptional advantages for the extension of the lumber district. In 1881 therefore, the firm purchased this island and, after much opposition, secured from the state legislature and from Congress permission to erect a drawbridge in order to provide the railroad facilities necessary for the adaptation of the island to its new purposes. The work of building docks and of clearing and leveling the ground, in fact of putting in adequate business facilities, was a large and expensive undertaking, but, under Mr. Fassett's personal direction, it was carried through successfully. In a remarkably short time eight large lumber yards were established there under various tenancies, carrying in pile an average total of about 100,000,000 feet of white pine. This was an important step in the development of the lumber business of the Tonawandas, and augmented the annual output from less than 54,000,000 feet when Mr. Fassett went there in 1872, to 718,650,000 feet of lumber eighteen years later. Since that time there has been a gradual decline in the volume of business, coincident only with the decline in the volume of the white pine trade in general, resultant upon the gradual exhaustion of the supply.

In this remarkable development Mr. Fassett has borne an important part, not only as one of the earliest members of the trade and by means of his personal successes and the prosperity of his own firm, but also in the general upbuilding of the market as well as in every question of good citizenship affecting the community.

In association work Mr. Fassett has long been a conspicuous figure and especially so as the principal organizer in 1875 of the Tonawanda Lumbermen's Association. He wrote its constitution and by-laws, and was its president for the first two years of its existence. He was one of the original directors of the State Bank of Tonawanda and served a term as president of the village during his residence there. Mr. Fassett has always been prominent in public affairs in Buffalo, where he has made his home for many years. He was an active member of the entertainment committee of the great Pan-American Exposition and is a leading member of the Chamber of Commerce of the city. Mr. Fassett's eminence in the lumber trade and his own executive ability have received suitable recognition by his associates in the National Wholesale Lumber Dealers' Association, where for several years he has been chairman of the board of managers of its bureau of information. He has never had political aspirations and in the old Niagara district refused the Democratic nomination for Congress at a time when a nomination at the hands of that party in that district practically meant election.

New York. This was supplemented by a
Normal School at Geneseo, Livingston

After leaving this school he received an
United States Military Academy at West
predilection, however, was for a business instead
career, and in a short time he left the academy
mercial pursuits. His first employment
Walter Horton, at Sheffield, Pennsylvania, where for
years he acted as clerk and general office
engaged for a short time in the
hubs at Berkshire, New York.

In 1884 Mr. Horton obtained a position with the firm
Davidge & Co., sole leather tanners at English Center, Pe
sylvania. His aptitude for and interest in the business ma
him superintendent of the Leicester tannery at that pl
one year later and 1887 found him a member of the firm.

In 1893 the business was acquired by the United Sta
Leather Company, which was organized at that time
the three operating concerns of this company was known

CHARLES S MINER HORTON

CHARLES SUMNER HORTON

Charles S. Horton

An important factor in the business activities of Pennsylvania, especially in lumber manufacture, and a leader in the social and civic life of Williamsport, is Charles Sumner Horton.

Mr. Horton is the oldest son of Lucien and Harriet Burr Horton, and was born January 3, 1863, at Lake Como, Wayne county, Pennsylvania, where his father was engaged in tanning hemlock sole leather. His ancestors were of virile English stock and the American branch can be traced back to 1635, when Barnabas Horton came to this country from Leicestershire, England, and settled at Southhold, on Long Island, New York.

Mr. Horton received his public school education at Berkshire, New York. This was supplemented by a course in the State Normal School at Geneseo, Livingston county, New York. After leaving this school he received an appointment to the United States Military Academy of West Point. His predilection, however, was for a business instead of a military career, and in a short time he left the academy to enter commercial pursuits. His first employment was with his uncle, Walter Horton, at Sheffield, Pennsylvania, where for two years he acted as clerk and general office man. He afterward engaged for a short time in the manufacture of lumber and hubs at Berkshire, New York.

In 1884 Mr. Horton obtained a position with the firm of Davidge & Co., sole leather tanners at English Center, Pennsylvania. His aptitude for and interest in the business made him superintendent of the Leicester tannery at that point one year later and 1887 found him a member of the firm.

In 1893 the business was acquired by the United States Leather Company, which was organized at that time. One of the three operating concerns of this company was known as the Union Tanning Company, which was established with headquarters at Williamsport. Of this company Mr. Horton was chosen general superintendent and soon after became president, moving his family to Williamsport and becoming at once prominent in the business and social life of the place.

Up to 1903 the tanning companies had operated their vast hemlock tracts for the bark alone, the timber having been disposed of from time to time to saw mill men. With the view that this lumber could be handled to better advantage by themselves, the Central Pennsylvania Lumber Company was organized to develop these lands, and in the summer of 1904 became one of the largest producers of hemlock lumber in the United States. In one year this company placed in operation eight saw mills, perfectly equipped, having a capacity of 1,000,000 feet daily. This most important business venture was launched May 25, 1903, with Charles Sumner Horton as president of the company. Associated with him as officers were C. B. Farr, vice president, R. G. Brownell, secretary, and F. E. Bradley, treasurer.

The timber territory owned and operated by the company aggregates 450,000 to 500,000 acres, located in the counties of McKean, Warren, Forest, Elk, Potter, Clinton, Lycoming, Sullivan, Bradford, Tioga, Bedford, Luzerne and Wyoming. It is undoubtedly the largest body of hemlock timber lands under single control in the United States.

The company also owns or controls 250 miles of railroad, which includes the Susquehanna & New York railroad and the Tionesta Valley and Leetonia railways, and several connecting lines of logging and tram railroads.

One of the largest of its plants is located in Williamsport, with others at Gray's Run, Laquin, Jamison City, Leetonia, Tiadaghton, Mina and Loleta, all in Pennsylvania. There are also some smaller operations on the line of the Tionesta Valley railway with headquarters at Sheffield, Pennsylvania.

In addition to handling this large production of lumber, the company is extensively engaged in peeling and delivering to the tanneries controlled by the United States Leather Company an enormous quantity of bark, estimated at from 250,000 to 400,000 cords yearly. For a large portion of the year the company carries on its pay rolls the names of 10,000 persons, and during the bark-peeling season the services of 5,000 additional employees are necessary.

The chief executor and moving spirit of this great corporation is Charles Sumner Horton, whose wonderful energy and prodigious capacity for work and organization have evolved an enterprise that moves with the greatest precision. Mr. Horton keeps familiar with every detail of his great operations, and no matter is so small or apparently unimportant that he does not consider it worthy his attention.

In addition to his interests in this company Mr. Horton is connected with various other concerns. He is a director of the United States Leather Company, and president of the several railroads controlled by it. He has investments in timber lands and several smaller industries and is identified with the banking interests of Williamsport. His real estate holdings are extensive and he has added materially to the architectural attractiveness of Williamsport by erecting several fine buildings.

Mr. Horton is one of the most active members of the Williamsport Board of Trade, and is energetic in helping to forward any movement looking to the advancement or industrial development of the city of his adoption.

Mr. Horton is particularly favored in his home life and even pressing exigencies of business do not lessen the devotion of a large portion of his leisure to his family. He married Miss Stella M. Jones, of Towanda, Pennsylvania, April 21, 1887, and they have been blessed with four children, Harriet Burr, Gifford Davidge, Charles Sumner, junior, and Harry J. The family occupies a beautiful home in Williamsport.

Mr. Horton is a devotee of sport. He is an expert automobilist and a great admirer of baseball. He is a thirty-second degree Mason and a Knight Templar and is a me of the Ross and Howard clubs as well as of the Ha Country Club.

Although but forty-two years of age, he has crowd great deal into his active and busy career. A man of st constitution and powerful physique, no matter what requirements of the time may impose it is said that h never been known to tire. He is of a genial and affable perament, a man whom it is a pleasure to meet, and his fri ship means much to those who are privileged to enjoy it.

LIBRARY
OF THE
UNIVERSITY
OF
CALIFORNIA

As a

DuBois stood as a type

in thought and action and determined in all that

He was born in Owego, Tioga county, New York, March 3, 1809. Mr. DuBois was the second of a family of

children, of whom only two brothers and one sister

His father was John DuBois, a descendant of the

Huguenots, and his mother was Lucy Crocker, daughter of Ezekiel Crocker, one of the earliest settlers of the Susquehanna valley. The younger DuBois, early in life, engaged in the lumber business near his home, and his inventive ingenuity soon devised numerous appliances which were

improvements on the methods of lumbering then in

The log slide that he built early in his youth is said

been the first constructed in that region.

disappearance of pine from his section of New York

Mr. DuBois to move his operations to Pennsylvania, where, in partnership with his brothers, David and Matthias, he purchased a mill site on Lycoming creek, together with a quantity of pine land. This business was carried on for several years and showed a steady and increasing prosperity. The profits realized therefrom were immediately invested in more pine lands and other real estate and were the foundation of the DuBois fortune. At this time two farms were purchased and platted and this property has since become the heart of the residence district of the city of Williamsport. Mr. DuBois also purchased 500 acres of land on the south side of the West Branch of the Susquehanna river, opposite Williamsport, and here in subsequent years were located his large saw mills and lumber yards.

John DuBois and his brothers were heavy purchasers of

JOHN DuBOIS

John DuBois

As a pioneer lumberman of Pennsylvania the late John DuBois stood as a type of rugged character—a man independent in thought and action and determined in all that he did. He was born in Owego, Tioga county, New York, March 3, 1809. Mr. DuBois was the second of a family of thirteen children, of whom only two brothers and one sister survive. His father was John DuBois, a descendant of the French Huguenots, and his mother was Lucy Crocker, daughter of Ezekiel Crocker, one of the earliest settlers of the Susquehanna valley. The younger DuBois, early in life, engaged in the lumber business near his home, and his inventive ingenuity soon devised numerous appliances which were distinct improvements on the methods of lumbering then in vogue. The log slide that he built early in his youth is said to have been the first constructed in that region.

The disappearance of pine from his section of New York caused Mr. DuBois to move his operations to Pennsylvania, where, in partnership with his brothers, David and Matthias, he purchased a mill site on Lycoming creek, together with a quantity of pine land. This business was carried on for several years and showed a steady and increasing prosperity. The profits realized therefrom were immediately invested in more pine lands and other real estate and were the foundation of the DuBois fortune. At this time two farms were purchased and platted and this property has since become the heart of the residence district of the city of Williamsport. Mr. DuBois also purchased 500 acres of land on the south side of the West Branch of the Susquehanna river, opposite Williamsport, and here in subsequent years were located his large saw mills and lumber yards.

John DuBois and his brothers were heavy purchasers of

timber land in Clearfield county, Pennsylvania, and these lands afforded them the necessary supply of logs for the operation of their Williamsport mill. They were also heavy purchasers of lands at that time inaccessible to lumbering operations. The wisdom of this investment was afterward demonstrated, for these timber lands rapidly assumed a value far in excess of their original cost and the added expenditure for taxes and other purposes.

David DuBois died while the brothers were still operating on Lycoming creek, and at this time John DuBois and Matthias DuBois moved to Williamsport, where they erected a large steam gang saw mill on the south side of the river, giving employment to hundreds of men and producing annually millions of feet of lumber. John DuBois survived his brother Matthias also, and purchased his share in their business and property, becoming thus sole owner of all the DuBois interests.

Mr. DuBois was at the very front of the movement which made Williamsport a great lumber center. With others he secured a charter for a boom on the Susquehanna river to serve as a place of storage for the logs brought down that stream. Mr. DuBois was not only one of the charter members of the Susquehanna Boom Company but for many years its president. He owned nearly all of its stock and his vigorous administrative policy was responsible for the rapid completion of the boom and its subsequent successful operation. Not only had the ordinary risks of booming operations to be met and overcome, but Mr. DuBois and his associates also had to contend with an adverse local sentiment which objected to the driving of saw logs on the Susquehanna. He subsequently retired from active management of the boom company and eventually disposed of all his boom stock and his mill to Ten Eyck, Emery & Co. He, however, immediately built another large saw mill which he continued to operate until the removal of his operations to DuBois, in the present borough of DuBois, on the western slope of the Alleghanies.

Reference has already been made to Mr. DuBois' inventive genius. On several of his inventions, by which he sought to expedite and simplify the manufacture of lumber, he secured letters patent, but others he did not protect and they were generally adopted by other concerns.

By 1872 he had practically exhausted his available supply of timber tributary to Williamsport and in that year he moved his operations to Sandy creek, on the western slope of the Alleghanies, where he erected a small circular mill. This was the beginning of the great mills and lumber interests at DuBois. The first small mill was followed by greater business ventures. Dams were built, land was cleared, roads were made and houses were erected, until the scope of his lumber transactions and the completion of the low grade division of the Alleghany Valley railroad drew a heavy population to the borough of DuBois. His industries afforded employment to a large army of workmen and in their train naturally followed merchants, mechanics and professional men with their families.

The present borough of DuBois in 1872, when Mr. DuBois began his operations there, contained but three houses, but in a little over a decade the population had increased to 7,000. Mr. DuBois built three saw mills, a box factory, a machine shop, a store, a hotel and a tannery, cleared a 1,200 acre farm and erected 100 dwelling houses, and it was in these enterprises that he was actively occupied during the closing years of his life. He died May 5, 1886, leaving behind him a record of over fifty years of active life in the lumber business.

LIBRARY
OF THE
UNIVERSITY
OF
CALIFORNIA

and died at Ridgway, Pennsylvania, June 30, 1883. His parents were Jacob and Comfort Hyde. He was one of nine children: Asenath, Joseph, [illegible], Maria, Eliza, Catherine, Henry. Of these only Eliza, Jacob and Portland were living in 1904.

At the age of nineteen, owing to his father's business embarrassment, brought about by injudicious indorsements for friends, Mr. Hyde was constrained to seek a living self. He went to Bangor, Maine, where he secured work in a saw mill at $13 [illegible] month. He remained in this vicinity for nearly five years, working in mills and in the lumber woods, during a large part of which time his wages were remitted to his father to aid in the support of the family at home. In the fall of 1836 he came to Baltimore, where he was employed for a year. He emigrated to Elk county, Pennsylvania, in 1837. He remained a short time at Caledonia and then drifted to Ridgway, where he secured work digging on an embankment for Enos Gillis. Afterward he ran Mr. Gillis' mill on contract, but this venture not proving profitable he went to St. Croix, Wisconsin, in 1840, where he continued as a laborer in

Joseph S. Hyde

The life sketch of Joseph Smith Hyde is a remarkable illustration of the fact, which cannot too often be repeated, that it is not helps, but obstacles; not facilities, but difficulties, that make men. His history of early struggles, laborious toil and eventual success is pregnant with meaning. It shows that the world, though rough, is the best school master —better than books, better than study— for it makes a man his own teacher and gives him that practical training which no schools, academies or colleges can ever impart.

Joseph Smith Hyde was born in the little village of Tamworth, Carroll county, New Hampshire, August 30, 1813, and died at Ridgway, Pennsylvania, June 30, 1888. His parents were Jacob and Comfort Hyde. He was one of nine children: Asenath, Joseph, Adaline, Maria, Eliza, Catherine, Jacob, Portland and Henry. Of these only Eliza, Jacob and Portland were living in 1904.

At the age of nineteen, owing to his father's business embarrassment, brought about by injudicious indorsements for friends, Mr. Hyde was constrained to seek a living for himself. He went to Bangor, Maine, where he secured work in a saw mill at $13 a month. He remained in this vicinity for nearly five years, working in mills and in the lumber woods, during a large part of which time his wages were remitted to his father to aid in the support of the family at home. In the fall of 1836 he went to Baltimore, where he was employed for a year. He migrated to Elk county, Pennsylvania, in 1837. He remained a short time at Caledonia and then drifted to Ridgway, where he secured work digging on an embankment for Enos Gillis. Afterward he ran Mr. Gillis' mill on contract, but this venture not proving profitable he went to St. Croix, Wisconsin, in 1840, where he continued as a laborer in the lumber woods for about a year. Illness overtook him and, a good deal disheartened, he returned to Ridgway, where he again went to work in the lumber woods.

When Mr. Hyde returned to Ridgway his sister Adaline joined him and set up housekeeping for him in the "Red House," an old landmark well remembered by the older citizens. Mr. Hyde's anecdotes of his poverty at that time and the makeshifts to which he resorted in order to gain a living partook of both the humorous and the pathetic.

On July 25, 1842, he married Jane, daughter of Enos Gillis and niece of Hon. James L. Gillis. He lived at Montmorency about two years and then moved to Sharpsburg, Pennsylvania. He there found work about the foundries, but not enough to keep him busy, and in 1846 he returned to Elk county for a third time, determined finally to cast his lot there.

In the meantime his father-in-law had moved by wagon to Marshall, Michigan, and when Mr. Hyde returned he took up his quarters at the Gillis & McKinley mill, which was then owned by the late B. F. Ely. The following year he bought the mill and about 400 acres of land adjoining, on credit. This venture marked the turning point in his business career, as prior to that time he had made a hard struggle for existence. Beginning with that step his untiring industry was rewarded and his indomitable will commanded success. At the end of three years he was worth $3,000, accumulated from his savings. He then opened a small store in which the trade was largely barter. He supplied the country people with goods in exchange for shingles and other forest products and these in turn he sold. He also began to buy timber lands as fast as his credit extended, and tract after tract and mill after mill were added to his possessions until he eventually became the leading lumberman of that section of Pennsylvania. In 1862 he built a residence on the home farm at Hellen, where he lived for many years.

From this time forward his history was to a large extent

the history of Elk county, as at the time of his death he was the wealthiest man in that section. His property consisted of timber and coal lands, factories, stores and mills in Elk county, and of large real estate interests in Louisville, Pittsburg, Freeport and other cities. Mr. Hyde was sagacious and enterprising in business affairs, as the numerous undertakings of which he was a projector and which he carried to a successful culmination will abundantly testify. He despised dishonesty and idleness, but loved honesty and faithfulness, however lowly the man in whom he found it. He was a man of the people, with a profound contempt for pride of riches or position, and he was extremely tender hearted and charitable. He was a man of magnificent physique and of fine personal appearance.

Mr. Hyde was twice married. By his first wife, who died in August, 1864, he had four children: Mrs. John G. Hall, Mrs. Esther L. Campbell, W. H. Hyde and Mrs. J. K. P. Hall. The son, W. H. Hyde, who succeeded to the business of his father, died some years ago. The daughters were all living in 1904. In 1866 he married his second wife, Mrs. Nancy B. Campbell, a widow, who died in January, 1882.

Mr. Hyde's funeral services, which were held at Ridgway, were attended by a large body of laboring men, a tribute to one who as an employer would do without food and sleep rather than that any one of his workmen should lack them. He was buried at Painesville, Ohio, by the side of the wife of his youth.

Mr. Hyde was never a candidate for office but was strong in his political convictions, and throughout his life was an earnest Democrat of the Jacksonian type. He was a man of strong prejudices and imperious temper, which seemed a necessary adjunct to that sturdy and courageous New England character which made his name synonymous with the material prosperity of Elk county. His life was a well rounded one and he died full of years and honors. He was the type of the

courageous, hardworking,
and his career is a monu
handed business integrity.

LIBRARY
OF THE
UNIVERSITY
OF
CALIFORNIA

which he made [illegible]
was established, [illegible]
They built a mill one mile north
Toby creek, in Jefferson county, on the
Alexander tract. In the next
15,000,000 feet of white pine lumber
ket at Pittsburg.

In 1875 Mr. Carrier moved to [illegible]
during the next two years as assignee [illegible]
concern. In the meantime, in 1876, he
yard at Turkey City, Clarion county, a[illegible]
interest in the North Fork Saw Mill p[illegible]

CASSIUS M. CARRIER

Cassius M. Carrier

Those who know and love "Cash" Carrier will be glad to have the opportunity to learn something of the career of that well known Buffalo man and to acquaint themselves with the progressive steps by which he has moved forward to success from his first humble business venture. He comes of pioneer ancestry. As long ago as 1810 one Darius Carrier migrated from Connecticut to western Pennsylvania, settling in Jefferson county. To Darius Carrier were born seven sons. Cassius M. was born in Summerville, Jefferson county, June 29, 1847. The father was a lumberman and farmer and the sons followed the paternal vocation.

Darius Carrier owned a little sash saw mill on Red Bank creek. This was built in 1840. He also erected and operated a small tub and pail factory, the product of which was shipped to Pittsburg on top of the sawed lumber rafts.

Cassius M. Carrier was brought up, in association with his father, in the woods and on the river. His first business experience on his own account was the purchase of two rafts from his father, on which he rode to Pittsburg and on the sale of which he made $300. In 1870 the firm of Carrier Brothers was established, consisting of C. M., E. G. and S. P. Carrier. They built a mill one mile north of Brockwayville, on Little Toby creek, in Jefferson county, on what was known as the Alexander tract. In the next four years they produced 15,000,000 feet of white pine lumber, which was rafted to market at Pittsburg.

In 1875 Mr. Carrier moved to Brookville and was engaged during the next two years as assignee of a bankrupt lumber concern. In the meantime, in 1876, he conducted a lumber yard at Turkey City, Clarion county, and in 1877 bought an interest in the North Fork Saw Mill property at Brookville.

The firm was originally Jackson, Carrier & Co., afterward Jackson, Moore & Co., and later Jackson, Versteine & Co. It operated at that point until 1890, Mr. Carrier eventually selling out to Versteine & Kline. The concern made about 4,000,000 feet of lumber a year, operating entirely upon 5,000 acres; and at length, after twelve years of operation, the property sold for as much as was originally paid for it.

During all this time Mr. Carrier had been slowly but steadily accumulating experience, capital and credit, but it was during the next ten years that he assured his position. In 1890 he established a saw mill plant on Little Toby creek, four miles north of Brockwayville. Around the plant he built a village which was named Carrier and which for years was a thriving little place. Here was first a water mill, which Mr. Carrier changed into a steam mill, installing a Stearns band. This is said to have been the first band saw mill in that section for cutting hemlock. His output here was almost exclusively hemlock, and during the next ten years he cut approximately 125,000,000 feet.

About 1900, having cut out his timber, he sold his saw mill, his remaining stock of lumber and his land and sought new fields. During the last few years of his Pennsylvania operations Mr. Carrier made his home in Buffalo, where he has a beautiful residence and from whence he has conducted his more recent operations.

Mr. Carrier always has been a believer in timber, and so, with the proceeds of his Carrier operation, he began to look for an investment. He found what he wanted in what is known as the Yazoo Delta in Mississippi. Here he bought about 40,000 acres of magnificent oak, gum and cypress. The timber was in the northwestern part of the state and in the extreme northeastern part of that famous timber belt. In addition to this tract he bought timber lands in Louisiana and North Carolina. In 1891 he built a mill at Sardis, Mississippi, on the line of the Illinois Central railroad, about fifty miles south of Memphis. This is said to be one of the finest hardwood mills in the South, of especially strong and permanent construction and equipped with an Allis band and a resaw. In connection with this plant he built fifteen miles of standard gage railroad, laid with sixty pound rails. He chose Sardis for the scene of his milling operations out of regard for the health and comfort of his men, thus rendering himself surer of faithful and continuous service than would be likely if his mills were built on the low land in the timber. In this enterprise Mr. Carrier's son, Robert M. was interested and the firm was C. M. Carrier & Son.

In June, 1903, the firm was transformed into a stock company entitled C. M. Carrier & Son, Incorporated, and Mr. Carrier retired from active participation in the enterprise. The present owners are Robert M. Carrier, M. B. Burke and J. A. Riechman. The company is a prominent and prosperous one.

Preliminary to turning over this business to his son, Mr. Carrier was selling timber and buying a little and becoming especially interested in Cuba. In January, 1903, Mr. Carrier made a trip to the island, and, after about three months of travel and study of the situation, bought 40,000 acres of land in eastern Cuba. It is located in Santiago province, thirty-eight miles from Manzanillo, and is near Bayamo, in the valley of the Canto river. The bottom lands and a considerable portion of the property are ranch land, especially adapted to grazing, though also suited to the growth of any sort of crops. The higher levels are well timbered with mahogany, cedar and other indigenous woods, including a native pine. At least 15,000 acres of the tract is as fine timber as ever grew in Cuba. A large part of it, however, is open land, of which he has 10,000 acres under fence.

Mr. Carrier, with his wife and daughter, resides in a modern mansion on West Ferry street, Buffalo, New York. He was bereaved in March, 1904, by the death of his eldest daughter, Miss Olive Evelyn, who was a young woman of remarkable beauty, charms and attainments. His dwelling place is one of the handsomest in that city of beautiful houses and was built by him several years ago and epitomizes beauty and comfort in a home.

Cassius M. Carrier is a unique character and his acquaintances are fond of telling stories of his thrift, the ingenuity of his methods and his quaint sayings. He is medium in stature and of spare build, though he has a firmly knit frame, hardened by constant exercise and unweakened by injurious habits. His mind is always on the alert. He is particularly curious as to anything affecting the lumber business. He is all the time looking for new methods and hunting for the odds and ends of information which he can turn to account in his business. He never forgets anything and has profited by the experience of others as well as by his own. He is punctilious as to business courtesies and equities, consequently no one, considering his means, stands higher with the commercial world that knows him than does Cassius M. Carrier.

JOHN LONSDALE ROPER

John L. Roper

In the modern development of the North Carolina pine trade Captain John Lonsdale Roper, president of the John L. Roper Lumber Company, of Norfolk, Virginia, has sustained a prominent part. His first acquaintance with the North Carolina pine forests was not as a manufacturer of lumber, but when, as a Union soldier in the Civil War and as an officer of the rank whose title is still by common consent accorded him, he was engaged in military maneuvers through this region. During even the exciting periods of campaigning Captain Roper was regarding with an eye of interest the trunks of the trees about him. Born in the town of Belleville, Mifflin county, Pennsylvania, in 1835, he was raised in the pine and hemlock district of the Keystone State, where he absorbed the instincts and inclinations of a lumberman. With the conclusion of the Civil War he looked for an opportunity to resume the arts of peace among the pines where he had done a portion of his fighting. In 1865, therefore, he removed to Norfolk, Virginia, and at the head of North Landing river in Princess Anne county, at the entrance to the Albemarle canal, twenty-four miles distant from Norfolk, he built a single circular saw mill with a capacity of about 6,000,000 feet annually. It is worthy of remark, however, that this mill at the time of its construction had a capacity equal to one-half the total of all of the North Carolina pine then manufactured and shipped from Norfolk.

The question of an improvement in the product was the first and most important subject Captain Roper encountered, and he early concluded that this must be secured through better dry kiln methods. He was one of the first manufacturers of this wood to introduce dry kilns, which then were of a decidedly primitive type. They demonstrated their usefulness, however, and were systematically and constantly improved.

Captain Roper since that early time has been continuously a manufacturer of North Carolina pine lumber; and, while intervening years have not been marked by any sensational event to enliven the story of his successful progress, each year has seen his product increased and his manufacturing plants improved. At Gilmerton, in the suburbs of Norfolk, the company is operating a band and a band resaw mill with a daily capacity of 65,000 feet and planing mills which exceed this mill capacity by 100,000 feet daily, this excess being utilized upon stock manufactured at other plants of his company or purchased outside. At Roper, North Carolina, the concern owns and operates a band and band resaw mill, with dry kilns, which has a daily output equal to that of the Norfolk plant. It also has at Winthrop a mill of the same type and capacity. The Roper operation includes a small saw mill plant which is devoted entirely to the manufacture of lumber from juniper, a variety of cedar. Still another plant at that point is manufacturing juniper shingles, which are known to all the Atlantic Coast trade as the Roper cedar shingles. Several other minor manufacturing plants are operated by the company at various points, with an aggregate capacity of about 50,000,000 feet of lumber annually. The John L. Roper Lumber Company is the absolute owner of over 200,000 acres of timber land, and a great many miles of railroad have been built in the development of its operations, among them the thirty miles of track which now constitute the Pamlico division of the Norfolk & Southern railroad.

Captain Roper has two sons, George W. and William B., respectively vice president and secretary and treasurer of the company, the first the company's outside man and the second its office manager. Although by birth a Pennsylvanian, he is by adoption a southerner of the highest public spirit in the consideration of any subject affecting the interests of his trade and of the city which is proud to claim him as a resident. He is an honored and active member of the Methodist Episcopal Church and has for over twenty years been president of the United Charities of Norfolk. His fraternal impulses find an outlet through the Masonic order, of which he is a member. He is a past officer in the various bodies and has attained the thirty-second degree. He is also identified with various commercial enterprises in Norfolk, notably as vice president of the Virginia Savings Bank & Trust Company, and as president or director of several other extensive concerns, including the Roper Storage Company, the Chamber of Commerce, the National Bank of Commerce, the Seaboard Fire Insurance Company, and the Norfolk Public Library.

The most important work of Captain Roper's life is that which he has done in behalf of North Carolina pine, and his services in this direction have benefited the entire trade. In the improvement of methods of manufacture he has blazed the trail of the pioneer, and others have followed him. In the matter of better price values for North Carolina pine, in which the tendency at times has been toward an undue demoralization and depression, he has been the preëminently strong man of the industry. As president of the North Carolina Pine Association he has wielded a great influence among his fellow manufacturers, and his excellent work and advice in this official capacity have done much toward obtaining a greater measure of respect, and better prices, for the excellent wood to the promotion of which this association is devoted. Captain Roper is exceedingly well informed upon all of the varied details of lumbering, and his wide knowledge and wise counsel are often of much assistance in the deliberations of the National Wholesale Lumber Dealers' Association, of which he is a member.

EDGAR CHARLES FOSBURGH

Edgar C. Fosburgh

The National Lumber Manufacturers' Association is a delegate body or federation of manufacturers' associations. Some comparatively unimportant sections are not represented and there are two or three woods which are not specifically included within its scope, but it well justifies its name. Territorially it covers the southern pine belt from Norfolk, Virginia, to Texas, Indian Territory and Missouri. It represents the hardwood belt lying north of the yellow pine, including the northern manufacturing district of Michigan, Wisconsin and Minnesota, in hardwoods, hemlock and pine; and then it crosses the mountains and includes the varied manufacturing interests of Washington, and in California the sugar pine and white pine. The only important lumber producing territories not represented in any way are Oregon, Montana and Idaho, New York and New England; the only important woods not included are redwood, cypress and spruce.

To be elected president of such an organization and therefore the primate among lumbermen of ability and influence is an honor of which any man might well feel proud. The man who first occupied this position was Edgar C. Fosburgh, of Norfolk, Virginia. He was chosen because of his high personal qualities and because, notwithstanding he is a comparatively young man, he is a leader in trade organization. The successful launching of such an association demands loyalty and enthusiasm as well as a high degree of ability. Such qualities were found in Mr. Fosburgh.

Edgar Charles Fosburgh is of English descent and was born at Lacolle, near the foot of Lake Champlain, province of Quebec, September 19, 1854. He was a farmer's son and until seventeen years old led the life of a farmer's boy. Breaking away from these connections, he first went to Detroit,

Michigan, thence to Chicago and then to St. Louis. There he found employment with Branch, Crookes & Co., saw manufacturers. That was in May, 1872, and with that institution he remained ten years, beginning as office boy and ending as cashier and confidential man.

Having reached the highest position possible to an employee, and his ambition not being satisfied with what he had already accomplished, he decided to seek new work. In the saw business he had been more or less intimately acquainted with the lumber trade and he had no difficulty in securing employment with J. Cummer & Son, of Cadillac, Michigan, then one of the most extensive concerns operating in white pine. Here he devoted himself to mastering all the details of the lumber business, with which he had been acquainted only in a general way. His ability and diligence met a sure reward, for he eventually reached the position of general manager of the internal office affairs and sales department of J. Cummer & Son, the Cummer Lumber Company and Cummer & Cummer, all of Cadillac. He handled a business representing 75,000,000 feet of product annually, all of which was shipped by rail into territory extending from the Missouri river to the Atlantic seaboard.

The Cummers were branching out. As their Michigan timber was cut away they made heavy investments in the Southeast and, needing some one to represent them, Mr. Fosburgh was selected as the man to take charge of the interests of The Cummer Company, as that branch was known, in and around Norfolk, Virginia. It was in the fall of 1892 that he took charge of this business as secretary of The Cummer Company and general manager of its North Carolina pine department.

In 1902 Mr. Fosburgh and The Cummer Company decided upon another change, and the Fosburgh Lumber Company was formed to take over the North Carolina pine department of the Cummer business centered at Norfolk. Of this new company Mr. Fosburgh was made vice president and general manager, associating with himself men of standing in financial and business circles. The Fosburgh Lumber Company is still young but it gives promise of attaining the same success which has characterized every business which has had the benefit of Mr. Fosburgh's ability and energy. It was as secretary and manager of The Cummer Company, and, more recently, as vice president and general manager of the Fosburgh Lumber Company, that Mr. Fosburgh became identified with North Carolina pine organization, and he has had much to do with the raising of that industry from the slough of despond in which it had been struggling for a generation and putting it on a sound and profitable basis. He is vice president of the North Carolina Pine Association.

The Fosburgh Lumber Company has very extensive holdings of North Carolina pine timber. It has a magnificent manufacturing plant at Berkley, Virginia, across the Elizabeth river from Norfolk, consisting of a double band saw mill, extensive dry kilns and planing mills. In addition to the general sales office maintained at Norfolk, the company has branch sales offices at New York and Boston.

Mr. Fosburgh has the good fortune to be associated with two of the leading businessmen of the Wolverine State, who are his partners and associates in the Fosburgh Lumber Company, Harvey J. Hollister, of Grand Rapids, Michigan, vice president of the Old National Bank, of that city, who is the president of the Fosburgh Lumber Company, and James M. Barnett, also a banker and representative businessman and property owner of Grand Rapids, who is the treasurer of the company. These gentlemen have been actively identified with Mr. Fosburgh in the North Carolina pine business since he first became associated with the Virginia proposition and during their entire business career have been prominent in the lumber industry of Michigan.

In Norfolk Mr. Fosburgh has long been recognized as one of the leading and most energetic citizens of that progressive city. Few men enjoy to a larger extent the respect, confidence and good will of their fellow citizens.

Among the various enterprises in which he is inte
he is president of the Lumbermen's Marine Insurance
pany, vice president of the North Carolina Pine Assoc
director of the National Bank of Commerce, the largest
cial institution in Norfolk, and director in the Norfolk
for Savings and Trusts.

Mr. Fosburgh's success is due to his ability, his ini
his industry and in no small degree to his personal pop
based on his broad and generous spirit, his good fell
and all those qualities which win and keep friends.
pleasure to extend this recognition to one of the still g
leaders in the great lumber industry.

LIBRARY
OF THE
UNIVERSITY
OF
CALIFORNIA

JAMES M. BARNETT

James M. Barnett

While the connection of James M. Barnett, of Grand Rapids, Michigan, with the lumber industry has been an important one, the historian is tempted to dwell more on his personal character than upon his personal achievements. Character is more than capital, and the recital of the good that a man has done contains more of human interest than a list of the great things he has accomplished.

Mr. Barnett is a native of western New York, having been born at Brockport, in 1832. He was educated at the Brockport Collegiate Institute and later went to Buffalo, where he took a course of study at Bryant & Stratton's Business College, which fitted him admirably to begin his commercial career. Later he followed the advice of a famous newspaper sage and went west to grow up with the country. It was in 1857 that he located at Grand Rapids, Michigan, and he has ever since made that city his home. His first manufacturing interest was an association with L. M. Sweet, in which they conducted a flour milling business. This partnership continued until 1869.

In 1870 began Mr. Barnett's connection with the lumber industry. He had already won his laurels in the western Michigan business world. He was connected with the Old National Bank and its predecessor, the First National Bank of Grand Rapids, from the foundation of the latter in 1864. He served this institution continuously as vice president until 1895, when he became its president, and he has served it in the latter capacity ever since. For several years he carried on lumber operations in various parts of Michigan and was associated with Harvey J. Hollister, a relationship that continues until this day. For forty years Mr. Hollister and Mr. Barnett have been in the banking business together and identified with the management of Grand Rapids banking institutions.

The lumber operations of Mr. Barnett and Mr. Hollister continued from 1870 for several years, until Mr. Barnett transferred his activities to other lumber interests. In company with Thomas Byrne and John Murray, under the style of John Murray & Co., he was engaged in lumbering in Roscommon and Crawford counties, with a mill at Muskegon for the manufacture of lumber.

In 1880 Mr. Hollister and Mr. Barnett again became associated in the lumber business. In that year Wellington W. Cummer, of Cadillac, Mr. Hollister and Mr. Barnett organized the Cummer Lumber Company, which carried on its business in and near Cadillac until 1894, when the timber holdings of the company became exhausted.

Like many other Michigan lumbermen, they then sought a new field in the South and active business operations were resumed in North Carolina and Florida. One company was located at Jacksonville and was known as The Cummer Lumber Company. The other was The Cummer Company, of Norfolk, Virginia. Under the name of the St. Tammany Land & Lumber Company the same interests also owned a large block of timber in Louisiana. This tract was sold in 1902.

In the same year Mr. Barnett and Mr. Hollister exchanged their holdings in the Jacksonville plant with Mr. Cummer for his share of the Norfolk business and the latter was reorganized under the name of the Fosburgh Lumber Company, of which Mr. Barnett is president, Mr. Hollister treasurer, E. C. Fosburgh vice president and general manager and McGeorge Bundy secretary. Mr. Barnett's lumber interests and those of his associates were thereby centralized.

The Fosburgh Lumber Company manufactures kiln dried North Carolina pine, and has eastern sales offices in the Exchange building in Boston and at 18 Broadway, New York.

Mr. Barnett is also identified with a number of local business interests at Grand Rapids. Besides being president and director of the Old National Bank of Grand Rapids, he is a director of the Grand Rapids Gaslight Company, the Michigan Trust Company and the Michigan Barrel Company and is a director and vice president of the Antrim Iron Company, of Mancelona, Michigan. One who has known him intimately for a quarter of a century said:

"In my judgment the state of Michigan has never numbered among its people a man of finer qualities than Mr. Barnett. His business career has been a remarkable one and he stands today as one of the most honored leaders of the great financial institutions of his state. Endowed by nature with a genial disposition that has endeared him to everyone with whom he comes in contact, he is rounding out a life that might be the envy of any man. During all the twenty-five years that I have known and been in close personal relations with him, I am free to say that I have never yet known his sunny disposition to be ruffled for even a single moment, nor have I ever known him to say an unkind word to anyone or of anyone. He is one of those men whom it is always a pleasure to know and those who have been associated with him in commercial and fraternal relationships fully appreciate his good qualities."

HARVEY J. HOLLISTER

Harvey J. Hollister

A man who combines the business of a banker and a lumberman with equal success is Harvey J. Hollister, of Grand Rapids, Michigan, well known to lumbermen as the treasurer of the Fosburgh Lumber Company, of Norfolk, Virginia, well known to bankers as the vice president of the Old National Bank in Grand Rapids, Michigan, known to the railway world as a director of the Grand Rapids & Indiana railway, known to the manufacturing world as the president of the Michigan Barrel Company, the treasurer of the Grand Rapids Malleable Company and other concerns, and, in spite of all these commercial activities, known to the people at large because of the business ability which he has brought to the administration of the affairs of charity organizations, educational institutions and a mass of other benevolent works. The life of such a man must be of interest to all who admire the busy American of today who is active for himself and for the public good.

Harvey J. Hollister was born at Romeo, Macomb county, Michigan, August 29, 1830. For his ancestry he goes back to the pioneers of Connecticut, the first settler of his family in this country being Lieutenant John Hollister, who came from England in 1642 at the age of thirty and settled in Weathersfield. The subject of this sketch is a representative of the eighth generation from Lieutenant Hollister, and the son of Colonel John Bently Hollister, who was one of the early pioneers in Michigan. Colonel Hollister gave distinguished service as a civil engineer in the territorial organization of that state.

Harvey J. Hollister seems to have made the most of the meager opportunities that a country village offered in his youth, being a hard worker on his mother's farm in summer and attending school in winter. When seventeen years old he taught school one winter near Romeo and then secured a position in a drug store in Pontiac. Two years later he joined his family, which had moved to Grand Rapids. For a few months he was a clerk in a mercantile house, then for a time he had charge of the old "Faneuil Hall" drug store owned by W. G. Henry. In 1853 he became confidential clerk in the banking house of Daniel Ball & Co., and later a partner in the firm. The troublous times of 1861 compelled Daniel Ball & Co., the last of the three banking houses in the city, to close out their business at a great loss to themselves, but their obligations were all met in full.

M. L. Sweet opened almost at once another bank, with Mr. Hollister as manager. This arrangement continued until 1864, when the First National Bank of Grand Rapids was organized. The Sweet bank was merged into it and its manager was made cashier and director. The bank was successful and when its charter expired was succeeded by the Old National Bank, with Mr. Hollister as a director and cashier and vice president. He is the pioneer banker in Grand Rapids and the oldest banker in continuous service in the state, having served more than fifty consecutive years in these relations.

Mr. Hollister is always a busy man, and besides his banking business has been identified with many other interests. He has been president of the Grand Rapids Clearing House, a position he has held since its organization seventeen years ago. He is a stockholder and director in the Grand Rapids & Indiana Railway Company and a director in the Michigan Trust Company. He is president of the Michigan Barrel Company and a director in the Grand Rapids Brass Company and the Antrim Iron Company, of Mancelona, Michigan. He is also treasurer of the Fosburgh Lumber Company, of Norfolk, Virginia, and treasurer of the Grand Rapids Malleable Company. He has been in the northern lumber business practically all his life and is interested also in North Carolina pine. He visits the mills two or three times a year and takes a genuine interest in them.

In addition to his business affiliations Mr. Hollister has been president of the Grand Rapids Charity Organization Society during the last eight years, and was formerly one of the board of control of the State Public School. He is a trustee of Olivet College, a trustee of Butterworth Hospital and president of the Michigan Social Science Association and is identified with many of the charitable and educational institutions of the state and country. He is a strong supporter of the principles of the Republican party and, although at no time actively engaged in politics, is closely connected with the councils of that party in the state.

Harvey J. Hollister has been a member of the First Congregational Church of Grand Rapids for fifty years. He is one of its deacons and has been its treasurer for thirty years. He has been identified with the Young Men's Christian Association since its organization, being its president for three years, and is greatly concerned in anything that can benefit young men and fit them for their life work.

Mr. Hollister is benevolent, cultured and refined and his family is one most delightful to know. He has many acquaintances all over the country, all of whom hold him in the highest regard.

which comp
white pine.
Mr. Shryoc
and has pra
of Columbi

THOMAS J. SHRYOCK

Thomas J. Shryock

The discovery and development of southern white pine as a commercial possibility should be credited to Gen. Thomas J. Shryock, of Baltimore, Maryland, and his valuable services in this regard are generally acknowledged, for they form a significant element in the history of the section in which his operations are located.

Mr. Shryock was born February 27, 1851, at Baltimore, Maryland. He is the son of Henry S. and Annie Ophelia Shryock, who were native Virginians. His great-grandfather was Henry Shryock, of Frederick county, Maryland, a member of the First Maryland Battalion, of Flying Camp, in the Revolutionary War, and who subsequently was a member of General Washington's staff.

Mr. Shryock was educated in the public schools and the Light Street Institute of the city of Baltimore. He left school when sixteen years of age and went into the lumber business as a yard clerk. At eighteen years of age he married and bought out his employers. He thus started in the retail lumber business in Baltimore, in which occupation he was engaged until twenty-seven years of age. He then entered the wholesale trade in the same city, in which business he continued alone for five years and then associated with himself George F. M. Hauck, who was formerly manager of the Lochiel Lumber Company, of Bloomington, Maryland.

About this time he became interested in southern white pine and was elected president of the St. Lawrence Boom & Manufacturing Company, of Ronceverte, West Virginia, which company has manufactured nearly 500,000,000 feet of white pine. This product has been handled entirely through Mr. Shryock's firm, Thomas J. Shryock & Co., of Baltimore, and has practically all been sold in Baltimore and the District of Columbia.

In 1892 he was elected president of the Iron Mountain & Greenbrier railroad, a standard gage road running from White Sulphur Springs, Virginia, at which point it connects with the Chesapeake & Ohio railroad, to Huntersville, West Virginia, the line passing through the timber holdings of the St. Lawrence Boom & Manufacturing Company. This road traverses a large wooded area. The timber therefrom is all railroaded to Ronceverte to be sawed. This road is said to penetrate the largest body of standing oak in this country and furnishes an outlet for the product of a number of other saw mills along the line. The road has also rendered accessible an immense iron deposit owned by the Sherwood Company, of West Virginia, which is allied to the St. Lawrence Boom & Manufacturing Company.

The house of Thomas J. Shryock & Co. possesses the largest wholesale lumber plant in Baltimore. The equipment consists of a large dock and an immense storage warehouse. A considerable branch establishment is carried on in Washington. The house does a business of upward of $1,000,000 a year, largely in white pine and oak, although the firm handles considerable quantities of yellow pine and miscellaneous hardwoods.

Mr. Shryock was president of the Third National Bank, of Baltimore, from which position he resigned to take the directorship of the Second National Bank, one of the strongest financial institutions in Baltimore. In early life he took an active interest in the state militia of Maryland and was captain in the famous Fifth Regiment. Subsequently he was appointed brigadier general and chief of staff by former Governor Henry Loyd. This was the first instance in the history of Maryland where a Republican was appointed to a position on a Democratic governor's staff, as party lines are drawn very closely in that state.

Mr. Shryock is a man of large civic spirit and has been connected with nearly all utilitarian movements in the city of Baltimore which have tended toward the development of the business interests of that city. He is a Republican in politics and public office has frequently been urged upon him. In 1895, when the Republicans came into power in Maryland, he was elected treasurer of that state and was reëlected in 1897. Under his administration of the finances of the state the state debt was refunded on a 3 percent basis and he sold the bonds at a premium of 2½ to 3 percent. Upon retiring from office, he left the state practically free from debt, the treasury having on hand in the sinking fund sufficient securities to wipe out all obligations. In the legislature of Maryland of 1897 Mr. Shryock was prominently spoken of as a candidate for United States senator to succeed Senator Arthur P. Gorman, but he retired from the contest in favor of Lewis E. McComas, who was elected.

Mr. Shryock has been at the head of the Masonic fraternity of the state of Maryland for the past twenty years, having been consecutively elected Grand Master for that period of time, probably longer than any other man has enjoyed this distinction in the United States. Naturally he is an active and enthusiastic Mason and has attained the thirty-third degree of the Ancient and Scottish Rite.

He has been an extensive traveler in the far East and Europe, and during his travels made his splendid collection of pictures and articles of virtu. On account of his knowledge of art and the interest he takes in it, he was for a long time president of the Art Club of Baltimore.

General Shryock is an illustration of the fallacy of the foreigner's judgment of the American businessman. His broad culture, artistic taste, patriotism and grasp of affairs outside the world of business make him representative of a class on which the wisest guidance and best development of our nation depends.

DAVID LINDSAY GILLESPIE

David L. Gillespie

Of the same sturdy, thrifty, Scotch-Irish blood as many of Pittsburg's most noted citizens is D. L. Gillespie, of D. L. Gillespie & Co., manufacturers and dealers in lumber, railroad ties and planing mill work. His parents, Mr. and Mrs. James Gillespie, came to this country and settled in 1840 in Pittsburg. They were both natives of the north of Ireland, near Belfast, where their families had resided for three generations. Prior to that the land of the bannock was their native heath and it is to the combination of thistle and shamrock, with the addition of American aggressiveness, that D. L. Gillespie owes his success.

David Lindsay Gillespie was born in Pittsburg, Pennsylvania, October 20, 1858. As is the case with perhaps the majority of successful American businessmen, Mr. Gillespie's school days were few. For six years, from 1865 to 1871, he attended the public schools, but at the age of thirteen started in business life as a messenger in the Western Union Telegraph Company's office. This marked the beginning of a hard, twenty years' struggle. After a year's experience in the telegraph office, Mr. Gillespie, from 1872 to 1875, worked for his father, James Gillespie, who was engaged in the planing mill business. The father was one of the largest retail dealers in western Pennsylvania, and until his mill was burned and serious financial difficulties followed, did the phenomenal business of those days, 3,000,000 feet a year.

After the destruction of his father's mill Mr. Gillespie was employed by Lewis, Oliver & Phillips, iron and steel manufacturers, as messenger boy. He worked there for about two years, and in 1877 he was engaged by A. Speer & Son, plow manufacturers, as telegraph operator and general office man. Speer & Son had an office in conjunction with the Pittsburg

Forge & Iron Company and Mr. Gillespie worked for these combined institutions until 1882. He then entered the employ of the Westinghouse interests, working in the gas department in the capacity of paymaster. He remained in this position until 1886, when he embarked in the lumber business. During the first year of this new venture the style of the firm was W. H. Thompson & Co., but Mr. Gillespie purchased his partner's interest at the end of the first year and changed the name of the firm to D. L. Gillespie & Co., which name it has borne ever since. From 1884 to 1890 Mr. Gillespie found it extremely hard sailing, but after 1890 the tide of fortune turned in his favor and he ranks now as one of Pittsburg's leading and very successful businessmen. During its first year in the lumber business the Gillespie concern handled less than 3,000,000 feet, but in 1902 its output was 70,000,000 feet.

D. L. Gillespie & Co. have made a specialty of large contracts and have executed some of the largest orders in the country. Their contracts with the Westinghouse Air Brake, the Westinghouse Electric and the Westinghouse Machine companies have aggregated about 50,000,000 feet and with the British Westinghouse Electric & Manufacturing Company about 15,000,000 feet.

The firm has made a great record in furnishing building material for the large skyscrapers of New York, seventeen of these large buildings having been finished mainly of lumber purchased from D. L. Gillespie & Co.

Mr. Gillespie's commercial interests are not confined to his own immediate firm but branch out in many paths. He is a director in the Pittsburg Reduction Company, of Pittsburg, aluminum manufacturers; the Commercial Sash & Door Company, of Pittsburg; the Iron City Trust Company, of Pittsburg; in two mining companies; in the West Penn and Dixmont hospitals; in the Pittsburg-Honduras Company, mahogany and merchandise operator in Honduras, and in the Pittsburg and Connellsville division of the Baltimore & Ohio Railroad Company. He is president of the Board of Education of Pittsburg, member of the Board of Managers of the Western Penitentiary of the state of Pennsylvania and a member of all of the different Masonic bodies, including Blue Lodge, Chapter, Commandery and Consistory. Notwithstanding the enormous strain which would naturally follow in the wake of these many demands, Mr. Gillespie finds time to devote to the social amenities of life. He is a clubman of prominence, belonging to the Duquesne, Monongahela and Union clubs, of Pittsburg, and to the Lawyers' Club and the New York Athletic Club, of New York City.

Politically Mr. Gillespie is a Republican and has been a most faithful adherent to the principles of his party. He has been treasurer of the state Republican organization and delegate from the state of Pennsylvania to the national convention on two occasions, the last one being when Theodore Roosevelt was nominated. Mr. Gillespie has been named for mayor and recorder, but declined to accept either office, owing to a deep rooted objection to shouldering the onerous responsibilities of public place. Moreover he prefers his own business to a political position.

Mr. Gillespie was married in 1885 to Miss Anna R. Darlington, of Wilmington, Delaware. They have one child, Miss Mabel, who is attending an eastern school. The Gillespies live in a beautiful home on North Highland avenue, Pittsburg.

ounty, about 60,000 a

John M. Hastings

When it was given out in July, 1903, that John M. Hastings, of Pittsburg, in company with business associates of the same city, had purchased the property of E. D. Davison & Sons, Limited, of Nova Scotia, for the exact amount of $1,000,000, there was made known not only one of the largest lumber and timber transactions of recent times but also one which in many features was unique.

Mr. Hastings' latest coup, which put him in the front rank of the lumber producers of British North America, was characteristic of the man in its daring and the speed with which it was consummated. It remains to tell something of the material facts and the men involved.

The history of the Davison lumber interests reaches back about sixty years. The late Edward D. Davison, senior, founded the business in the early '40's of the last century and erected two mills at Lunenburg. He built, in 1845, the first steam saw mill erected in Nova Scotia and in 1850 built another one. It is said that at the outset of his career Mr. Davison cherished as his pet idea the consolidation of all the lumber interests in the southern counties of Nova Scotia, and he worked steadfastly until there was developed the great business which has now been purchased by Mr. Hastings and his associates. Various operators, including a number of Americans, began business in that section but found it unprofitable, and the Davison interests acquired their properties, the last transfer of 25,000 acres having been made in 1900. The result was a property including about 200,000 acres of fine timber, of which about 120,000 acres were in Annapolis county, about 60,000 acres in Kings county, about 16,000 in Lunenburg county and a smaller quantity in Queens county. The Davisons' headquarters for years have been at Bridgewater, on La Have river, with their saw mills at Alpena on the Nictaux, at Bridgewater, at Mill Village on the Medway and one at Greenfield. They are all water power mills and those at Bridgewater and on the Nictaux have a capacity of 250,000 feet a day. It was these great properties which Mr. Hastings acquired and reorganized in harmony with thoroughly modern ideas.

John M. Hastings was born of Scotch-Irish parents at Allegheny City, Pennsylvania, August 16, 1859, his father being James Hastings, of Belfast, Ireland, and his mother Mrs. Margaret McBride Hastings, whose birthplace was Glasgow, Scotland. In early life they located in Allegheny, where the old homestead is still standing. Mr. Hastings, senior, followed the contracting business, in which he was eminently successful. His son John received his early education in the First Ward school, Allegheny, after which he spent a term at the Iron City College at Pittsburg.

At fifteen years of age he entered the employ of the William Dilworth Saw Mill Company, located on the Allegheny river, where he had charge of the timber along the river. After one year's employment he went with DuBois & Fuller in their yard in Allegheny where he learned the business so quickly and thoroughly that at the age of nineteen he purchased the interest of J. E. DuBois. The yard was then run under the name of Sidney Fuller, Mr. Hastings having gone in on a combination basis. After five years under this title the name was changed to Cowan & Hastings, but three years later Mr. Hastings purchased Mr. Cowan's interest and shortly afterward disposed of the whole concern to Joseph H. May. He then started in the wholesale lumber business in Pittsburg and conducted a successful trade which withstood all financial crises during its existence. This business continued for twelve years under the name of J. M. Hastings. In 1901, Mr. Hastings, wishing to lighten his burden of responsibilities, formed the J. M. Hastings Lumber Company, of which he is president. He is also the chief executive of the Commercial Sash & Door Company and of the Pittsburg-Honduras Company, a director in the Moreland Trust Company, the Valley Water Company, the Youngstown Street Railway Company, the Bellaire Bridge Company, the Pittsburg Plate Glass Company and the McClure Timber Company. He was president of the late Queen & Crescent Company, is the president of the Davison Lumber Company, Limited, of Nova Scotia, and is a member of the Duquesne, Union and Monongahela clubs of Pittsburg.

Mr. Hastings was married in 1886 to Miss Katherine Brown, of Jefferson county, Pennsylvania, and in a few short years was left a widower. In 1895 Mr. Hastings married Miss Mary E. Gillespie, sister of D. L. Gillespie. He resides with his wife and three daughters on North Highland avenue in one of the handsomest homes in that district of beautiful residences. In religion he is a consistent member of the Presbyterian Church; in politics he has always voted for the "best man" regardless of partisanship, except in national elections, when he votes the straight Republican ticket.

Nothwithstanding his devotion to business he finds time to inform himself on all municipal and civic affairs, and to enjoy the comfort and culture of his home as well as the company of his friends.

LIBRARY
OF THE
UNIVERSITY
OF
CALIFORNIA

Edward V. Babcock

Graduates of the Michigan lumbering school can be found in every section of the country, and even the East has gone to it for some of the most successful men in the ranks of lumberdom. Edward Vose Babcock was born January 31, 1864, at Fulton, New York. He worked on his father's farm in the summer time and in the winter attended school until seventeen years of age, when he began to teach school. Arriving at his majority he started west with the deliberate intention of learning the lumber business from the ground up. He began work with the Robinson Bros. Lumber Company, at Detroit, Michigan, as a lumber shover. Two years later he secured a position as inspector and shipper with Henry Stephens & Co., at St. Helen, Michigan. A year later he became salesman for Switzer & Eastwood, of Bay City, Michigan, selling their white pine for three years in Ohio, Pennsylvania, West Virginia, Maryland and New Jersey.

January 1, 1890, the present firm of E. V. Babcock & Co. was established in Pittsburg, Pennsylvania, the "company" being E. V. Babcock's brother, Fred R. Babcock. A carload business was first essayed, being well adapted to the consuming needs of that heavy manufacturing district and also requiring at the outset no more than the limited amount of capital which the brothers had for investment. Slowly the capital grew, and along with it the list of customers and the volume of annual sales. In 1899 the firm handled lumber, and its equivalent in shingles and lath, amounting to 120,000,000 feet.

In 1898, the Babcock Lumber Company was incorporated with E. V. Babcock as president and F. R. Babcock as secretary and treasurer. A standard gage railroad was constructed and each year it is extended farther into the timber. Logging camps were put into operation, managed by the company, and around the mill grew up a thriving town called Ashtola. The hum of the saws continues without cessation night or day the year around, and 450 men are given steady employment.

This is the business to which E. V. Babcock has of late years given practically his entire time. Four-fifths of the stock of the Babcock Lumber Company is owned by the partners in the firm of E. V. Babcock & Co., who handle the output of the mill. The original 7,000 acres of timber land soon were increased, by additional purchases, to 34,000 acres, conservatively estimated at 400,000,000 feet of stumpage, and all tributary to the Ashtola plant.

In 1901 the Babcock Lumber Company became the operator of two other band mills in Pennsylvania, purchasing outright the entire town of Arrow, in the same county with Ashtola, together with a new saw mill of 70,000 feet daily capacity, 8,000,000 feet of lumber in pile and in log and 60,000,000 feet of standing timber. Almost simultaneously a mill property at Foustwell was acquired and improved by the installation of a modern band machine, giving the Babcock Lumber Company an annual output of over 50,000,000 feet, principally the famous Pennsylvania hemlock.

This, however, is but a fraction of the business annually handled by the selling concern, E. V. Babcock & Co. April 2, 1901, the Babcock Brothers Lumber Company was incorporated in the state of Georgia for the development of 30,000 acres of choice timber land estimated to contain 200,000,000 to 250,000,000 feet of the finest timber in the state. The new town of Babcock was founded upon Lake Boykin, in the center of the timber tract, about twenty miles from the Alabama line and sixty miles from the Gulf, and a mill, with a daily capacity of 75,000 feet, is operated entirely upon flooring and ceiling, with rift-sawed flooring as a specialty. The entire output of the mill is marketed by E. V. Babcock & Co. Of the Babcock Brothers Lumber Company, F. R. Babcock is president and E. V. Babcock is secretary, treasurer and general manager.

In all these various interests, E. V. Babcock is the executive head, although he leaves almost all of the affairs of E. V. Babcock & Co. to his brothers, F. R. and O. H. Babcock, whose high abilities in salesmanship here have full scope. E. V. Babcock devotes himself chiefly to the manufacturing enterprises, being assisted at Ashtola by a fourth brother, C. L. Babcock. A great quartet are the Babcock brothers, and E. V. Babcock is their chief. A stalwart, clean cut, genial, lovable young man, he makes friends fully as easily as he makes money, and his best friends are those from whom he has made his money, because the business relations have been profitable to them as well as to him.

E. V. Babcock, while still a young man, has not only numbered himself among the millionaire lumbermen of the country, but has laid carefully and gradually a solid foundation for even greater operations in the future.

His progress has been along well defined lines and his operations, while varied, have all been in connection with the eastern trade. His Michigan experience was largely with lumber destined for eastern shipment. His first venture as a salesman had to do with portions of the eastern territory. As a wholesaler in Pittsburg his trade lay largely to the east of that city, and his manufacturing enterprises in Pennsylvania and Georgia all had reference to the demands of that great territory lying on the eastern slope of the Alleghanies and embracing Pennsylvania, New York, New Jersey and the New England states. A business of such magnitude as that conducted by Mr. Babcock leads out naturally in many directions, but by basing it on the requirements of the region with whose needs he is familiar and in which he is so favorably known, he insures himself a business stability which is not always secured by those who seek from the beginning to cover too wide a territory.

This great wholesale lum
a matter of evolution. It w
mission lumber salesmen m
ually and in a limited way th
of lumber, which he resold
single car purchases the wh
in block of the wholesale t
from the large manufacturi
[illegible] and Minnesota.

Afterward yellow pine
trade and the Pittsburg wh
large blocks of these wood
larger and larger buyers of
Virginia and Michigan. T
to be a very catholic one
American woods.

One of the oldest and
lumber houses is that of E

FRED RAYMOND BABCOCK

Fred R. Babcock

The Pittsburg district is one that produces scarcely any lumber and yet it is the wholesale distributer of so vast a quantity as to be exceeded by few lumber centers in the country. The Pittsburg wholesale and manufacturing contingent includes but a little more than a score of dealers, yet in 1902 this coterie of energetic and enterprising lumbermen marketed approximately 1,200,000,000 feet. While the Pittsburg wholesale lumber trade to a large degree confines its distribution to the Pittsburg district, these figures in no wise represent the consuming demand of that district, as scores of foreign lumber houses either maintain offices in Pittsburg or through their traveling representatives regularly canvass the trade.

This great wholesale lumber business of Pittsburg has been a matter of evolution. It was practically started by the commission lumber salesmen more than twenty years ago. Gradually and in a limited way the commission man became a buyer of lumber, which he resold in the Pittsburg district. From single car purchases the wholesalers eventually bought lumber in block of the wholesale trade along the chain of lakes and from the large manufacturing concerns of Michigan, Wisconsin and Minnesota.

Afterward yellow pine and cypress became factors in the trade and the Pittsburg wholesalers branched out and bought large blocks of these woods. All this time they have been larger and larger buyers of hemlock from Pennsylvania, West Virginia and Michigan. The trade in this section has grown to be a very catholic one and today comprises a full line of American woods.

One of the oldest and foremost of Pittsburg's wholesale lumber houses is that of E. V. Babcock & Co., established

January 1, 1890, by F. R. and E. V. Babcock. It is a concern that by dint of industry, honorable dealing and great enterprise has built up a trade approximating 130,000,000 feet a year, and since inception has had a continuously prosperous career. The active head of the business is Fred Raymond Babcock.

Mr. Babcock was born at Fulton, Oswego county, New York, April 16, 1865, of good old fashioned Yankee parentage. He was brought up on a farm and at the age of twenty-two made his first venture in commercial pursuits by becoming a general utility man for B. B. & R. Knight, the great cotton manufacturing institution of Providence, Rhode Island. In the spring of 1888 he severed his connection with the Knights and went to Bay City, Michigan, at the suggestion of his brother, where he found employment with Ross, Bradley & Co., of that city, at $1.25 a day. He served his apprenticeship and gained a practical knowledge of the lumber business, filling various positions from dock walloper to that of shipper. At the beginning of 1890 he joined the firm of Switzer & Eastwood, of West Bay City, Michigan, as shipper and was three months later sent into the Pittsburg district to assist his brother in selling lumber for that firm.

As before stated, the firm of E. V. Babcock & Co. was organized at Pittsburg at the opening of 1890. From the first day the business was a success, 1,300 carloads of lumber having been sold the first year. F. R. Babcock was the chief salesman of the concern and eventually became its executive head.

In 1898 Mr. Babcock, in connection with his brothers, organized the Babcock Lumber Company, an independent concern, and made a purchase of 7,000 acres of hemlock timber land near Ashtola, Pennsylvania. This expanse of timber property has gradually been increased to 34,000 acres.

The original Somerset county mill—a Filer & Stowell single band—has been supplemented by an Allis double cutting telescopic band, and by the purchase of the single band mill plant of John Curry & Son, at Arrow, Pennsylvania, and the mill plant of the Cambria Lumber Company at Foustwell, Pennsylvania. The Arrow plant has been reconstructed and converted into a double band and gang mill. During 1904 the company produced approximately 200,000 feet of lumber daily, largely hemlock.

In 1901 the Babcock interests organized a third concern known as the Babcock Brothers Lumber Company and bought 30,000 acres of virgin longleaf timber near Bainbridge, Georgia, on the Georgia, Florida & Alabama railroad, where they constructed during 1902 one of the most complete yellow pine plants in the South, comprising an Allis double cutting telescopic band and rift gang mill, dry kilns, planing mill and stock sheds. In 1903 they added to this a timber mill, timber surfacer and dry kilns, and they now have a capacity of 25,000,000 feet annually, making rift flooring a specialty.

Mr. Babcock is secretary and treasurer of the Babcock Lumber Company and president of the Babcock Brothers Lumber Company. He has been president of the Pittsburg Wholesale Lumber Dealers' Association, not because he wished the office but because his confreres were unanimous in their choice. He is a director of the National Wholesale Lumber Dealers' Association, a member of its executive committee and a director of the Federal National Bank of Pittsburg, Pennsylvania.

In addition to his active participation in the lumber trade, Fred Raymond Babcock is a broadgaged citizen, with close relationship to public affairs. He is a worker in the Merchants' & Manufacturers' Association, an organization formed in Pittsburg in 1900 to look after the general commercial interests of the cities of Allegheny county and to keep outside merchants and businessmen in touch with Pittsburg and her interests. Mr. Babcock is a member of the association's executive committee and is on its board of directors. He is chairman of the entertainment and reception committees of the association, which promises to be one of the strongest organizations of the kind in this country. He married in 1895 Miss Frances St. Ledger Jacobs, of Charleston, West Virginia. Miss Jacobs was a musician not unknown to fame, as she was West Virginia's prima donna at the Chicago world's fair in 1893. Two children have been born to them.

In appearance Fred Raymond Babcock is a man of youthful features and stalwart proportions. He is an indefatigable worker. It is seldom that a call can be made at his offices, 910-914 Frick building, and Mr. Babcock not be found at his desk, with a welcoming smile and cordial grasp of the hand for every visitor. His manner is the personification of frankness and cordiality, and perhaps it is to these attributes more than to any other cause that his popularity and success can be traced.

LIBRARY
OF THE
UNIVERSITY
OF
CALIFORNIA

John B. Flint

The Pittsburg lumber district contains an exceptional number of successful men who are young. One who has attained a high position among them is John B. Flint.

Mr. Flint was born at Rochester, New York, July 31, 1853. His parents were both natives of Cambridgeshire, England. They came to America in 1851, during the great London exposition, and settled in Rochester, where his father pursued his trade of cabinet making. They remained there until 1855 when they removed with their family to the flourishing little town of Stouffville, Canada, near Toronto. There young Flint attended the common and high schools and remained until he was fifteen years old, establishing a reputation as an apt student and acquiring the rudimentary knowledge which afterward enabled him to cope with the exigencies of the business in which he has become an important factor. He then entered into factory work as an engineer in a rake-bending and turning factory, where he was employed for two years. He learned the turning trade thoroughly, giving it his entire attention for the next five years. In 1869 his father opened a planing mill and sash factory where young Flint was employed in an important position until 1879, when his father moved to Toronto.

Mr. Flint secured a position with the S. Hadley Lumber Company at Chatham, Canada, working in this company's planing mill for two years. He was engaged at the munificent salary of $8 a week. The cost of living in Chatham, or in any town of similar size at that time, cannot be compared with that of the present day, but the fact that Mr. Flint saved $100 of his first year's salary may "point a moral or adorn a tale" for the gilded youth of today. This trait of thrift has predominated throughout Mr. Flint's career and has proven itself to be one of the vital qualifications by virtue of which he attained success.

Mr. Flint's next step in the business world was, as always before, higher than the last. He engaged with H. A. Patterson & Co., of Chatham, as salesman and yard superintendent, serving in this combined capacity for two years. Here he assimilated the additional knowledge necessary to the education of the lumber dealer. After his service with Patterson & Co., Mr. Flint was employed by the J. Piggott Lumber Company as manager and superintendent, and such was his efficiency in that position that he was retained by the Piggott company for twelve years at an ever increasing salary. When he decided to leave Canada for the States he was earning the largest salary of any man in Chatham.

An inviting offer from one of the most promising young lumber firms of Pittsburg—E. V. Babcock & Co.—was accepted by Mr. Flint and preparation was immediately begun for his departure from the land of "Our Lady of Snows." Mr. Flint had been too important a citizen of the town of Chatham, however, too vitally interested in the development of its industrial and civic resources, too prominent in his efforts for the advancement of the good of that busy little town, to be allowed to leave unnoticed. His departure was an occasion at which every member of the community tendered his regret at the loss, and as a tangible tribute to Mr. Flint's worth the citizens presented him with a purse of $500 in gold, a beautifully written testimonial, and to Mrs. Flint a gold watch and chain. Mr. Flint had served faithfully for many years as the secretary of the Liberal Association (the liberal party) and as secretary of the Free Library Board of Chatham, and his interest and zeal in these affairs made his departure an almost irreparable loss.

Still his guiding star pointed to the States, and September, 1892, found him established in Pittsburg with E. V. Babcock & Co., as salesman in the Pittsburg territory. In the three years in which Mr. Flint served in this capacity he secured for himself the reputation of being able to sell more lumber than any other man in the vicinity.

Realizing the vastness of the future of Pittsburg's lumber industry, Mr. Flint determined to embark for himself in his chosen field, and in January, 1896, the firm of Flint, Erving & Lindsay was formed, with offices in the Ferguson building. The enterprise was prosperous from the start. The lines handled by the new firm comprised all kinds of lumber—white pine, yellow pine, hemlock, poplar, hardwoods, shingles and lath; and the retail yard trade was catered to exclusively. After five years of steady climbing toward good fortune Messrs. Flint, Erving and Stoner purchased the interests of J. H. Lindsay, and the firm name was changed to Flint, Erving & Stoner. This company is a member of the National Wholesale Lumber Dealers' Association and of the Pittsburg Wholesale Lumber Dealers' Association and is one of the most valued firms on the rosters of these two organizations.

In 1874 Mr. Flint married Miss Ruth S. Revis, of Markham, Ontario, and five children were born to them—Dr. Willard Flint, a graduate of the University of Michigan; Miss Minnie, a graduate of the Female Seminary of St. Catherines, Ontario; Miss Edith, a graduate of De Mille College, Oshawa, Ontario; George, now attending the University of Pennsylvania at Philadelphia, and Stanley, attending Cornell University at Ithaca, New York. Mr. Flint with his family resides in a beautiful home on Hill street, Wilkinsburg, Pennsylvania, a borough adjoining Pittsburg. Their summers are spent at their charming country place at Jackson's Point, on Lake Simcoe, Ontario. Mr. Flint owns considerable real estate in Chatham as well as in Pittsburg. He is vice president of a leading manufacturing company of Pittsburg and is a director and owns stock in many other local enterprises. He is a member of a number of societies, the Ancient Order of United Workmen, Ancient Order of Foresters, Independent Order of Odd Fellows and others. Mr. Flint's tastes are decidedly of a domestic order and preclude his being a clubman.

WILLIAM DAVID JOHNSTON

William D. Johnston

All businessmen are interested in every experiment which involves a different application of old principles or the exercise of new ones. A certain lumber handling institution in this country has by its novel methods attracted the attention of the trade at large. This business house is comparatively young, as it was established during the period of business depression following the panic of 1893, but it has steadily grown by the use of a system which is unique in lumber history. It is an example of selling ability coupled with the use of new business methods. This concern is the American Lumber & Manufacturing Company, of Pittsburg, Pennsylvania.

The presiding genius of the institution, the man who is largely responsible for its methods and for its success, who has furnished the motive power as well as directed its course, is William David Johnston, born at Pittsburg, August 9, 1866. His parents were natives of Ireland and emigrated to Canada in 1864. His father was employed there as a woodsman for a year and then went to Pittsburg to engage in the window glass business, an industry that was then in its infancy in that city. W. D. Johnston graduated from the commercial department of the Pittsburg high school at the age of thirteen, the youngest in a class of forty-two. Almost immediately, in December, 1879, he entered the employ of the Davis-Chambers Lead Company as office boy. He became in turn bookkeeper, assistant manager and then general manager of the office. The Davis-Chambers Lead Company was merged into the National Lead Company in 1891 and Mr. Johnston was appointed chief auditor for the six concerns which made up the Pittsburg branch of the National company.

Mr. Johnston's active connection with the lumber industry

began in June, 1892, after he had decided that it afforded him a better field and a more promising future than did service with a great corporation. In 1892, therefore, he became identified with the retail lumber business of the William Anderson Company, of Pittsburg, and in 1893 he purchased a controlling interest in this company and became its general manager. In the latter part of 1894 it was determined to close out the retail business conducted by this concern and to engage in the wholesale trade exclusively. The name was changed to the American Lumber & Manufacturing Company, which made a notable beginning as a wholesaler, for its business in 1895 amounted to 20,000,000 feet, gradually increasing to a little over 115,000,000 feet in 1899. At first the operations of the company were confined to Pittsburg, but now they reach into every state in the Union and to Canada, Mexico and Europe. The company handles all kinds of hard and soft wood lumber and veneers.

The American Lumber & Manufacturing Company has a white pine department with an office at Menominee, Michigan, which ships about 150 cars a month. Its yellow pine department at Montgomery, Alabama, ships over 100 cars a month. The North Carolina pine department has an office at Norfolk, Virginia. The hardwood department has a branch at Buchanan, West Virginia, which ships from seventy-five to 100 cars a month. The oak timber, car timber and export oak shipments average 100 cars a month. Pennsylvania hemlock and hardwoods are handled from the Pittsburg office and aggregate 100 cars a month. In addition seventy-five carloads of cypress and thirty-five carloads of redwood are handled every month by the Pittsburg office.

One of the valuable features of the management of this company is an organization within its working force called the "board of managers," of which W. D. Johnston is chairman. The men of this organization constitute the executive board of the company and outline its general policy. By this method of conducting a large and varied business the different departments are kept closely in touch with each other and there is a personal intimacy among the individuals which brings results that would probably be impossible under other circumstances. The American Lumber & Manufacturing Company sells chiefly by mail, fully 85 percent of the sales of the company being made by this method. When the company first attempted the sale of lumber in this way, serious misgivings as to its practicability were felt. It was then that the superior qualifications of Mr. Johnston as the head of a great enterprise were evidenced. He and his confreres evolved a system for conducting such a business that has been found to be nearly perfect.

Mr. Johnston is also president of the Florala Saw Mill Company, of Paxton, Florida, owning 300,000,000 feet of virgin longleaf yellow pine. Its capacity is 150,000 feet a day.

W. D. Johnston's success is measured by the prosperity of the American Lumber & Manufacturing Company, of which he has been a vital factor almost since his induction into the lumber business. He is entitled to a large share of credit, as in the good fortunes of this company, which has not only been a wise buyer but a clever seller, he is the moving spirit. Its capital was limited at the start, but a steady growth in the volume of its business, coupled with almost uniformly profitable results, inspired confidence in the trade and built up both its actual capital and its credit. To accomplish this by methods which differ materially from those commonly in use, required a man of brain, originality, determination and executive power. The remarkable success of this company proves that W. D. Johnston is such a man.

LIBRARY
OF THE
UNIVERSITY
OF
CALIFORNIA

WILLIAM McCLELLAN RITTER

William M. Ritter

Within the space of a very few years William McClellan Ritter, of Columbus, Ohio, has made for himself a place in the history of the lumber industry as one of the foremost hardwood lumbermen of the United States. His achievement is the result of careful planning, indomitable industry and sagacious management.

Mr. Ritter was born on a Pennsylvania farm near Hughesville in 1864, and was brought up on that farm until he was eighteen years old. He acquired an elementary education in the schools of his native state. His first business venture was the purchase and operation of a small thresher of the old fashioned type in the community in which he was born. Afterward, for several years, he conducted a small country hotel. This was the extent of his business experience until he entered the lumber trade.

In 1891 he was induced by Colonel Polhemus, a successful Pennsylvania lumber operator, to visit West Virginia. In company they inspected the southern part of that state. At that time this section of the United States was one of the wildest and crudest east of the Mississippi river. The Norfolk & Western railroad, which now traverses this part of the country, was not completed to Cincinnati and Columbus, but stopped short in the Pocahontas coal fields. Mr. Ritter was quick to anticipate the opportunities that the future offered in this vast undeveloped section and fully appreciated the value of the markets that would be opened up on the completion of the railway system to the consuming regions east and west.

He returned to Pennsylvania, disposed of his small holdings and went back to West Virginia with about $2,000 in ready money, with a clear and well defined plan for his future and an abiding faith in his ability to turn conditions and circumstances to his advantage. He entered the lumber business as half owner of a small portable mill, in partnership with W. J. Denman. This mill was located near Bluefield, West Virginia, on a small tract of poplar and oak timber which the firm had purchased. After a year or two Mr. Denman died and his interest in the business was absorbed by Mr. Ritter. From the very start the lumber business grew and was prosperous. He worked as an individual operator in lumber up to 1902, when he organized the W. M. Ritter Lumber Company, which since that time has resolved itself into one of the largest (possibly the largest) hardwood manufacturing institutions in the United States. Mr. Ritter went to West Virginia, as before stated, handicapped only by a paucity of capital. He had youth, a splendid physique, strength, courage and integrity of purpose. Somehow or somewhere in his early career he had learned the inestimable value of system and organization in successful business enterprises and he had learned the paramount advantage of doing things well. Organization and system are the essentials of Mr. Ritter's commercial success.

The timber holdings of the Ritter corporation, or such portions of them as are now in operation, consist approximately of 1,000,000,000 feet of standing timber. The corporation, or individual components thereof, owns other undeveloped timber properties which will probably extend the present operations to approximately 100,000,000 feet of lumber annually for a period of at least fifteen years.

Mr. Ritter's principal office and home are at Columbus, Ohio, and his lumber operations are carried on in the extreme southwestern section of West Virginia, the extreme northwestern corner of Virginia, and the extreme eastern tip of Kentucky, the whole lying on the southern watershed of the Tug fork of the Big Sandy river. Within this area are operated five band saw mills and several portable circular mills. These mills are employed almost exclusively in the conversion into lumber of the splendid yellow poplar and white and red oak of the region. But in addition to this series of plants, the company of which Mr. Ritter is the head is an extensive operator in white pine, with a sprinkling of hemlock, in western North Carolina.

Mr. Ritter is not only distinguished as a successful lumberman but has achieved great success in the promotion of organization in the hardwood industry of the country. He was one of the principal movers in the organization of the Hardwood Manufacturers' Association of the United States and was its first president. Later he was distinguished as being the chairman of the executive board of that association. The resultant good to the hardwood manufacturing industry that has been brought about by this association is inestimable, and he is still carrying forward plans looking toward the betterment of hardwood conditions.

As a part of the ramifications of the organization of Mr. Ritter's individual enterprises, he has widened and extended the trade of his corporation, not only to all parts of the United States but abroad as well. For a number of years he has been a prominent exporter of American wood goods to Great Britain and the continent. He has introduced American methods in the disposal of his product abroad. With that end in view he has organized a corps of salesmen, part English and part American, with an experienced English manager, and opened his principal foreign office at Liverpool. At London he has taken a long time lease of a dock, upon which he has built a storage house, and there receives direct from the steamers his American grown and sawed lumber. While a large portion of his foreign dispositions is sold previous to shipment and arrival, he maintains a stock of American woods at London in order to be able not only to show the buyer exactly what he is to receive in future shipments but also to fill orders for stock upon demand if it is required.

Mr. Ritter and his wife live in a beautiful home at Ohio's capital city. The only interest the former has outside of his home and business life, is in a stable of fine road horses which he owns. Mr. Ritter is of stranger's first impression of especial measure, integrity of nature.

Robert H. Jenks

The lumber operator who, with headquarters elsewhere, consigns direct from the mill to the retailer without bringing the product to a central yard to be reassorted is one of the later evolutions of the trade.

It is of the foremost man in this line that this article is written—Robert Henry Jenks, president of the Robert H. Jenks Lumber Company, of Cleveland, Ohio.

Mr. Jenks was born at Crown Point, New York, July 26, 1854. His father was Benjamin L. Jenks, a pioneer lumberman, farmer and hotel keeper of Vermont and New Hampshire. In 1856, when Robert was two years of age, his father moved with his family to St. Clair, Michigan, buying a farm and putting in several winters in lumbering operations on the Huron shore. The family next moved to Forester, Sanilac county, the senior Jenks being connected with Smith, Kelly & Co. in their logging business and saw mill interests. The family lived at Forester until Robert H. Jenks was six or eight years of age. A few years later Benjamin L. Jenks went to the John L. Woods mill, five miles below Forester.

When Robert H. Jenks was fourteen years old his father died and his mother returned to the farm at St. Clair, young Jenks engaging his services for that winter to Brad & Smithbeck, of Tawas, who were engaged in lumbering. When eighteen years old he went to Cleveland, Ohio, and entering the employ of Woods, Perry & Co. developed such business ability and grew into such importance to the institution that when the firm was reorganized in 1886 it was styled Woods, Jenks & Co., and Robert H. Jenks became managing partner. This house went out of business in 1892, and in July, 1893, Mr. Jenks began business under his individual name as a buyer and seller of forest products. Having in mind a distinct theory of business, Mr. Jenks proceeded to put the theory into practice. He immediately began assorting stock where produced and distributing it to the trade direct. Mr. Jenks himself confesses that when he entered this line of trade he had no idea of the enormous development possible in it.

The growth of the business was so large from the very start that Mr. Jenks found it necessary two years later to organize the Robert H. Jenks Lumber Company, of which he was president and treasurer, John H. Jenks, his cousin, vice president and Samuel R. Griener secretary. During the progress of a vastly increasing business the officers of this company have been ably assisted by A. B. Lambert, now the treasurer of the Robert H. Jenks Lumber Company, who has acted in the capacity of head bookkeeper and cashier. While the first year's transactions of the Robert H. Jenks Lumber Company showed a business of about 15,000,000 feet, within five years the volume of lumber handled exceeded 115,000,000 feet. Of this immense quantity, by far the larger part is shipped to consumers by rail direct, from points of production.

The interests of the Robert H. Jenks Lumber Company involve a very wide line of lumber production. It is one of the largest handlers of hemlock, in both lumber and shingles, in the United States. The company is the buyer of the total product of more than a score of hemlock mills in Michigan and Pennsylvania. White pine and norway lumber are other important items in the company's handlings. In the sale and distribution of yellow pine, both longleaf and shortleaf, it is the most important house in the middle West. In poplar and various hardwoods also it is an important factor.

In addition to these many and important enterprises, Mr. Jenks is heavily interested in the manufacture of yellow pine. In 1901 he organized the Tremont Lumber Company, at Tremont, Louisiana, and became its president; W. G. Collar was vice president and H. H. Denison secretary and treasurer. The Tremont Lumber Company has about 600,-000,000 feet of yellow pine timber, from which it was in 1904 cutting at its two mills at the rate of from 36,000,000 to 40,-000,000 feet a year. The Tremont Lumber Company owns also the Tremont & Gulf railroad, a standard gage line that runs from Tremont a distance of twenty-five miles into the timber, along which several towns have been established that contribute a handsome volume of general traffic. This road was from its inception the work of Robert H. Jenks, and he is its president and general manager. It has nothing to do with the logging road which the company operates, but is a traffic line pure and simple. Mr. Jenks expects to extend the Tremont & Gulf road into a traffic line fifty miles long and of unusual importance, considering its short length.

Outside of his distinction in the lumber business, in his particular line of which he is dean, Mr. Jenks is intimately associated with three important Cleveland banking institutions, being a director of the Union National Bank of Cleveland, the Central Trust Company and the Colonial National Bank. He is on the loan committees of the two last named. In addition he is president and a director of the Lake Erie Lumber Company and of the Cuyahoga Lumber Company, two large retail lumber concerns of Cleveland. Of course Mr. Jenks is a Hoo-Hoo, and a loyal one. It is largely due to his efforts that the concatenations held in Cleveland have been attended with such success. He is also a member of the Union Club.

As to the private life of Robert H. Jenks: He was married to Miss Clara Brampton, of Cleveland, twenty-four years ago, and has twin daughters who are now eighteen years old. There is a well defined legend that when "Bob" Jenks, as everybody affectionately calls him, was a small boy he sat for his portrait. The man who engineered the daguerreotype machine suggested that Robert "look pleasant." That smile of healthy and hearty good nature has never left his face. It is a smile that is at once winning and infectious.

In 1901 the company

JOHN HENRY JENKS

John H. Jenks

Beloved as a good fellow and admired as a businessman is John Henry Jenks, of Cleveland, Ohio, vice president of the Robert H. Jenks Lumber Company, of that city. Mr. Jenks was born at St. Clair, Michigan, December 4, 1866. His father, Robert H. Jenks, was an old time Saginaw valley lumber operator. Young Jenks received a common school education at the little village of his birth on the St. Clair river and entered the lumber business in 1885, when he went with Woods, Perry & Co., of Cleveland, of which firm his cousin, Robert H. Jenks, was then chief employee. Mr. Jenks, during 1887, acted as white pine buyer for Woods, Perry & Co. at Muskegon, Michigan. When the firm of Woods, Perry & Co. was changed to Woods, Jenks & Co., by the admission of Robert H. Jenks in 1886, John H. Jenks continued as an employee of the firm. He was a general utility man, acting as buyer, salesman, or in whatever capacity his time and talents could be used to the best advantage.

In 1895 the Robert H. Jenks Lumber Company was incorporated, John H. Jenks becoming vice president. The success of this great lumber company, now one of the foremost in the United States, has been commensurate with the ability of its projectors. For several years it has manufactured and bought and sold an average of more than 10,000,000 feet of lumber each month. Its handlings cover practically the entire range of American wood growth; it is regarded as an important factor in the distribution and sale of both Pennsylvania and Michigan hemlock; is well known in the white pine trade, and is even better known in the yellow pine industry.

In 1901 the company made an extensive yellow pine timber purchase in Louisiana and organized an allied institution known as the Tremont Lumber Company. A large mill, dry kilns and planing mills were built at Tremont and extensive logging operations installed. This company is a growing and successful one.

In connection with these two enterprises John H. Jenks still modestly continues in the position of general utility man. If an important purchase is contemplated, he is the one selected to make it. If a large sale is to be negotiated, he is the man who does it. He is an extremely busy man and his work involves a vast amount of travel. His friends meet him one day in New York, the next week in St. Louis; one week at Duluth, the next week at New Orleans. Notwithstanding the immense amount of work he does, there never is an occasion on which he has not time to greet a friend or acquaintance and say a kindly word to him.

Besides Mr. Jenks' connection with the Robert H. Jenks Lumber Company and the Tremont Lumber Company he is also largely interested in the Lake Erie Lumber Company, an important retail institution at Cleveland, of which he is a director. Another concern in which he holds the position of director is the Commercial & Savings Bank of St. Clair, Michigan, one of the foremost financial institutions of that section of the state.

Mr. Jenks married March 27, 1900, Miss Mary Davidson. Mr. and Mrs. Jenks occupy an enviable social position in Cleveland and their home is the center of a circle of Cleveland's best people.

Personally Mr. Jenks is a tall man with square shoulders and of robust build. He has a kindly eye and greets friends with a hearty grasp of the hand. He is thoroughly likable and probably has the largest array of warm personal friends of any man engaged in the lumber industry in the country. He is not only an ideal good fellow but an ideal businessman as well. Friend or stranger cannot receive the hearty grasp of the hand of John Jenks without feeling at once that here is a man of earnest life, warm heart and deep feeling, whose kindly nature has the simplicity of truth. Much of the prosperity of John Jenks is due to this very simplicity of purpose. In all of the conflicts with individuals and interests that the successful businessman must have, he has always been just, because he is big enough to see from the other man's point of view as well as from his own. He has nothing in common with those who look back with regret or try to pierce the future. He lives the present honestly, consistently; each day's battle is ended with that day. In this way John Jenks has been able to do more work that counted than the majority of men, and he has not only added to the sum of American wealth—which is very different from American riches—but he has also added to the total of American manhood.

LIBRARY
OF THE
UNIVERSITY
OF
CALIFORNIA

was six years old and [illegible]
1831 the family moved [illegible]
man continued his stu[illegible]
entered business life a[illegible]
in Cincinnati. Before [illegible]
Martha Hart, of Penn[illegible]
qualities of he[illegible] and [illegible]

In [illegible] Mr. [illegible]
Dunlap organized the [illegible]
in the local lumber [illegible]
but was [illegible]
York and [illegible]
separated [illegible]
business as co[illegible]
between them [illegible]

In 1850 T[illegible]

Jethro Mitchell

Few men have contributed more to the history of the lumber industry of America than the late Jethro Mitchell, of Cincinnati. He was among the pioneers in the moving, sorting and distributing of Michigan white pine lumber in Ohio.

Mr. Mitchell was born on the Island of Nantucket, Massachusetts, August 17, 1817, and died in 1895. His forbears reached this country from Scotland in 1630 and for many generations the elder son was named Richard. Five generations ago one of the Mitchells married a Starbuck. Among the Starbucks "Jethro" was a family cognomen, and it came to be a patronymic in the Mitchell family. The last to bear the name is Jethro G. Mitchell, of Toledo, Ohio, eldest son of the late Jethro Mitchell.

Mr. Mitchell's parents moved to New York City when he was six years old and remained there about seven years. In 1831 the family moved to Cincinnati, Ohio, where the young man continued his studies in the public schools. He first entered business life as an employee in a wholesale grocery in Cincinnati. Before reaching his majority he married Miss Martha Hart, of Pennsylvania, to whose tactfulness, sterling qualities of heart and mind and devotion Mr. Mitchell owed much of his success.

In 1838 Mr. Mitchell borrowed $5,000 and with James Dunlap organized the firm of Dunlap & Mitchell and engaged in the local lumber trade of Cincinnati. The concern's lumber was secured chiefly in Pennsylvania and western New York and rafted down the Ohio river. When the partners separated after three years, both continued in the lumber business as competitors in adjoining yards; yet the relations between them were always friendly until death separated them.

In 1850 Thomas C. Rowland, a former employee, joined

Jethro Mitchell in business under the name of Mitchell & Rowland and established a yard on Vine street, Cincinnati. The firm also had yards on Colerain Pike, on Freeman street and in the Mill Creek section of the city.

In 1862 Mitchell & Rowland organized a yard at Sandusky, Ohio, receiving lumber from the St. Clair river, Saginaw bay and Huron shore districts, which was shipped to interior points on the pioneer Ohio railroad known as the Mad River road; but they soon after removed to docks along Swan creek at Toledo, seeking the better distributing facilities afforded by the Miami & Erie canal. In 1866 the firm was reorganized into the Mitchell & Rowland Lumber Company and made extensive purchases of undeveloped water front along the Maumee river, which it docked and improved so that it afforded facilities for storing more than 100,000,000 feet of lumber. For many years this was known as the lumber district of Toledo.

The company originally began to move white pine from the upper St. Clair and Black river districts by vessel, but during the latter part of the Civil War tonnage became very scarce and freights advanced to $7.50 to $10 a thousand feet. Mr. Mitchell, being familiar with the system of rafting lumber on the Ohio river, for several seasons utilized this system with success in moving lumber from Michigan to his Toledo yard. With the reduction of lake freights to a normal amount, however, he returned to transporting lumber by steam and tow barges.

The company eventually built a saw mill at Toledo to utilize the crib timbers employed in building lumber rafts. This timber was soon afterward augmented by log rafts from the Black river and other points, which were made up of full length trees and converted at the Toledo mill into logs of the lengths demanded by the company's orders. The saw mill business increased with the distributing trade and the milling plant was enlarged several times. After the Toledo mill had exhausted the supply of white pine tributary to it, the mill plant was sold. For years the Mitchell & Rowland Lumber

Company had an annual output of about 50,000,000 feet, one year reaching 60,000,000 feet, and the company was recognized as the largest producer of square timber on the lakes. During 1904 the entire plant was destroyed by fire and the company retired from the white pine distributing business.

Mr. Mitchell early foresaw the value of white pine stumpage, of which he became a large purchaser. In 1869, with Wellington R. Burt, of Saginaw, he organized the firm of W. R. Burt & Co., which continued until 1879, when Mr. Mitchell purchased Mr. Burt's interest and reorganized it, with the late John A. Hamilton and the late W. C. McClure, as Hamilton, McClure & Co. While Messrs. Hamilton and McClure had an interest in the enterprise, the capital was furnished entirely by Mr Mitchell. This concern continued until the death of Mr. Hamilton, when it was again reorganized as Mitchell & McClure and continued business at Saginaw until its timber resources were exhausted, when extensive white pine timber purchases were made in northern Minnesota and the business perpetuated at Duluth. The largest and best equipped mill on the lakes was built by the firm at that place. It was sold, together with the timber, in 1903.

Of Mr. Mitchell's large family three sons and four daughters reached maturity, although of the sons, Jethro G. Mitchell, the eldest, was the only survivor at the time of his death. This son continued at the head of the enterprises established by his father.

Mr. Mitchell was the leader in numerous business enterprises. He was one of the founders of the original board of directors of the Ohio & Mississippi railroad, which now forms a part of the Baltimore & Ohio system. He was a man whose forethought ran ahead of his times, and it is recorded that he urged upon the Board of Directors of the Ohio & Mississippi railroad the desirability and feasibility of running through coaches from St. Louis to New York, at a time when the idea was scouted as chimerical. He was one of the organizers and a director of the Merchants' National Bank of Cincinnati. He was also the moving spirit in many small saw mill operations in southern Ohio and Indiana.

Mr. Mitchell was the architect of his own fortunes. He was dauntless in business enterprises. His ability to compass a vast amount of work and do it well was in full keeping with his ambition. His brain never ceased its activity. Originally necessity spurred his ambition, and later there was no commercial proposition too great for him to consider. He is described as having been fond of fun and anecdote, and although his temper was quickly aroused by any act he considered unjust, he was as quick to forgive as to condemn.

The capital involved in his many investments required the raising of immense sums of money, but he had the confidence of capitalists and was always able to secure the necessary funds.

Mr. Mitchell was much interested in the Presbyterian denomination and planned and superintended the building of the original Mt. Auburn Presbyterian Church at Cincinnati. On removing from Cincinnati to its suburb of Wyoming, he contributed liberally toward the building of the Presbyterian Church at that place, of which he was also a trustee. He was a most generous man. His known benefactions attest his kindness of heart and liberality and these would be still more emphasized if all his benevolences were known. It can truthfully be said of him that his "charity was as wide as want."

Even up to the close of his life Mr. Mitchell was a tremendous worker, though suffering from cataracts of the eyes and for long periods nearly blind. However, he never faltered in his work and in his service to others. He was an extremely modest man and was the kindest of husbands and fathers. He loved his home, which was at Cincinnati, with a paramount intensity, and his family was always first in his thoughts.

Mr. Mitchell's first wife died August 15, 1889, and he was married again, March 24, 1892, to Miss Helen Handy, of Cincinnati, who survived him. He died respected and beloved by all who knew him, and left behind an enviable record for probity, industry, acumen and kindliness.

RALPH A. LOVELAND

Ralph A. Loveland

The Saginaw valley has been peculiarly fortunate in the possession of men of exceptional ability in its chief industry—lumbering—for nearly a half century. No locality in America in proportion to population has been blessed by more men of great capacity for general affairs than has this district. The greater number of them were of New England and New York lineage, and they came into Michigan at an early date, naturally engaging in the lumber business because it offered the greatest returns for the capital and labor invested. In the Saginaw lumbering district, from 1850 to 1890, the period in which the industry most flourished, the lumbermen as a class were noted for their business capacity and virile citizenship. They were not only strong men in the industry in which they were engaged, but they were strong in all of those essentials of character which the great and growing West demanded. They were bold, broad gaged, public spirited men, who were engaged in large transactions and looked at things with a comprehensive vision. They laid the foundations of a prosperous and progressive community and made possible the splendid civilization that it now enjoys.

Ralph A. Loveland, the subject of this sketch, came into the Saginaw valley late in its period of lumber production, but he quickly took rank among his fellows, and his business capacity, his unblemished character and his helpful temperament won for him the unreserved respect and confidence of his neighbors and friends. In the history of the Saginaw valley his name is borne in loving memory. Not only is his personality impressed upon the community in which he once labored, but the story of his career is singled out as an example to later generations.

Mr. Loveland was born at Westport, New York, January

17, 1819. His father was a prominent owner and operator of shipping upon Lake Champlain and the Hudson river. His summers were spent on the lake and river and his winters in the public schools, and later in Essex Academy. He thus acquired the education of experience as well as of books. He gradually secured personal interests in the navigation business, which, in 1845, he consolidated with the interests of the Northern Transportation Company. He was for several years connected with that company.

In 1857 Mr. Loveland formed a partnership with D. L. White and S. W. Barnard and opened a lumber business in Albany under the name of White, Loveland & Co. The firm became the consignees of the Gilmours, then the largest lumber operators in America. He continued in this partnership, the operations of which proved to be profitable, until 1863, when he was obliged to retire because of impaired health. He went to Janesville, Wisconsin, and adopted as his business the outdoor work of sheep raising. He went through southern Michigan, picked up 4,000 sheep, which he drove to Iowa, and in a year had the largest flocks of any man east of the Missouri. Having recovered his health, he went into the lumber business again, this time in Chicago. In 1876 he moved to Michigan, where he remained until his death.

His first operations in Michigan were in Montcalm county, where he purchased a small mill and operated it until the contributory pine timber was exhausted and a change of base made necessary. In looking over the advantages offered to investment he eventually selected a tract of white pine timber located on the Au Gres river in Iosco county, and estimated to contain 150,000,000 feet. This was the beginning of the career of the Saginaw Lumber & Salt Company, which Mr. Loveland was instrumental in organizing and of which he was president from 1893 until his death.

This company, formed in 1881, purchased what was at that time known as the Sibley & Bearinger lumber and salt plant at Crow Island, three miles below the city of Saginaw, Michigan, on the east side of the Saginaw river. The mill was operated successfully by the Saginaw Lumber & Salt Company. The lumber plant at Crow Island had a cutting capacity of 25,000,000 feet in a single season, and the company contracted with other saw mill owners to cut from 10,000,000 to 20,000,000 feet a year additional. The salt works operated by the company in connection with the saw mill had an output of 50,000 barrels of salt annually during all the years in which the company operated them. South of the Crow Island mill property were located several thousand acres of marsh land which were overflowed each spring, lying as they did along the Saginaw river and but little above the level of it. The productiveness of the soil of this marsh was early recognized by Mr. Loveland, and his practical mind at once evolved a project for bringing it into use. With his sons and son-in-law he purchased 2,000 or 3,000 acres. On this farm, which is still owned and operated by the Lovelands, there are grown annually about two hundred acres of cabbage, three hundred acres of sugar beets and several hundred acres of Hungarian grass, wheat, oats, corn and vegetables.

In 1893 the timber owned by the Saginaw Lumber & Salt Company in Michigan became exhausted. In the meantime the company had purchased a large body of timber in the Georgian Bay district of Canada.

With his sons, Ralph and Daniel K., and his son-in-law, R. H. Roys, Mr. Loveland secured a large body of timber in the Georgian Bay district, independent of the company's holdings, and they engaged extensively in getting out board pine for the Quebec and European markets. This business is still continued, amounting to about 140,000 cubic feet annually.

The lumber and salt manufacturing business, in which Mr. Loveland became prominent and in which the last twenty years of his life in the Saginaw valley were passed, has been transferred to Sandwich, Ontario, the Crow Island mill and salt works having finished their career on the Saginaw river with the close of 1901. They were moved to Canada, where a new plant was erected. The operations are carried on by the old company under the same name, and it has business enough in sight to enable it to continue its corporate career twenty years yet.

While a resident of New York state Mr. Loveland was successively elected a member of the Assembly and the Senate and performed the duties of these positions in a manner creditable to himself and satisfactory to the people and to his party. He was one of the pillars in the First Baptist Church Society in Saginaw.

Mr. Loveland married Miss Harriet M. Kent, of Benson, Vermont, March 25, 1840, and eight children were born to them. Mrs. Loveland died in 1887, and seven years later Mr. Loveland was united in marriage to Miss Helen Crittenden, of San Francisco, who survived him.

On November 9, 1899, Mr. Loveland, after a brief illness, passed to the realm of the hereafter. He was a patriotic citizen, and an earnest worker in every cause that tended to promote the welfare of his fellow man. Courteous, considerate of others, just and sympathetic, he made many friends. His life was rich in good deeds, and his death was sincerely mourned by all who knew him. When it can truthfully be said of a man, as it can of Ralph Loveland, that the world is better for his having lived, no higher tribute can be paid.

LIBRARY
OF THE
UNIVERSITY
OF
CALIFORNIA

CHARLES WILSON KOTCHER

Charles W. Kotcher

Charles Wilson Kotcher, of Detroit, Michigan, has the distinction of being the largest individual operator in lumber at retail in the United States. Mr. Kotcher is of German ancestry two generations removed, and was born in Detroit, July 2, 1862. He received his education in the public schools of that city. At the age of fifteen years he began his life work as general utility boy in a drug store in Detroit, from which business he retired nine years later after having risen to the position of manager of the store. In 1886 he entered the retail lumber trade, taking a business established in 1864 by Japes & Dietrich, who had been succeeded by Larkin & Wallich. Mr. Kotcher bought the Wallich interest and soon after acquired the entire business. At that time Detroit was a city of about 150,000 inhabitants, and Mr. Kotcher's lumber transactions amounted to about $40,000 a year. The growth of Mr. Kotcher's business in Detroit has been steady from the time he took hold of it until the present and he gradually increased its operations until in 1903 he handled a total output of 60,000,000 feet of lumber and did a business which amounted to $1,240,000.

At the foot of Adair street, in Detroit, Mr. Kotcher has a lumber storage dock on which he piles and keeps constantly in stock 20,000,000 feet of lumber. This dock has a water frontage of 4,500 feet. From this storage yard a large proportion of his contracts are delivered direct. Within a mile of the business center of Detroit, on Gratiot avenue, he has a retail yard which covers the space of three city blocks. This is fenced in and covered with substantial warehouses and storage sheds, from which his dressed stock and miscellaneous small items are delivered. Here he keeps stored more than 7,000,000 feet of lumber. At the Gratiot avenue plant he has a well equipped planing mill and sash, door and blind factory. Mr. Kotcher has never handled hardwoods, but is a dealer in every other kind of lumber building material produced in the country. In his yard are white pine, hemlock, spruce, longleaf and shortleaf yellow pine and the full range of Pacific Coast building woods.

During the last six years Mr. Kotcher has produced through logging and lumber manufacturing enterprises a large proportion of the stock he has sold in Detroit but his timber holdings are now entirely exhausted and he buys his stock on the open market. A large percentage of his lumber is received by water and he is the owner of eight lumber carriers, four being steam and four tow barges. These vessels have a total trip capacity of 4,500,000 feet.

As being incident to the prosperity of the retail lumber business in Detroit and contributing largely to the success of Mr. Kotcher's great enterprise there, it is worthy of mention primarily that Michigan has an excellent lien law and that retailers in Detroit are strongly organized in the line of protection of their trade. Mr. Kotcher has been prominently identified with the work of the local association, which handles every detail of procedure looking to the betterment of retail lumber conditions in the city. Irresponsible contractors and carpenters have been so thoroughly eliminated from the market that Mr. Kotcher's total losses from bad debts since he has been in business have aggregated less than $3,000.

When this article was prepared Mr. Kotcher was vice president of the Detroit Retail Lumber Dealers' Association and a director in the Michigan Retail Lumber Dealers' Association.

He is a man of medium height and betrays his German ancestry only by a slight rotundity. He is the personification of good nature and invariably greets friend and stranger alike with a hearty grasp of the hand and a welcoming smile. Socially he is a man of delightful characteristics and naturally he has dropped into nearly all of the social orders that have a following in Detroit. He is a pioneer Hoo-Hoo, a prominent member of the Fellowcraft Club, a Mason and owes allegiance to scores of other fraternal orders. He is very fond of yachting and owns one of the most beautiful yachts on the lakes. As he is the soul of hospitality his friends enjoy the boat quite as much as its owner. Mr. Kotcher is also fond of travel and he arranges his business so that a part of each year may be spent in this kind of rest and recreation.

Mr. Kotcher is married and has one son and two daughters. The son is now completing his education at a military school at Faribault, Minnesota, and it is Mr. Kotcher's hope that he will soon become identified with his father's great and growing business in Detroit.

"Charley" Kotcher, as every one knows him in Detroit, is entirely worthy of his success. Besides his tremendous forcefulness he has an inheritance of excellent health, which he has preserved by his habits of life, as he is a total abstainer from all intoxicants and from tobacco. His voice has the ring of sincerity and one hears in it the quality belonging to the man who, as Emerson says, "trusts himself" and therefore trusts his fellow man. He enjoys the confidence of his fellow citizens and of the entire lumber fraternity.

LIBRARY
OF THE
UNIVERSITY
OF
CALIFORNIA

David Whitney, Jr.

Standing forth like a giant in a community of men who achieved greatness in lumber operations such as is possessed by no other group of individuals in any state of the Union, stood the late David Whitney, junior, of Detroit, Michigan.

Mr. Whitney was born at Westford, Massachusetts, August 23, 1830. He sprang from New England ancestors and was one of a family of four brothers, Charles, Hiram and Albert being the names of the others. He gained a common school education and afterward was a student at the Westford Academy, from which he graduated. At the age of twenty-one years he began his life work as clerk in a box factory. In 1854, when twenty-four years old, he started a lumber business at Lowell, Massachusetts, and built up a prosperous trade which soon became wholesale in its character and extended throughout New England. The forests of the upper Connecticut river were then a profitable source of lumber supply.

With his constantly expanding trade he soon found need of assistance, and was joined by his brother, Charles Whitney, and others in establishing sorting and distributing yards at Albany, New York, and Burlington, Vermont, and at a later date at North Tonawanda, New York, the principal office of the concern being located at Boston. The corporate name of the institution was the Skillings, Whitneys & Barnes Lumber Company, under which title it still exists. Of this company Mr. Whitney was president up to the time of his death, when he was succeeded by his son, David C. Whitney, of Detroit.

In 1857, in searching for a future lumber supply for his wholesale yards, he began an investigation of the timber resources of Michigan and was not slow to discern that they were destined to become a most important factor in the lumber trade of the nation. He secured the services of expert and trusted cruisers and began making investments in the splendid white pine tributary to the Tittabawassee and Saginaw rivers. Soon afterward he interested with himself men of large and practical experience in timber, and bought other tracts of most valuable forest lands upon these and other streams in central Michigan. At one time he owned by far the largest timber acreage ever possessed by any individual in the Wolverine State. Later he bought timber lands in Wisconsin and the northern peninsula of Michigan, on the waters of the Menominee river, and even made some purchases on streams tributary to Lake Superior.

In connection with his associates he owned and for many years operated one of the largest saw mills in the country, located on the Saginaw river. Among the individuals associated with him in lumber operations were D. N. Skillings, Jacob W. Stinchfield and his son, Charles Stinchfield, J. F. Batchelor and his son, H. A. Batchelor, and Royal C. Remick and his son, James A. Remick. In his direct investments Mr. Whitney was known as the foremost manipulator of good white pine in the country, and he undeniably handled more "good end" white pine stock than any other man ever associated with the industry.

In the later years of his life Mr. Whitney and several of his associates made large investments in timber properties in Washington, Oregon and northern California. In these purchases Charles Stinchfield and the estate of R. C. Remick participated. The corporation is known as the Whitney Company, Limited, and its holdings consist of fir, cedar, California white pine, sugar pine and spruce, and aggregate more than 40,000 acres.

For many years prior to his death Mr. Whitney was a resident of Detroit and contributed very largely to the material prosperity of that city. He was a large owner of real estate, which he improved handsomely with fine business buildings and other structures. His interests did not lie entirely in lumber and real estate, as at one time he owned ten steam barges and consorts, which he employed in the ore and lumber trade and which made him an important factor in the lake marine. He was president of the Whitney Transportation Company, which owned five large lake vessels. He was also the principal stockholder in the Merida Transportation Company, owning the large steel steamer Merida, and in the Marshall Transportation Company, owning the big steamer Oglebay. At the time of his death he had another large steamer on the stocks in the Wyandotte yards of the Detroit Shipbuilding Company. He was also the owner of much Michigan farm property as well as Detroit city residence property. He had a handsome home on Detroit's famous boulevard, Woodward avenue.

He was president of the Michigan Fire & Marine Insurance Company, a director of the Union Trust Company, a heavy stockholder in the People's Savings Bank and in the Preston National Bank; he was a large stockholder in Parke, Davis & Co., and in the local Edison Electric Light Company, all of Detroit.

Mr. Whitney's commercial operations, by means of which he amassed one of the few great fortunes achieved largely within Michigan, were marked by extreme care and great conservatism. As a young man he was frugal, but in his later years he lived richly. His private charities during his life were numerous and large and his benefactions to hospitals were generous. His giving was without ostentation, as an incident related by his associate, Charles Stinchfield, shows. Mr. Stinchfield made an unexpected visit to Harper Hospital one afternoon and returned to his office thoroughly imbued with the idea that great good was being done by the institution. So interested was he in the hospital that he said to Mr. Whitney:

"Do you know, Mr. Whitney, I wish I were a rich man, as I would like to give some money to the Harper Hospital. I think it is one of the most deserving charities in Detroit."

"Do you really think it is a real charitable institution?" asked Mr. Whitney.

"I certainly do," affirmed Mr. Stinchfield.

"I am glad to hear that," said Mr. Whitney, "for I sent them a check yesterday for ten thousand dollars."

"Under any other circumstances neither I nor any one else would ever have known of this gift," said Mr. Stinchfield when telling the story.

Mr. Whitney was an even tempered man, easy to approach and agreeable to both friend and stranger. He was exceedingly modest in his tastes and was revered by those who were honored by his personal friendship. As has been stated, the word of David Whitney, junior, was always equivalent to his bond, and several instances are known in which year after year lumber producers shipped their stock to the big wholesale concern of which he was the head, without contracts and without orders, securing payments from time to time on the shipments and in the fall receiving a final settlement. One lumberman was known to have followed this custom with Mr. Whitney for years and was never disappointed when the final settlement came, as he was invariably paid more money for the stock than he had anticipated was due.

In 1869 Mr. Whitney married Mrs. Flora A. Veyo, nee MacLauchlin. Mr. and Mrs. Whitney had four children—David C. Whitney, who is now at the head of the vast business enterprises left by his father; Grace Whitney, now Mrs. John J. Hoff, of Paris, France; Flora Whitney, now Mrs. Rudolph Demme, of Detroit; and Katherine Whitney, the wife of Tracy McGregor, of Detroit. Mrs. Whitney died in 1882 and some years later Mr. Whitney married Miss Sarah MacLauchlin, a sister of his first wife, who survives him.

Mr. Whitney died on November 28, 1900, in the midst of his family at his home in Detroit. He was a great man and his memory will be revered for many generations, for in his passing departed a man who contributed more to the history of the lumber trade of America than any other man who ever cast his fortune with the great industry of Michigan.

LIBRARY
OF THE
UNIVERSITY
OF
CALIFORNIA

William C. Yawkey

For nearly a century the name of Yawkey has been identified with the lumber history of the middle West. It was from this ancestry of lumbermen that William C. Yawkey was descended.

He is the second son of John Hoover Yawkey and Lydia Clyman Yawkey and was born at Massillon, Ohio, August 26, 1834. His public school education ended when he attained the age of fourteen years, at which time he began active employment as a clerk in a hardware store at a salary of $6 a month. He secured a very good education, however, through the medium of a private school and by much industrious night study. He did not remain long in the hardware business, because he inclined naturally toward his father's occupation, that of lumberman.

He became a clerk in his father's lumber office and remained there until 1851, when he moved to Flint, Genesee county, to which place his father followed him in 1852. He entered his father's firm and was placed in charge of the manufacture of lumber at the firm's mill near Flint. By this time, although he had not attained his majority, he had acquired a good knowledge of the lumber business; not only in manufacturing lumber but in properly estimating timbered lands. This knowledge, together with the belief that a fortune might be made in Michigan pine, formed the foundation of his future success.

He was one of the earliest operators in the Saginaw valley. In 1855 he located at Lower Saginaw, now known as Bay City, and became a clerk in the employ of S. W. Yawkey & Co., his brother being the head of this concern. He was its principal inspector and shipper and served the firm during its entire partnership existence. In 1857 he bought an interest in C. Moulthrop & Co. and had charge of their main office at East Saginaw until 1859, when he entered business for himself and began buying logs and lumber for a Chicago firm.

He was soon buying and inspecting lumber not only for Chicago but for Albany and other points in the East and for numerous markets in the West. This agency was operated under his personal name and did much to establish the fame of the Yawkey interests in the West. In 1863 his father and brother Edwin entered into partnership with him and began the active manufacture of logs into lumber. In 1865 Samuel Yawkey, another brother, was admitted to the firm which, from the purchase and inspection of lumber, came to deal in shingles, lath and pine lands also. Mr. Yawkey was a buyer not only for himself but for other important concerns. He was recognized as an adept in the lumber business and one of the best inspectors of lumber and judges of standing timber in Michigan. The volume of business which the firm handled reached during some years 75,000,000 feet, or more than the entire business of all the other lumber firms in the Valley at that time. Mr. Yawkey invested the profits in pine lands on the Saginaw river and its tributary streams. By 1868 his operations had become mammoth, and from that time on they extended from the Saginaw valley over a much larger territory. In time he was the owner of thousands of acres of timber lands in Michigan, Wisconsin, Minnesota, Alabama, Florida and other states.

In 1888 Mr. Yawkey organized the Yawkey & Lee Lumber Company, Limited. Its mills were erected at Hazelhurst, Wisconsin, and their capacity was 20,000,000 feet of lumber a season. Mr. Yawkey was president of the company. It was dissolved in 1893 and was succeeded by the Yawkey Lumber Company, of which W. C. Yawkey was president, Cyrus C. Yawkey treasurer and manager and William H. Yawkey secretary. This company purchased all the interests of the Yawkey & Lee Lumber Company, Limited, and about 300,000,000 feet of standing timber which W. C. Yawkey had in Wisconsin.

The Yawkey interests at Hazelhurst became very large. The plant at this point included a band saw mill, a planing mill, a box factory and a railroad which not only served to assist in logging operations but to get the manufactured product to a trunk line for shipment to market.

Lumber and timber did not command all of Mr. Yawkey's attention and energy. He early recognized the possibilities of northern Michigan mines and secured valuable interests in mineral lands in the Iron Range of the Northern Peninsula, a district which included the Bessemer, Commodore and Alpena mines. He had mining interests also in Minnesota and on the Pacific Coast. In 1891 he erected at Detroit the Western Knitting Mills, which required three hundred employees, and he had a yarn mill at Rochester, Michigan.

Mr. Yawkey was united in marriage to Miss Emma Noyes, of Guilford, Vermont, in 1869. She died December 2, 1891. The two children born to them, a daughter, now Mrs. Thomas J. Austin, and a son, William H. Yawkey, both reside at Detroit. W. H. Yawkey is engaged in looking after his father's estate, which in addition to the ramifications of his lumber and timber properties consists of interests in other financial and industrial concerns.

William C. Yawkey died in Detroit November 23, 1903. The remains were taken to Brattleboro, Vermont, and there laid to rest by the side of his wife.

With his death ended the career of a lumberman who was one of the first to recognize the value of the white pine forests of Michigan. He possessed qualities necessary for making the most of his opportunities, and left behind him not only a record of successful business operations but the recollection of a personal character which retained its charitableness and gentleness through all the changes of an active life.

[illegible] he [illegible]

clerk, [illegible]

the bus[illegible] ghly. When [illegible]

entered the hardware business

being Yawkey & Corbyn, and [illegible]

1888, in association with his [illegible]

organized at Hazelhurst, Wisconsin, [illegible]

lumber Company, Limited, which

reorganized as the Yawkey Lumber Comp[illegible]

it now has a saw mill, a planing mill and a logging

This railroad, which is twenty-five miles in length, is on

on a large scale and is incorporated

Southeastern Railway Company, of which Mr. Yaw[illegible]

president. One of its branches connects Hazelhurst w[illegible]

Chicago & North-Western railway at Tomahawk lake

town of Hazelhurst has been built in the woods on the

the St. Paul road on the shore of Lake Katherine, wh[illegible]

Cyrus C. Yawkey

The faithful performance of every promise he makes has caused to be applied to Cyrus Carpenter Yawkey, of Wausau and Hazelhurst, Wisconsin, the good old phrase, "His word is as good as his bond." He is a son of Samuel W. Yawkey, one of the pioneer lumbermen of the Saginaw valley. The senior Yawkey moved to Chicago in 1858, where he engaged in the lumber business with Thomas M. Avery. He returned to East Saginaw in 1864. C. C. Yawkey was born in Chicago, August 29, 1862, while his father was engaged in the lumber business there. Subsequent to his father's return to East Saginaw, the youth became a student in the common schools, in which he continued to study until about 1879, when he was sent to the Michigan Military Academy, at Orchard Lake. He graduated from that school in 1891, when eighteen years of age. Upon leaving school he went into a hardware store at East Saginaw as clerk, serving several years and learning the business thoroughly. When twenty-one years of age he entered the hardware business on his own account, the firm being Yawkey & Corbyn, and prospered for five years.

In 1888, in association with his uncle, W. C. Yawkey, he organized at Hazelhurst, Wisconsin, the Yawkey & Lee Lumber Company, Limited, which not long thereafter was reorganized as the Yawkey Lumber Company. At that point it now has a saw mill, a planing mill and a logging road. This railroad, which is twenty-five miles in length, is operated on a large scale and is incorporated as the Hazelhurst & Southeastern Railway Company, of which Mr. Yawkey is president. One of its branches connects Hazelhurst with the Chicago & North-Western railway at Tomahawk lake. The town of Hazelhurst has been built in the woods on the line of the St. Paul road on the shore of Lake Katherine, where the plant is located. The company has been adding to its original holdings ever since its organization and has manufactured over 300,000,000 feet of lumber at that point. Besides the equipment mentioned the Yawkey Lumber Company has a box factory which turns out about 6,000,000 feet of box material each year. The company logs entirely by rail the year around.

Since the death of W. C. Yawkey, in 1903, C. C. Yawkey has been president of the company. W. H. Yawkey, of Detroit, son of W. C. Yawkey, is vice president. Thus the only remaining male members of a distinguished lumber family of several generations are associated in the Hazelhurst enterprise. The company is now getting out between 30,000,000 and 35,000,000 feet a year.

The president of this company is the one who has built it up, for he is the only one of the proprietary members who has lived in Wisconsin, where the operations have been conducted; and his initiative, backed by indomitable energy, has culminated in splendid results during the last fifteen years. This company was one of the first in Wisconsin to log with horses exclusively, and its members were among the first saw mill people of the North to put in band mills, to run a logging railroad and to operate their mill winters as well as summers and to keep an open pond the year around. Their concern was one of the first in the valley to establish box factories in connection with mills, and every one of these innovations has been a success.

None of Mr. Yawkey's associates has been active with him at the mill and, aside from the initial purchase which was made before the plant was established, C. C. Yawkey has bought all of the timber. He has looked after the logging and manufacturing and sold the product of the mills for the last fifteen years. He has outside relationships of a commercial character; he is vice president of the Wisconsin & Arkansas Lumber Company, which has vast interests at and near Malvern, Arkansas; he is president of the Yawkey-Crowley Lumber Company, a line yard concern operating retail yards in southern Wisconsin, and he owns considerable stock in several other lumber and land companies. He is vice president of the Wausau Quartz Company, Wausau, Wisconsin; a director of the First National Bank, of Rhinelander, Wisconsin, and a director of the Comptograph Company, manufacturer of adding machines, at Chicago. Mr. Yawkey is also president of the Globe Mining Company, which owns valuable iron lands near Birmingham, Alabama.

One of the traits of a thoroughbred lumberman is to be everlastingly looking out for more timber, and the Yawkey Lumber Company, through Mr. Yawkey, has not only added extensively to its holdings in Wisconsin, but has been a liberal purchaser of yellow pine timber in Florida and has added to its holdings considerable quantities of Pacific Coast stumpage within the last few years. Mr. Yawkey spent part of 1903 on the Coast, adding materially to the timber possessions of the company.

In addition to the substantial work of building up so great an industry at Hazelhurst, and incidentally purchasing timber lands all over the country on behalf of his associates and himself, Mr. Yawkey has devoted much time to association work for the general good of the lumber industry. He was elected president of the Wisconsin Valley Lumbermen's Association in 1904.

In 1888, some time after leaving the Michigan Military Academy at Orchard Lake, he was captain of a company in the Michigan National Guard. He afterward became a major in the Third Regiment and kept that position until he embarked in business in Wisconsin. In 1894 he had so impressed himself upon the people of his community and district in Wisconsin that he was sent to the legislature. Prior to his selection for this station, which he filled with credit to himself and honor to the state, he had, as chairman of the county board of Oneida county during 1891, 1892 and 1893, demonstrated his fitness for public office.

Mr. Yawkey, although an exceedingly busy man, has

found time to devote to fraternal fell
Templar and a thirty-second degree
Mr. Yawkey makes his home at
sisting of his wife, who was Miss
Ann Arbor, Michigan, and one dau

Walter S. Eddy

The often repeated phrase, "Blood will tell," is manifestly verified in the history of the Eddy family. Walter Stanley Eddy can trace his lineage back hundreds of years. His great-great-grandfather, Colonel Jonathan Eddy, was born in 1726 and was prominently identified with English and Colonial forces in the French and Indian War of 1755-63. Colonel Eddy died at Eddington, Maine, in 1804, the tract of land whereon Eddington was built having been granted to him by the government of Massachusetts for services which he rendered during the Revolutionary War. Mr. Eddy's great-grandfather, William Eddy, was born in Mansfield, Massachusetts, August 16, 1752, and was killed by a shot fired from a British warship near Eastport, Maine, May 3, 1778, during the War of the Revolution. Mr. Eddy's grandfather, William Eddy, junior, was born in the province of New Brunswick, July 1, 1775, and in 1796 was united in marriage to Rachel Knapp, who was of English descent. The youngest of the eight children born to this couple was Charles K. Eddy, the father of Walter S. Eddy. C. K. Eddy was born in Maine and resided there until 1858, when he moved to Canada and engaged in lumbering. In 1865 he located in Saginaw, Michigan, where he continued in the same business.

Walter S. Eddy, who was one of four children, was born June 17, 1855, on his grandfather's farm, close to the village of Exeter Mills, township of Corinth, Penobscot county, Maine. His father had been born in the same house. Mr. Eddy's mother was Albina Dunning Eddy, of Charleston, Maine. Young Eddy attended the public schools in Saginaw, and finished his education in 1873 at the Highland Military Academy, at Worcester, Massachusetts. He then began his business career, his first position being that of bookkeeper for his father, by whom he was afterward taken into partnership under the firm name of C. K. Eddy & Son. The firm was subsequently incorporated under the title of C. K. Eddy & Sons, and Walter S. Eddy is now president of this company, which for many years was one of the important lumber manufacturing institutions on the Saginaw river. Several years ago the concern cut out all of its timber tributary to the Saginaw river and its mill was dismantled and sold, but the company still continues and is the owner of valuable real estate in Saginaw, including a half mile of river frontage in the business district. It also owns the Eddy building, a modern six-story office structure which is one of the finest in the state.

Mr. Eddy is identified with large and varied commercial interests and is quick to discern the merits of any proposition submitted to him. He invariably gives his opinion "straight from the shoulder," and his judgment is quick and accurate. When he once undertakes an enterprise he gives it untiring energy and support.

Mr. Eddy has been president of the Michigan Salt Association since 1898. This company handles about 75 percent of the salt product of Michigan, and is made up of salt manufacturers of the state, the state producing 30 percent of the entire salt output of the United States. He is vice president and a director of the Second National Bank of Saginaw, one of the strongest financial institutions in the state. He is president and owner of a controlling interest in the Saginaw Milling Company, a concern operating a large flour milling plant, besides handling hay, grain and farm produce in quantities.

The corporation of C. K. Eddy & Sons, while primarily organized in 1893 to take over the active lumber business of C. K. Eddy & Son, was continued as a large manufacturer of lumber and salt until 1899. Since then the nature of the business has changed to that of a holding company for the many different interests in which Mr. Eddy is engaged, becoming each succeeding year more and more like a banking institution.

Prominent among the concerns in which a controlling interest is held by the Eddys is that of Eddy & Glynn, operating from 1889 until 1904 in logs, land and lumber in Minnesota and Wisconsin. The interests of Eddy & Glynn are now, in 1905, entirely on Georgian bay, Ontario, where their holdings of pine timber constitute many hundred millions of feet of the best located and finest timber remaining in that district. Another interest is that of the Galloway-Pease Company, operating largely in pine and hardwood lumber in Tennessee, with headquarters at Johnson City.

Mr. Eddy is president of the Consolidated Coal Company, which operates five mines in the Saginaw district and produces upwards of 500,000 tons of bituminous coal annually. Mr. Eddy and his associates have been operators in coal, at first in a limited way, from the time of the earliest discovery of that fuel in the Saginaw valley. He has felt his way carefully in the enterprise and during 1903 and 1904 acquired large coal land areas, the possession of which places him in a position to rank with the leaders in that industry. This business is fast developing in the Saginaw valley and bids fair to outrank its immediate great predecessor—the production of white pine lumber.

In both inclination and training Mr. Eddy is essentially a businessman. Coming from a family of men who have had to fight for home and country it is only natural that he should find in the every day battles of business his most solid satisfaction. No businessman today has been successful who has not loved the game for itself, outside of the money he sees piling up as the result of his executive ability and commercial foresight. This has been Walter S. Eddy's greatest interest outside of his comfortable but modest home at Saginaw and his attachment for his little niece and nephew, the children of his sister, Mrs. M. B. Mills, of Detroit. He has never married.

Mr. Eddy has never aspired to any political office and is not a member of any fraternal organization, although he takes an active part in politics and is a staunch Republican. At times he has served as a member of the Republican State Central Committee. He is always most interested in every project calculated to advance the material welfare of the community in which he lives, and every legitimate enterprise has received his hearty encouragement and aid. Saginaw, which now ranks third in importance among Michigan cities, owes much of its modern development to Mr. Eddy, and in 1904 he was planning several new enterprises for its advancement. Among these was the extensive permanent improvement of the river front property owned by his company, to be used for business houses and manufacturing institutions.

It is to men of the caliber and worth of Walter S. Eddy that America owes her supremacy. He truly belongs to that element which is noiselessly and with deliberate structural accuracy raising the United States above all other nations, not only in business affairs but in the dignity and importance of that simplicity of life which is a synonym for truth.

William B. Mershon

William B. Mershon has many activities but they are all closely related to the lumber industry—a natural result of his ancestry, training and ambitions. His father, the late A. H. Mershon, and his grandfather were lumbermen. Mr. Mershon therefore represents the third generation of his family in the lumber business. In the later history of the lumber industry of Saginaw, Michigan, he has played an important part. He is Saginaw through and through. He was born in that favored lumber city January 16, 1856, and received a common school education in its public schools.

In 1876, before he was of age, he entered the lumber trade on his own account. This business was continued for three years, when it was consolidated with that of Mershon, Brown & Co. and the corporation of W. B. Mershon & Co. was formed. This company had a very prosperous existence; but, fully recognizing the value of large, allied interests in a single line, it was consolidated, in 1901, with William Schuette & Co., of Saginaw, S. L. Eastman & Co., of Saginaw, and the Eddy-Sheldon Company, of Bay City, into a corporation known as Mershon, Schuette, Parker & Co., of Saginaw. The paid up capital of the new corporation was fixed at $1,000,000 and, in recognition of his high business qualifications, William B. Mershon was elected its president. He is president in fact as well as in name, for he is the business head of the corporation and personally handles every important detail connected with it.

The principal office of the company is at Saginaw, Michigan, where it has a large yard on the Saginaw river, connected by railroad tracks with all of the railway lines entering the city. The plant consists of an immense planing mill and box factory, an equally large cutup factory and two other spacious factories devoted to the making of doors, sash and blinds, mouldings, shingles resawed from boards and at least a hundred wood specialties. In addition there is a large salt block.

Plant No. 2 of the company is located on the Saginaw river at Bay City, fifteen miles distant from Saginaw, where it has one of the most extensive receiving docks in the country. This dock has a capacity for unloading a fleet of ten large vessels at one time. In connection with this plant is a large and modern planing mill and a salt block.

While the aggregate handlings of a good many lumber houses of the United States may exceed that of Mershon, Schuette, Parker & Co., there is no other institution that converts so immense a quantity of lumber into minor cutup material for use in so great a variety of ways. It is owing to this feature that the concern is so important to the Saginaw valley, as the company employs more than 1,500 men and boys. It has branch sales offices in all the great trade centers of the East and a large portion of its output is distributed throughout Michigan, Ohio, Pennsylvania, New York, New Jersey and New England.

The business exemplifies the science of the finer manipulation and conversion of lumber, and the company's standing and trade are based very largely upon the intelligence, industry and perseverence of its dominant factor, William B. Mershon.

Mr. Mershon has commercial ventures outside of Mershon, Schuette, Parker & Co. Together with E. C. Mershon, his brother, he is concerned in the house of W. B. Mershon & Co., builders of the Mershon band resaw, which in its various types is known to practically the lumber trade of the world. He is also prominently identified with the Saginaw & Manistee Lumber Company, large timber owner and lumber manufacturer at Williams, Arizona. Besides these enterprises he is interested in several mining concerns in the West. He is also of the firm of Mershon & Morley, of Saginaw, builders of portable houses.

At least twice a year Mr. Mershon throws business aside and appears in an entirely different guise. For a month at a time he does not permit himself even to think of business. Then it is that he is "Billy" Mershon, one of the country's most noted amateur sportsmen, an all-around good fellow and famous story teller. May finds him casting the fly for the wary speckled trout of Michigan streams. June usually sees him down on the Grande Cascapedia river, in Quebec, where he has leased a fishing cottage and sundry salmon pools. In October he will be found with a party of genuine sportsmen friends in North Dakota in the private car, "W. B. Mershon," of which he is part owner, shooting ducks, geese and deer. Then he returns to Michigan just in time for a few days of the good quail and partridge shooting that abounds about Saginaw.

While Mr. Mershon has never had any political ambitions he has always deemed it his duty to discharge the obligations of citizenship and has served his city four terms as alderman and once as mayor.

He occupies at Saginaw a handsome, modern house which is surrounded by a large yard filled with trees and flowers. This home is presided over with grace and intelligence by Mrs. Mershon. They have four children—three sons and a daughter—all handsome and sturdy. It is a home where respect, happiness and love rule supreme.

It is difficult even for one who is intimate with William B. Mershon to write comprehensively of him. He is a many faced diamond. However, his days are lived with a truthful vigor that would please the apostle of "the simple life," Charles Wagner, and his voice has in it the ring of sincerity. One hears in it the forceful quality of a man whose fathers shouted vehemently in the ancient forests as they felled the trees and chopped the wood. Of him it may be said that his friends love him, his enemies respect him and no one is indifferent to him.

Edward Germain

A splendid type of the selfmade American businessman is Edward Germain, of Saginaw, Michigan. He was born at Kingston, Ontario, October 30, 1846, educated at St. Peter's Academy, Detroit, and in 1863 moved to Saginaw, where he worked in a shingle mill and at the carpenter's trade for three shillings a day. However, this modest wage was not all that he obtained, for he mastered the details of the business and equipped himself to engage in the building operations which claimed his activities until 1874.

Then he established a small planing mill plant and sash, door and blind factory in the city of East Saginaw, the consolidation of the two Saginaws into one municipality not taking place until 1890. The plant was a modest one, housed in a frame structure, and the operations of Mr. Germain at the outset attracted comparatively little attention, as the planing mill business at that time occupied about the same relative position to the saw mill industry as the operations of a peanut vender do to those of the wholesale merchant.

It was not many years, however, until the proportions of the business had outgrown the circumscribed area of the little wooden building. In 1886 Mr. Germain transferred his business to a modern plant, consisting of large four-story brick buildings just off Genesee avenue, near the southeastern limits of Saginaw, where he had purchased thirty-eight acres of land for the location of the plant and its lumber yard. This required a large investment of operating as well as of fixed capital, as the capacity of the plant was greater and the force of men and material was vastly augmented.

The manufacture of sash, doors, blinds, mouldings, box shooks and dressed lumber of every kind was carried on extensively and the business expanded rapidly. Mr. Germain investigated the manufacture of doors for the export trade, foreseeing attractive possibilities in that direction, and soon had large contracts secured. White pine lumber was much cheaper then than it was some years later, and stock that he bought easily under $15 can hardly be secured at any figure now. The export door business grew to large proportions and for several years he did a heavy and profitable business in that line. Subsequently other American manufacturers engaged in the business, until it became a trade that was carried on under fierce competition, and consequently was less profitable.

A disastrous fire swept over Saginaw May 20, 1893, and destroyed a vast amount of property. Among others the plant of Mr. Germain was destroyed, together with many millions of feet of lumber. His warehouse alone was saved. Within a few hours' time the flames inflicted a loss of $350,000—enough to have paralyzed one less resourceful. But fire could not daunt this tireless, enterprising man. The ashes had not cooled before plans were being prepared for another and larger plant. And here the value of a name and an established and localized business was recognized by Mr. Germain, and the confidence of the Saginaw people in his business sagacity, public spirit and loyalty to the city was justified. He received flattering offers to locate his business plant elsewhere. West Superior offered him $200,000 to move there. But he reasoned that "Ed" Germain at any other point would not be the "Ed" Germain of Saginaw, where he had built up his business reputation and credit and whose name was linked with his own in the minds of thousands of people, and he decided to remain. His judgment in so doing has been vindicated again and again. Before the snow fell that year his plant was again in full motion and, despite the financial depression that ensued throughout the country, his business developed still larger proportions.

Some time prior to 1897 Mr. Germain reached the conclusion that the day was not far distant when the white pine industry, which had been subject to varied changes incident to the diminishing supply of raw material, would soon materially decline, and he began an investigation for the purpose of determining to what use a portion of his plant could be devoted. His attention was attracted to the manufacture of pianos, which could be carried on very well in connection with his other business. He visited piano factories all over the country, noted the methods of manufacture and asked questions. If a certain rule obtained he found out why it was followed, and determined in his own mind if other methods were not superior. Out of all this patient, sagacious investigation, which occupied eighteen months of time, the Germain piano, embodying some features new in piano design, was evolved. He erected a fine conservatory of music on South Washington avenue in Saginaw, where the Germain piano is daily in evidence and where the best music is brought to the people of the city and state.

Mr. Germain is recognized as one of the most forceful men in the community in which he lives. But there is nothing of the dress parade feature in his makeup. No man is more intensely practical. He possesses the rare faculty of organization and executive talent in a high degree, as well as the ability to grasp the intricate problems of the most exacting business ramifications.

He married Miss Emma Taylor, June 9, 1870, and his home on South Washington avenue, Saginaw, is noted for the hospitality of its master and mistress.

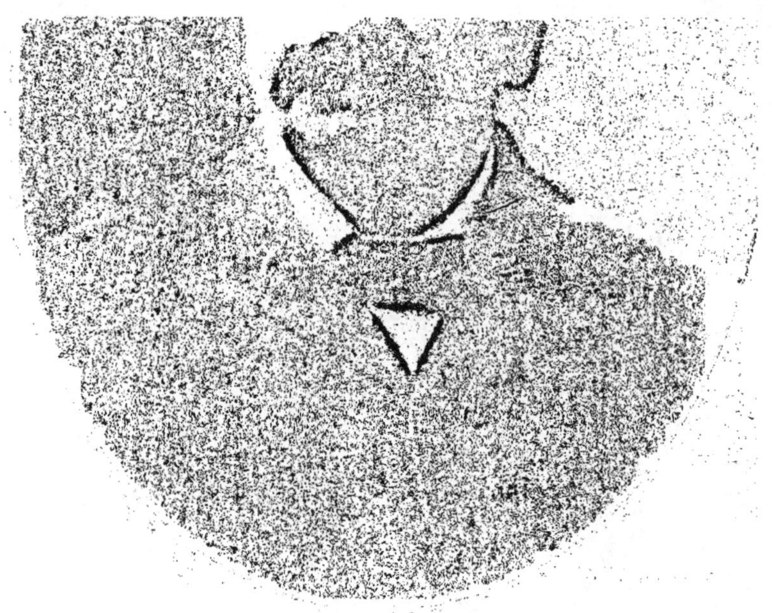

FRANK WILLIAM GILCHRIST

Frank W. Gilchrist

Occasionally an honest and kindly man wins success without breeding enmity. Such a man is Frank William Gilchrist, of Alpena, Michigan. Mr. Gilchrist was born at Concord, New Hampshire, February 27, 1845. His father was Albert Gilchrist, a New Hampshire lumberman who went out into the then great West to seek his fortune in Michigan pine. This was in 1850, when F. W. Gilchrist was five years old. The family located at Marine City, Michigan, and at that point the elder Gilchrist for several years was engaged in the manufacture of lumber. Young Gilchrist received a common school education at Marine City in the rather primitive schools of that time, and, the family moving to Oberlin, Ohio, in the early '60's, he had the advantage of two years of the college training afforded by the excellent educational institution there.

Following his student days, Mr. Gilchrist served a two years' apprenticeship in the handling of lumber in the yards of Cleveland. As a youth he had considerable training in lumber production in connection with his father's enterprises, and this experience gave him an insight into the other end of the trade. In 1867 he moved to Alpena, Michigan, and started in the business on his own account, under his own name, and has operated as Frank W. Gilchrist ever since. Immediately after his Alpena advent he erected a saw mill which he has kept in operation up to the date of this work.

As early as 1870 Mr. Gilchrist became interested in the transportation of lumber by vessel to various points on the Great Lakes, and began his career as a vessel owner. This part of his business has developed into the Gilchrist Transportation Company, the second largest owner of shipping on the chain of lakes, having about seventy vessels in service. These ships are all freighters and are utilized for the transfer of lumber, ore, grain and coal during the season of transportation on the lakes. About fifteen years ago the company began the building of large boats, and those now in operation carry double the average amount of freight of those of former years.

Mr. Gilchrist's lumber operations at Alpena began originally with the manufacture of white pine; later more or less norway was manufactured, and at a still later period he produced a large quantity of hemlock and hardwood lumber. At present his Alpena mill is running largely on hardwoods and a good portion of this is maple which, in a modern factory there, is transformed into flooring famous for its high quality.

Outside of Mr. Gilchrist's Alpena lumber operations he was associated for many years with the late William A. Rust in several timber and lumber deals. Nearly twenty years ago a large purchase of white pine timber at Drummond, Wisconsin, was made and the Rust-Owen Lumber Company was organized. In this company Mr. Gilchrist is a heavy stockholder. The company is still in active operation and has been one of the most successful enterprises of the kind in the country. Mr. Gilchrist is the chief factor in the Rust Land & Lumber Company, handling southern timber lands; he is also interested in the Three States Lumber Company and the W. E. Smith Lumber Company, both of Cairo, Illinois, but now having their chief offices in Memphis, Tennessee.

In addition to Mr. Gilchrist's active lumber and transportation operations, he has been a buyer of timber lands in the North, South and West for many years, never having lost sight of the value of timber properties, and he has large holdings of various woods.

Mr. Gilchrist is president of the Alpena National Bank and is also the principal owner in a cement manufacturing plant in Alpena, which is one of the largest of its kind in the United States. He is also extensively engaged in the beet sugar business with other lumbermen and business friends of Michigan; but his business interests are so multitudinous as to preclude the possibility of enumerating them all.

Mr. Gilchrist has always been allied with the Republican party. For three successive terms he has been mayor of Alpena and probably will be reëlected for as many terms as he will consent to give his time to the guidance of the municipal affairs of that city.

In 1868 Mr. Gilchrist married Mary Rust, a daughter of Aloney Rust, who was one of the pioneer lumbermen of the Saginaw valley. The children of Mr. and Mrs. Gilchrist are Frank R., who is the treasurer of the Gilchrist Transportation Company, William A., Ralph E. and Miss Grace Gilchrist.

As a pioneer lumberman and producer for forty years Mr. Gilchrist has had continuous success and during that time has manufactured between 3,000,000,000 and 4,000,000,000 feet of lumber, largely white pine. At his Alpena mill he has cut as high as 200,000 feet of white pine daily, and he still cuts about 50,000 feet of hemlock and hardwoods. He has had much to do with the development of Alpena and the commercial interests of the Thunder Bay district generally.

In discussion of the early history of lumber affairs on the Huron shore of Michigan, and in comparing former conditions with those existing today, Mr. Gilchrist delights. He can recall the time when he bought, on the basis of twenty cents a thousand, white pine timber which could not be duplicated at all today, but which, if it were possible to obtain, would readily command $10 to $12 a thousand.

Mr. Gilchrist is a Hoo-Hoo, and also stands high in the ranks of Free Masonry.

He has always had an aim in view and in reaching it he has never lost courage, nor relaxed his energy nor changed his fixity of purpose; consequently he has attained his ends. Usually there is a thorn in the flesh of success—enmity—but such is not the case in the experience of Frank Gilchrist. The reason for this may be the bigness of his soul. Too noble to be other than just in all of his dealings, too kind to win to himself anything but esteem, he seems to have made only friends.

Lewis Penoyer

Among the pioneer lumbermen who made a name and won lasting fame for the lumber industry of Michigan, Lewis Penoyer stands out prominently and will long be remembered. He was for many years a resident of Saginaw county, locating there when a young man of but twenty years of age and closing a well rounded and industrious career February 1, 1897, at the age of sixty-nine years. He was one of the foremost of the well known pioneers who hewed a fortune from the "forest primeval" of pines in the Saginaw lumbering district.

Lewis Penoyer was born at Manlius, New York, March 3, 1828, being the son of David Penoyer, one of the pioneers of Michigan. In 1834, at a time when the western country, and particularly Michigan, was attracting the attention of the people of the eastern states, Mr. Penoyer moved his family to Michigan and located on a farm on Flint river near Flushing, Genesee county. When Lewis was sixteen years old his father died and life took on a serious phase as far as he was personally concerned. He worked on a farm and for one year was employed by the late Governor Bingham.

When he was twenty years old he went to Saginaw, where he found employment in the Emerson saw mill and on the river. He was an observing man, and turned every experience to good account. After some years' employment, by saving his earnings and laboring with untiring industry, he succeeded in accumulating a little money. His great ability and capacity were so deeply impressed upon the minds of those with whom he came in contact, that in the early '50's he was given charge of the lumbering business of Frost & Bradley, at St. Charles, Saginaw county, a small hamlet on Bad river. In 1862 he moved his family to St. Charles, at which point he was engaged for many years in the manufacture of lumber.

Mr. Penoyer was in several respects in advance of the times in which he lived. He was the first lumberman to foresee the advantages of handling and distributing lumber by rail, although for years the railroad companies doing business in the Saginaw valley could not be made to see the advantages to be gained in freighting lumber by fixing rates on a basis that would enable it to be handled in that way. Mr. Penoyer, however, sold a good deal of his lumber in markets that were more conveniently reached by the railroads than by lake or by lake and rail, and this fact, together with the faculty which he had by nature and by means of which he was able to see farther into the future than the majority of men, may have been responsible for his advocating rail shipments. His mill manufactured 7,000,000 to 12,000,000 feet annually and its capacity was increased as the developments of the industry progressed. Subsequent to his residence in St. Charles, he moved to Saginaw.

About 1880 a number of Saginaw lumbermen invested largely in timber land in Louisiana, in Calcasieu parish, forming the Bradley-Ramsay Lumber Company and erecting a large lumber manufacturing plant at Lake Charles. The active management of the property was intrusted to young men, but back of them were such sturdy and sagacious businessmen of long experience and recognized financial ability as Lewis Penoyer and Nathan B. Bradley. Mr. Penoyer was president of this company and a heavy stockholder.

The personal character of Lewis Penoyer was that of a man who occupied the highest plane of integrity and honor. He was honest to a degree vastly beyond that ordinary commercial honesty that every businessman must have, and during the sixty-nine years of his active and useful life he enjoyed the dignity and importance that moral worth always brings. In disposition he was a quiet man. However, the violent is not necessarily the strong, and restraint is but the tacit acknowledgment of reserve power. He possessed a fund of humor that delighted his friends. He kept good horses, for which he had a marked fondness. He found great enjoyment in witnessing tests of equine speed and was an interested though unassuming spectator at the annual races in Saginaw. His social side was one of the pleasantest, although never obtrusive. Those who knew him loved him for his many virtues and recognized the value of his friendship and felt the purity of his character. Few citizens in the Saginaw valley possessed a larger circle of friends and none was more thoroughly respected or more sincerely mourned when gone.

In 1857 Mr. Penoyer was united in marriage to Miss Emeline Wisner, and was the father of two sons, Hiram S. and Chauncey W., and two daughters, Mrs. W. E. Ramsay and Mrs. S. S. Roby. The domestic life of Mr. Penoyer was a peaceful and happy one. He was ever a most affectionate husband and father and his home circle was one from which emanated genuine and charming hospitality to all who were fortunate enough to come within its sphere.

As a man of business and of family, as a neighbor and as a useful citizen, Lewis Penoyer adorned these respective relations, and his life of industry, strict integrity and usefulness is one to which those who came after him can point with just pride. When he laid down the burdens of living and, wrapping the mantle of an honorable career around him, passed to eternal sleep, it was well with him. He had so lived that, while his loss was regarded by hundreds of his fellow citizens as a personal bereavement, they realized the fullness and beauty of his life. He had earned the repose which came to him at last.

LIBRARY
OF THE
UNIVERSITY
OF
CALIFORNIA

Wellington R. Burt

Among the favored few who have witnessed the rise and decline of the great white pine industry of the Northwest, who have been identified with it for half a century and who, through the utilization of natural gifts and by unceasing toil, have reached a position of prominence among their fellows in the business world, is Wellington R. Burt, of Saginaw, Michigan.

Mr. Burt was born in the state of New York in 1831. When he was eight years old his family moved to Michigan, locating in Jackson county. He attended the district school, then attended school at Albion and subsequently studied for a short time at Michigan Central College, now Adrian College. Desiring to see something of the world, he spent five years on a trip through Central and South America and Australia.

Returning to the United States, he hired out in the lumber woods in Gratiot county, Michigan, through which Pine river flows, traversing a region then containing large areas of fine white pine timber. It is said that during the first winter he engaged at $15 a month and that when spring came his employer either failed or in some way was unable to pay his help, and Mr. Burt received nothing for his winter's work but the experience which it afforded. In 1860 he formed a business partnership with Thomas Snell, the firm name being Burt & Snell. In 1865 Mr. Burt purchased the interest of another in a partnership with U. S. Gilbert and Mr. Gelpie, the concern being known as Gelpie & Gilbert. Two years later this house failed.

In 1869, Mr. Burt, associating with himself Jethro Mitchell, of Cincinnati, and T. C. Rowland, of Toledo, under the firm name of W. R. Burt & Co., erected a large saw mill and salt works six miles below Saginaw, the place being designated by

Mr. Burt as Melbourne. The concern in the meantime acquired large timber properties on the tributaries of the Saginaw and Tittabawassee rivers. The plant manufactured 25,000,000 feet of pine lumber annually and about 100,000 barrels of salt. In 1877 this vast hive of industry was totally destroyed by fire, the partners losing about $100,000 over and above the insurance. The firm then bought what was known as the New York Saw Mill & Salt Company's works, a short distance south of the property destroyed, which plant was operated two years, when Mr. Burt disposed of his interest in it to his partner, Jethro Mitchell, the deal including the saw mill and salt works, 8,000,000 feet of lumber on the mill docks, 22,000,000 feet of pine logs cut and banked and 300,000,000 feet of standing pine timber, the trade representing an outlay of $432,850 in the purchase price paid for Mr. Burt's one-half interest.

This virtually closed out the interests of Mr. Burt in lumber in the Saginaw valley, at least as a manufacturer. He then established a lumber yard at Buffalo, operating a large planing mill in connection, and continued this business nearly ten years. He also operated a saw mill several years at Grand Marais.

When the pine timber in eastern Michigan began to diminish, Mr. Burt was induced to help stake a landlooker of some experience in Minnesota, and the result was the purchase at a low price of several thousand acres of pine timber land on the Mesaba range. Subsequently Mr. Burt bought out his partner's interest and a few years later disposed of the timber on the land at a handsome profit on the investment. The discovery of iron ore in that range came in due time, although it was said that prior to that event Mr. Burt would gladly have disposed of the cutover lands at a nominal figure. In January, 1900, Mr. Burt executed a lease of the iron ore privileges of his Minnesota possessions to the Lake Superior Consolidated Iron Mines, for which he receives a royalty on the ore output during the fifty years' life of the lease, the minimum amount of which is $50,000 annually.

Mr. Burt became interested, with M. I. Brabb, of Romeo, Michigan, and others, in the establishment of a large lumber manufacturing plant at Ford, Kentucky, now under the ownership of the Burt & Brabb Lumber Company. Mr. Burt has acquired the interests of some of his original associates, and the industry is largely owned and operated by Mr. Burt, its treasurer, and his son, Charles W. Burt, the vice president and general manager.

When the Michigan Salt Association was formed, in 1870, Mr. Burt was elected its president. He held this position nearly a score of years and the success of the organization was largely the result of the masterly executive ability of the president. Mr. Burt also organized the Home National Bank, of Saginaw, and was its president for fourteen years, until it became a part of the Second National Bank. He was also one of the organizers of the People's Bank, of Buffalo, in which he was a heavy stockholder.

In 1888, Mr. Burt, in association with A. W. Wright and three or four other Saginaw men, organized the Cincinnati, Saginaw & Mackinaw Railroad Company and built a road from Durand, Michigan, to Saginaw and thence to West Bay City. It was nearly fifty miles in length. Subsequently he became identified with the Ann Arbor Railroad Company, being receiver and president of the company for several years.

He was one of the original stockholders of the Alma Sugar Company. In connection with his son, George R. Burt, he purchased, in 1904, the old Michigan Alkali Company's quarry property at Bellevue, Eaton county, Michigan. The largest cement chimney in the world was erected on this property. The output of the plant is 300,000 barrels a year. An investment of $800,000 was made in this property by the Burts.

In 1903 Mr. Burt made a proposition to the Board of Education of Saginaw to donate $150,000 toward the erection and equipment of a manual training school; the generous offer was promptly and gratefully accepted. His charities have been numerous. There is no institution in his hom has not been the beneficiary of his generosity.

In other public affairs Mr. Burt has been promi was mayor of East Saginaw in 1867. In 1888 he was nee of the Democratic party for governor of Mic polled a large vote, though failing of election. I was elected to represent the twenty-second district i Senate. In 1900 he reluctantly accepted a nomi Congress in the eighth district.

Mr. Burt has been twice married, and occupies dence on Genesee avenue in Saginaw.

LIBRARY
OF THE
UNIVERSITY
OF
CALIFORNIA

ISAAC BEARINGER

Isaac Bearinger

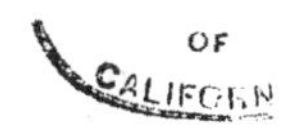

On November 3, 1904, death claimed a well known capitalist of Saginaw, Michigan. It came suddenly and unheralded, bringing to an end the career of a man who by dint of tremendous work, keen insight and excellent judgment had accumulated a fortune, and through the influence of whose personality a record was made in the lumber affairs of the state.

Isaac Bearinger was born January 4, 1847, at Hamilton, Ontario. He was the son of William and Margaret Bearinger and was of Pennsylvania-Dutch descent. He arrived at Saginaw when he was sixteen years old and his advent into the then new lumber manufacturing center was coincident with the arrival of a raft of cork pine logs from up the Flint river. He did not come down the stream as a passenger on this raft but as the cook's helper, or, in the vernacular of the times, as the "cook's devil."

Thus early in his career life's responsibilities were thrust upon young Bearinger and the necessity of gaining a livelihood confronted him. In fact, it was a case of work or starve, and the idea of starving never entered his head. He loved work for work's sake and all through life he displayed an energy almost dynamic in its intensity.

He became a saw mill employee and learned to do his work quickly and well and it was not long before he became a saw filer and took charge of the saws at the old Rochester mill on the Saginaw river, later becoming a filer at the Sanborn mill. He husbanded his means, his ability was soon recognized by Saginaw mill men, and the firm of Bearinger, Bliss & Sanborn came into existence. This concern rented the mill of George Sanborn and engaged in cutting white pine logs for various lumbermen. When the partnership was dissolved Mr. Bearinger rented the Crow Island mill on the

Saginaw river from Hiram W. Sibley, and made a great financial success of it.

In the following year the firm of Sibley & Bearinger was organized and it bought, on the Cedar river, its first tract of timber. This tract was operated for about two years and was then sold to the Saginaw Lumber & Salt Company. The next venture was the purchase of a large tract of pine land on the Au Gres river, which the firm operated for some time and also finally sold to the Saginaw Lumber & Salt Company. It bought from Joseph Chandler a tract of timber land near Ely, Minnesota, on the Vermillion range. On this property was developed one of the finest iron mines in the United States, which for years has been known as the Chandler Iron Mine. It was eventually disposed of for a very large sum.

The firm also owned a large mill at East Tawas, Michigan, whose log supply was secured from the Au Gres river in Michigan and the Spanish river in the Georgian Bay district. Logs were towed in rafts to stock this mill from 1880 to 1890. The firm had the distinction of bringing across Lake Huron in safety the largest raft of pine logs ever made into a single tow. This raft consisted of 9,000,000 feet of logs.

The firm of Sibley & Bearinger was also the owner of pine lands in the Upper Peninsula near Marquette, Michigan, and made the purchase of a large poplar and oak timber property near Panther, West Virginia. On the Tug river, at the mouth of Panther creek, was established the town of Panther, on the line of the Norfolk & Western railroad, and here was erected, in 1893 and 1894, a model, modern double band saw mill and a complete equipment of dry kilns and planing mills. A logging railroad was built up Panther creek to tap the firm's timber and one of the foremost hardwood lumber operations in the mountain country was inaugurated. This property was sold a few years later to the W. M. Ritter Lumber Company, of Columbus, Ohio, which still continues it, and it has proven one of the best financial propositions in the south country, thus confirming the judgment of Mr. Bearinger.

The Panther enterprise was the last important lumber venture entered upon by Mr. Bearinger for several years. Previous to the selling of this property he had become interested in the possibilities of interurban railways, and entirely through his own efforts and largely by means of his own capital he built a line fifteen miles in length, connecting Saginaw and Bay City, at a cost of upward of $500,000. This road was splendidly built and equipped with the best electric cars manufactured. It has proved very successful and was sold in 1898 to the Saginaw Valley Traction Company.

In 1891 and 1892 Mr. Bearinger erected the finest business building in Saginaw, known as the Bearinger Fireproof Building. It is an ornate, six-story, brick and steel, fireproof structure. The first two floors are occupied by a great merchandise establishment and the upper stories are devoted to office purposes.

Mr. Bearinger was the founder of the American Commercial & Savings Bank of Saginaw, of which he was president until it was merged into the Bank of Saginaw. For years before his death he was largely interested in Saginaw real estate of various sorts.

In 1903, Mr. Bearinger, in connection with F. B. Chapin, organized the firm of Bearinger & Chapin, and in the Bay Chaleur district of New Brunswick, at Dalhousie, purchased a saw mill and 100,000,000 feet of spruce timber. Since that time this enterprise has been conducted by Mr. Chapin and Mr. Bearinger's son, Frederic, who succeeded his father in the firm of Bearinger & Chapin as general manager of its business.

In 1888 Mr. Bearinger built the steam yacht Wapiti, one of the finest yachts on the Great Lakes. During the Spanish-American War this yacht was sold to the United States government.

Mr. Bearinger married, in 1877, Miss Nellie Treadwell, of Saginaw, the daughter of a well known merchant. They had one son, Frederic, born in 1879, who inherited in a marked degree his father's good judgment in commercial affairs. Mrs. Bearinger died, and Mr. Bearinger's second wife, whom he married in 1897, was Adelaide McCormick. A son was born to them in 1900.

At the time of his death Mr. Bearinger held an important interest in the Saginaw Paving Brick Company, of which he was vice president. This company has the largest plant in Michigan devoted to making paving brick. He was also owner of Union Park, a race track at Saginaw, which interest came to him through his pet hobby—fine driving horses. This park afforded a place of recreation for himself and friends and an opportunity at regular spring and fall intervals to gather together the leading horsemen of the country. This penchant for horses was practically Mr. Bearinger's only hobby and even that he did not carry to an extreme.

Mr. Bearinger was forceful to a degree and his judgment was analytical. In all his business transactions he reasoned well. He was thoroughly likable and much appreciated by his friends. He was a man with his "heart in the right place." Want and distress invariably appealed to him and there were few men in the Saginaw valley whose charity was wider or more unostentatiously displayed than his.

LIBRARY
OF THE
UNIVERSITY
OF
CALIFORNIA

Ammi W. Wright

The lumber craft can boast many members conspicuous for their philanthropy. It is doubtful if any other occupation has, through the acts of its individual members, evinced a greater degree of public spirit or been more liberal in the distribution of private charity. In the list of lumbermen-philanthropists the name of Ammi Willard Wright, of Saginaw, Michigan, stands high upon the roll of honor. Mr. Wright first saw the light at Grafton, Windham county, Vermont, July 5, 1822. His parents were natives of the Green Mountain State. Early in Mr. Wright's life the family moved to Rockingham, in the same state, where he pursued his education at the district school until he was seventeen years old. The next three years he passed in working on the farm of his father.

When he was twenty-one years of age, Mr. Wright went to Boston, starting out in life on his own account. He returned to Vermont in 1844 and engaged in the carrying trade between Rutland and Boston, this date being before the era of steam cars in that section, taking produce to the metropolis of the Old Bay State and carrying goods back to the merchants. He was in this business two years, and then managed a hotel in Bartonsville, Vermont, for Jeremiah Barton. March 6, 1848, he married Miss Harriet Barton, the eldest daughter of his employer, and leased the hotel. One year later he moved to Boston and leased the Central hotel, on Battle square.

In 1850 he located at Detroit, Michigan, going to Saginaw a year later. His good judgment enabled him to select some valuable tracts of timber and he began his lumbering operations on Cass river, noted for producing the best white pine that has ever been carried to the saw. His first winter's operations were near the present seat of Tuscola county. The logs were driven down to Saginaw, where they were manufactured, and the lumber shipped to market.

From 1859 until 1865 Mr. Wright was associated in business with Messrs. Miller & Payne, and this firm purchased from its Vermont owners what was known as the "Big Mill," at Saginaw, Michigan, which was refitted with the best machinery available at that time. This concern did business until 1865, when it was succeeded by A. W. Wright & Co., the late James H. Pearson, of Chicago, becoming a partner of Mr. Wright. The same year their saw mill was destroyed by fire, but soon a larger one was erected on the same site. In 1871 the firm of Wright, Wells & Co., was established at Wright lake, Otsego county. In 1882 the A. W. Wright Lumber Company was organized at Saginaw, with a capitalization of $1,500,000, Mr. Wright being the president. This concern operated in Clare, Gladwin and Roscommon counties, having a logging railroad and handling about 30,000,000 feet of logs annually, which were rafted to Saginaw for manufacture.

About this time the lumber firm of Wright & Ketcham was doing a heavy business in Midland and Gladwin counties, having also a logging road and putting into the water 25,000,000 feet annually. It lumbered about 300,000,000 feet of timber, and the A. W. Wright Lumber Company handled about 500,000,000 feet during the period of its activity. When the timber owned by these concerns had become exhausted the attention of Mr. Wright and his associates was directed to the lumbering district of Minnesota, and Wright, Davis & Co. picked up a large quantity of pine stumpage. A railroad was constructed and the Swan River Logging Company was organized, composed of the associates of Mr. Wright. This company handled from 70,000,000 to 100,000,000 feet of logs annually for several years. This timber was sold, and the iron discovered beneath the surface was later purchased by James J. Hill, president of the Great Northern Railway Company, for a large sum.

Mr. Wright was also a member of a mercantile concern, the Wells-Stone Company, which did business at Saginaw for a score of years. A company of five gentlemen, of whom Mr. Wright was one, organized the Cincinnati, Saginaw & Mackinaw Railroad Company and constructed a railroad from Durand to Saginaw and Bay City, which was subsequently leased to the Grand Trunk system. Mr. Wright was one of the incorporators of the Tittabawassee Boom Company, a logging concern that rafted and delivered during the thirty years of its corporate existence a greater quantity of pine logs than has ever been rafted out of any other lumbering stream in the world. He was also for many years interested in a planing mill and factory at Oswego, New York, and he was one of the stockholders in the Saginaw Valley & St. Louis railroad, now operated by the Pere Marquette. He is a large stockholder in the Advance Thresher Company, of Battle Creek, Michigan, of which he is president, and is interested in the extensive dry goods house of Taylor, Wolfenden & Co., of Detroit. Mr. Wright is also much interested in live stock and has ranches in Texas and in the Dakotas. A few years ago he turned his attention to southern pine, and the gentlemen who form the company with which he is associated secured over 250,000 acres of fine pine timber in Louisiana. He is also extensively interested in timber properties on the Pacific Coast.

Alma, Michigan, is a town of his creation mainly. It has water works and electric lighting systems, high school, seven churches, two elevators, a large flouring mill, creamery and a beet sugar factory in which Mr. Wright is a large stockholder and president. It has also a fine college which owes its origin and prosperity largely to Mr. Wright's generosity, the principal buildings being gifts from him to the Alma College Society. The leading hotel in the place was erected by him and he has created a medical and surgical sanitarium which is one of the most complete in the world.

Mr. Wright's love of agricultural pursuits is illustrated by the fact that he owns nearly twenty fine, large farms surrounding Alma. He is a stockholder, director or other official in banking institutions in Detroit, Saginaw, Alma and Battle Creek, Michigan; Saratoga, New York; Minneapolis and Duluth, Minnesota; and in the Chemical National Bank of the city of New York. He is also interested in oil lands in Texas and mineral lands in Missouri; is president of the Peerless Portland Cement Company, of Union City, Michigan; of the Central Michigan Produce Company, of Alma, Michigan; of the Shepherd Canning Company, of Shepherd, Michigan, and has other interests. He is a liberal patron of religious institutions, and churches at Alma and in other places owe much to his thoughtful liberality.

Jacob Cummer

If it were desired to select from among the many who have been identified with lumber manufacture at Cadillac, Michigan, the one whose career would be most significant in connection with the rise and decline of pine manufacture in that region, the unanimous choice would probably be the man who was affectionately though respectfully known by every man, woman and child of that locality as "Uncle Jacob," not only because of the place he assumed in the trade and the magnitude of his operations, but also because of his relation to the community of which he was the almost patriarchal head.

During the seventeen years from 1876 to 1892, inclusive, the firms or companies in which Jacob Cummer and his son, Wellington W., were interested cut not far from 700,000,000 feet of white pine lumber, or over one-half of the amount which statistics credit to Cadillac during that period.

Jacob Cummer was born in 1823 at Toronto, where his father, John Henry Cummer, who was the first white child born in that place, was born in 1797. There Jacob Cummer attended school until eighteen years of age. After a short apprenticeship in his father's saw and flouring mill, he spent two years at Lockport, New York, in one of its flour mills, where he finished learning his trade of miller.

Returning to Toronto, he succeeded his father in the operation of the saw and flouring mill. In 1857 he moved to Watertown, Canada, and engaged in the saw mill and flour mill business with his brother. Shortly afterward he started a new flour mill at Delaware for its Toronto owner, and in 1860 moved from Canada to Michigan. At Newaygo he rented a saw and flouring mill. After three and a half years he went to Croton and rented a flour mill which he operated for three years. Then he engaged in buying pine timber land and logging as a side operation, the logs being sold to Beidler Bros. and Hackley & McGordon, of Muskegon.

Upon the completion of the Grand Rapids & Indiana railroad to Cedar Springs, in 1869, Mr. Cummer moved to that point and embarked still more heavily in the buying and selling of lumber. With the extension of the railroad he followed it up to Morley the ensuing year, and with his only son, Wellington W. Cummer, formed a partnership to manufacture the timber previously purchased in that vicinity.

During the next two years the Cummers purchased numerous tracts of timber, a number of which were in the vicinity of Clam Lake; and in 1876 they moved to that point, now known as Cadillac, the firm being J. Cummer & Son. A mill was purchased by Wellington W. Cummer in the winter of 1878-9 for the purpose of manufacturing the J. Cummer & Son timber. Jacob Cummer meanwhile had turned his attention very largely to timber lands, and every dollar of the earnings which could be spared from the business was invested in additional purchases.

The life of Jacob Cummer up to 1881 had been replete with hard work and many vicissitudes, but now began the period of the greatest prosperity in the lumbering industry of Michigan, an epoch which will probably never be duplicated in any other lumber producing section, and Mr. Cummer had by his foresight placed himself and his associate in a position where they were enabled to reap from it the greatest possible advantages.

The timber which there they utilized was of exceptional quality and yield, single sections being known to have produced 27,347,146 and 32,706,381 feet, mill tally, each. In the manufacture of this magnificent timber the most modern methods were used. The first band mills for sawing pine are said to have been installed in the Cummer saw mill (although that honor is claimed for two other mills), which also was the first mill to adopt the steam carriage feed with cutoffs in cylinder for sawing long or short logs with economy. Logging railroads were early adopted by the Cummers in their operations, and some of these were operated also for general freight and passenger traffic.

By 1893 white pine manufacture at Cadillac was nearly ended and other fields were sought. Investments were made in timber in Virginia, North Carolina, Louisiana and Florida. In these investments the Cummers were joined by James N. Barnett and Harvey J. Hollister. In 1901 the Louisiana tract was closed out at a large profit, and the interests of the parties in the remaining holdings were divided among them in 1902, the Virginia and North Carolina property going to the Barnett and Hollister interests and the Florida holdings to the Cummers.

Operations were commenced in Florida in 1896. Upon the lands lumbered numerous phosphate deposits had been discovered and the development of these beds added a new industry to their enlarging operations. In 1897 the Cummer Lumber Company was organized in Michigan to operate the Florida holdings. Jacob Cummer was made its president and a member of its directorate; W. W. Cummer, vice president; A. G. Cummer, second vice president; W. E. Cummer, secretary and treasurer. The last two are Jacob Cummer's grandsons and virtually the managers of the business.

Soon after the commencement of operations in Florida the company found itself forced to pay too much for the transportation of logs from the forest to its mill at Jacksonville, and a railroad was deemed a desirable adjunct to its operations. Accordingly the Jacksonville & Southwestern railroad was built, with Jacob Cummer as its president and principal stockholder, and subsequently the stock was all acquired by the Cummers. Over this road, ninety miles in length, of standard gage, equipped with first class rolling stock for freight traffic, and extending well toward the Gulf, a vast quantity of the products of the forest and the phosphate mines have been transported to Jacksonville. The foresight of these people had laid the course of their road so that a short extension would make the line a valuable feeder and short cut for some great southern railroad system. This fact was not long overlooked, and soon negotiations were undertaken which resulted in the sale of the line to the Atlantic Coast system, which is now operating it. This road opened up a new and unsettled territory where experiment proved the soil to be adapted to fruit; and now it is lined with new and thriving farming and truck settlements and orchards containing hundreds of thousands of peach and pecan trees.

Jacob Cummer always believed that a thing worth doing at all is worth doing in the best possible manner. Of improvements, new ideas and possibilities in side products, none were ever too small or insignificant to demand his careful and painstaking investigation.

November 7, 1904, Jacob Cummer passed quietly and peacefully to the ranks of the waiting majority, death being the result of a gradual breaking down of his splendid physical forces by the all conquering hand of time. The end came while he was surrounded by his relatives in his home at Cadillac, Michigan. During his long and successful career he had made friends by the thousand, and the news of his decease brought sorrow to the hearts of all who had been so fortunate as to enjoy his friendship or acquaintance.

LIBRARY
OF THE
UNIVERSIT
OF
CALIFORNIA

factory wer
successive
ton and the
ber Comp
50,000,000
up a consid

Justus S. Stearns

The story of what Justus S. Stearns has done for himself is an interesting one, but of greater interest is the story of what he has done for the city of Ludington, Michigan. The history of a success fairly won is in itself worthy of recital, but when that success has been used for the benefit of others its right of perpetuation is increased fourfold.

Justus S. Stearns, of Ludington, was born April 10, 1845, in Chautauqua county, New York. As a boy he worked in the saw mill of his father, H. S. Stearns. After a public and commercial school education, he became associated with his father in the lumber business at Conneaut, Ohio. Afterward, on his own account, he handled hardwood lumber at Toledo, at which time he had a saw mill in the Black Swamp district southwest of that city.

It was in 1876 that the lumbering instinct within drew him, as it did many others, to Michigan. His first year's experience with portable mills near Big Rapids was disastrous, as the result of bad markets, and his slender capital was swallowed up. Then he was a clerk for a time in the Ward store at Ludington, and for a time acted as cashier for Thomas R. Lyon. Here he saved a little capital, with which he again started out for himself by organizing the Stearns Lumber Company. He built a mill at Stearns Siding, on the Pere Marquette railroad a few miles east of Ludington. This small saw mill was afterward enlarged and a planing mill and a cutup factory were added to the plant. The business grew by successive stages and later the plant was removed to Ludington and the company reorganized as the Stearns Salt & Lumber Company. This plant has a double band mill of about 50,000,000 feet annual capacity, a planing mill which works up a considerable portion of the saw mill production, a grainer salt block with an annual output of about 300,000 barrels of salt and a large cooper shop supplying the barrels for the salt.

The growth of this enterprise has by no means absorbed all the activities of the man to whose foresight and energy its existence is due. J. S. Stearns is heavily interested in Wisconsin lumber operations through the J. S. Stearns Lumber Company, of Odanah, and the Flambeau Lumber Company, of Lac du Flambeau. The J. S. Stearns Lumber Company, in addition to its large white pine lumber production at Odanah, on the Bad River Indian Reservation, manufactures pine lumber at Ashland, Wisconsin, and also has a considerable hardwood interest at Jonesboro, Arkansas. The Stearns Salt & Lumber Company has a big hardwood and coal mining operation at Stearns, Kentucky. The Stearns & Culver Lumber Company is another institution of which Mr. Stearns is the presiding genius. It produces longleaf yellow pine at Bagdad, Florida. The selling institution which markets the production of Mr. Stearns' mills in Michigan, Kentucky, Tennessee and Florida is the Stearns Company, of Grand Rapids, Michigan.

In addition to his lumber enterprises Mr. Stearns has found time to be many different kinds of a public servant and a private promoter of the interests of Ludington and of Michigan in general. He is president of the Ludington & Northern Railway Company; president of the Electric Light & Power Company of Ludington, and is identified with many other enterprises, to which his genius for organization has been directed for the benefit of the community rather than for private gain.

He was prominent in the development and in the financial support of the Epworth League summer resort near Ludington on Lake Michigan; he is president of the J. S. Stearns Improvement Company; he is a stockholder in the First National Bank at Ludington; he owns the historic Ward saw mill plant and the company's store, in which he was formerly a clerk; he is senior member in the firm of Stearns & Mack, a mercantile institution at Scottville, Michigan; he is the owner of a beautiful model hotel at Ludington, and is also the owner of a fine Turkish bath house in the same city.

Mr. Stearns' public services have extended beyond his own city. For years he was chairman of the Republican County Committee and in 1888 was a Harrison elector for the Ninth Congressional District. In 1898 he was nominated by the Republican party of Michigan for Secretary of State and was elected by a rousing majority. Mr. Stearns has been a candidate for governor of Michigan; but, being strictly a non-machine politician, he has not yet succeeded in achieving his ambition in that direction.

One of Mr. Stearns' striking qualities is his genius for organization. He will inaugurate an enterprise, map out its policy and set it going. He will then leave it and turn his attention to something else, but the impress of his forcefulness and system is upon it and it keeps on going. He has the faculty of choosing able lieutenants and imbuing them with his ideas. He keeps closely in touch with his enterprises through a system of daily reports, but his supervision is of the most general character and he relieves himself of the burden of the details by leaving them to be executed by others according to the principles which he has established. Each enterprise and each department is specialized and carried on under distinct management. But there is also efficient co-operation among them, through periodical meetings where new and progressive ideas are eagerly sought and discussed. The most up-to-date appliances for lumber production are carefully analyzed and anything that promises to cheapen the cost of production or improve the quality is immediately purchased and installed.

In early life Mr. Stearns married Paulina Lyon, sister of Thomas R. and J. B. Lyon, of Chicago, and the one grief of Mr. Stearns' life is her death, which occurred in 1904. He has one son, Robert L., who, while an artist of quality and

distinction, has a
with his father in
lieutenants.

LIBRARY
OF TH
UNIVERSITY
OF
CALIFORNIA

E. GOLDEN FILER

E. Golden Filer

The operations of father and son have made the name of Filer already historic in the northern portion of the lower peninsula of Michigan, and particularly in the lumber industry of that section of the premier lumber state. Not only is the name celebrated in business annals and in local tradition, but it is officially affixed to a township in Manistee county and to a suburb of the city of Manistee, known as Filer City. It has a peculiar individuality, also, because of the family ownership of a long continued business.

The family is of Scotch descent, Delos L. Filer, father of E. Golden Filer, having been born in Herkimer county, New York, in 1817, of Scotch parents. He was a man of large native ability and of aggressive character. At various times he earned a livelihood as farmer, teacher, merchant and lumberman. After his removal to Manistee he became a physician and played an important part in ministering to the physical needs of the pioneer settlers of that section. He was married three times, the second marriage, in 1840, being to Miss Juliet Golden, who was the mother of E. Golden Filer and gave him her family name.

It is E. Golden Filer of whom this sketch particularly treats. He was born in Jefferson county, New York, December 4, 1840. In 1850 the family moved to Racine, Wisconsin, where young Filer was educated in the public schools and at Racine College, then one of the leading educational institutions of the West.

The elder Filer had entered the employ of Roswell Canfield, which led to his removal to Manistee in 1853, where the members of the Canfield family had established themselves in the lumber business.

This was Mr. Filer's opportunity. He was then in middle

life and had acquired but limited means; but at Manistee he invested what he had in milling and lumber interests and made accessions to his resources which soon grew into a considerable fortune. He came to own much of the territory on which Manistee now stands and was a liberal doner of money and lands for the erection of churches and public buildings as they were demanded by the growth of the new city. He was otherwise active in the development of this new lumber town. Most of his Manistee interests centered in the firm of D. L. Filer & Sons, in which Delos L. Filer and his sons, E. Golden and D. W., were partners. The management of this firm he gave over to his sons when he moved his residence to Ludington, where he had made heavy investments and where he died July 26, 1879.

After the removal of the Filer family to Manistee in 1853, E. Golden Filer received much practical training and experience. In 1860, in company with T. J. Ramsdell, he visited Lansing, the capital of the state, and secured a clerkship in the auditor general's office. He remained there in that capacity until 1862, when he enlisted in Company A, Twentieth Michigan Volunteer Infantry, serving two years in the Army of the Potomac. He was honorably discharged in 1864 and returned to Manistee, where he was needed by his father in the growing business of the Filer interests.

In 1866 the firm of D. L. Filer & Sons was organized. It consisted of D. L. Filer, the father, and E. Golden and Delos Warren, the sons. They purchased 2,500 acres of timber at the south end of Manistee lake, three miles from Manistee. Here, near the mouth of the Little Manistee river, they built a double circular saw mill. It had a capacity of 50,000 feet of lumber every twelve hours, and in 1867 it cut 8,500,000 feet. A portion of the land was platted and became known as Filer City. It is still known by that name, although it is under township government and is a suburb of Manistee, with which place it is connected by an electric road.

This mill was the first to use paper friction pulleys, and was the first in Manistee to introduce steam feed and the steam log turner. It was also the first in that vicinity to utilize the band saw. It is the oldest mill in the city and the only one now manufacturing pine exclusively.

In 1869 the father, D. L. Filer, became heavily interested in the Pere Marquette Lumber Company, of Ludington, the two sons assuming the Manistee business and continuing it with success, E. Golden Filer having charge of the office. The Manistee mill was improved until it produced 100,000 feet of lumber, 250,000 shingles and 50,000 lath daily. The refuse and poor run, which formerly went into lath or waste, were utilized after 1880 as staves and headings for the salt product and for fuel for generating steam for the salt block. A barrel mill was added to the plant and put in operation in 1904.

E. Golden Filer, after coming out of the army, was married, in 1865, to Miss Julia Filer, daughter of Alanson Filer, of Racine, Wisconsin. He is a director of the Manistee Booming Company, of which he was president for twelve years. He is president of the Manistee County Savings Bank and director and treasurer of the Grand Rapids & Manistee Railroad Company. He is a director in the Michigan Trust Company, of Grand Rapids, Michigan; the Pere Marquette Lumber Company, of Ludington, Michigan; the Michigan Salt Association, and the New York Land Company.

In addition to his lumber interests in Michigan he is largely interested in timber lands in Minnesota and California and to a less extent in Arizona and South Carolina. Mr. Filer is the resident member of the firm of D. L. Filer & Sons at Manistee. He has made the most of the opportunity presented to him by his father, and has demonstrated that he inherits his father's business sense and public spirit.

The lumber industry was one of the pioneer callings of this country. Together with the agricultural settler and the general trader it followed close on the heels of the hunter and trapper. But the pioneer days of lumbering in Michigan were over years ago, and many of those now engaged in it

have enjoyed all the advantages of
herited wealth and opportunity, an
held by some to be disadvantages;
those who in character and acco
that they may be advantages in fact.

LIBRARY
OF THE
UNIVERSITY
OF
CALIFORNIA

James Dempsey

James Dempsey, of Manistee, Michigan, was born in Ireland and came to this country when he was about fifteen years of age. The family located at Scranton, Pennsylvania, at which place his father died in 1857. James Dempsey was a son of his father's first wife, Mary Ward, who died while he was a child. James lived for a number of years with Judge Nathaniel B. Eldred, of a well known family of Pennsylvania, founders of the town of that name and interested in the lumber industry of that section. He left Pennsylvania early in 1852 and spent the two succeeding years in traveling through the country, engaged in a variety of occupations. Then followed his connection with the lumber industry of Michigan.

Thus he passed through the lower grades of the hard school of life—a school whose rewards are only for the strong and ambitious. Of the many thousands who enter it only a few graduate. The vast majority remain in the primary grade—they stay where they started. The woodchopper remains a woodchopper; the raftsman remains a raftsman; the millhand remains a millhand—which is to say that most men are born to be privates in the ranks. And it is fortunate that it is so, as for every captain there must be many privates, but we may say, "All honor to the private!" The good woodchopper, or raftsman, or millman is as necessary as he of higher station—and all the more honor to him if he fill his place well, and better as the years go on. But there must be leaders as well, and most of them are made of the erstwhile privates, of those who by virtue of bigger brains and higher ambitions rise to generalship. Of such caliber was James Dempsey. His was the dissatisfaction with small accomplishment that spurs on to higher; his the mastery of mind that ever remains uncontent with subordinate position.

His experience, gained in the logging camps, resulted in the formation of the partnership of Dempsey & Cartier, which took a contract for driving, sorting and booming logs on the Manistee river. Later the firm secured a similar contract for the logs on the Pere Marquette river at Ludington, Michigan, the home of Mr. A. E. Cartier. In 1873, four years after the formation of the partnership, the firm purchased a saw mill on Manistee lake, formerly known as the Green & Milmo property, and engaged in the manufacture of lumber. Ten years later the business was incorporated under the name of the Manistee Lumber Company and Mr. Dempsey was made president, the other stockholders being A. E. Cartier, his first associate, G. Wiborn and William Wente. Large bodies of pine timber in Kalkaska county and along the Manistee river were purchased.

In 1880, in company with John F. Brown, of Big Rapids, Michigan, he began the erection of a saw mill on the east side of Lake Manistee. Before this mill was completed Mr. Brown died and his interest in the venture was purchased by E. B. Simpson, of Milwaukee, Wisconsin. After the mill was finished it was operated under the firm name of Dempsey, Simpson & Co. until 1887. when it was destroyed by fire and never rebuilt.

Mr. Dempsey's other lumber interests are represented by large timber holdings on the Pacific Coast—about 20,000 acres in Skagit and Pierce counties, Washington, and several thousand acres in Oregon. He is also a stockholder and director of the Saginaw & Manistee Lumber Company, operating a large saw mill with planing mill attached, at Williams, Arizona.

Mr. Dempsey had much to do with the formation of the State Lumber Company, which was organized in 1887 for the purpose of purchasing and operating the plant theretofore known as the Davies & Blacker mill. The Manistee Lumber Company took one-third of the stock of this new company and was represented in its management by Mr. Dempsey, who assumed the vice presidency of the company.

Mr. Dempsey was president of the Eureka Lumber Company, which was organized in 1890 to purchase the plant and accompanying timber lands of the Manistee Salt & Lumber Company. The property of this company was absorbed in 1900 by the Manistee Lumber Company. The annual output of this company is now about 45,000,000 feet of lumber, 15,000,000 lath and 150,000 barrels of salt.

Early in his Manistee career, Mr. Dempsey embarked in the tug business, and in 1880 the Dempsey Tug Line was formed, which was operated until 1887, when the boats were sold and the company dissolved.

The Dempsey Lumber Company was organized June 2, 1904, and took over the Washington and Oregon lands. The company is composed of L. T. Dempsey, president; James Dempsey, vice president; J. W. Dempsey, secretary and treasurer; J. J. Dempsey and N. Dowen. Mr. Dowen was logging superintendent of the Manistee Lumber Company for twenty years.

Mr. Dempsey was the first Democratic postmaster of Manistee, being appointed during President Buchanan's administration and serving until its close. He was again appointed postmaster during Cleveland's first administration. While not seeking political honors, he served one term as mayor of Manistee, but declined to accept a nomination for a second term. He is a staunch Democrat, but during the split in that party over the money question he sided with the adherents to the gold standard. He is a director and the vice president of the First National Bank of Manistee.

Mr. Dempsey was the second son of his father's first marriage, there being also two daughters by this marriage. His own family is large. He was married June 30, 1861, to Miss Mary Mullen, daughter of Michael Mullen, of Racine, Wisconsin, and his family consists of five daughters and seven sons: Mrs. John F. Clancy, of Racine, Wisconsin; Mrs. Dr. James J. Murphy, of Pontiac, Michigan; Mrs. James W. Duncan, of Manistee, Michigan; Mrs. Augustus Fitzgerald, of Detroit, Michigan; Estelle Josephine Dempsey; Lawre T., superintendent of mills for the Manistee Lumber C pany; James W., bookkeeper and private secretary to father; John J., who is in charge of the Washington and gon business; Frank M., connected with the railroad and ging department of the Manistee Lumber Company; who is attending the University of Notre Dame, and L C. 'The youngest child, Walter M., lived but three ye dying September 20, 1886. In religion Mr. Dempsey faithful adherent of the Roman Catholic faith, as are all members of his family.

three
mill h
a capa
25,000

ROBERT R. BLACKER

Robert R. Blacker

Many men have attained as great wealth as Robert R. Blacker, of Manistee, Michigan, but it is doubtful if any has ever exerted a greater influence in his particular community.

Mr. Blacker was born at Brantford, Ontario, October 31, 1845. When nineteen years of age he went to Michigan and after a few years spent at Buchanan, moved to Manistee. The lumbering industry, with its limitless possibilities, fascinated him, and, his wits supplying the stock in trade that his purse refused, he entered it in the capacity of lumber inspector.

His faculty for absorbing detail soon made him thoroughly acquainted with all the various phases of the business, and in 1875 he became associated with R. G. Peters, the partnership being known as R. R. Blacker & Co., for the purpose of operating a shingle mill which had been erected. Four years later Mr. Blacker formed a partnership with E. T. Davies and Patrick Noud, which concern was known as Davies, Blacker & Co. The firm built and operated a saw mill and shingle plant, which was conducted successfully and without interruption until 1887, when the State Lumber Company was organized in place of the older concern and a salt block was added to the equipment.

The State Lumber Company's mill and yard site occupies about twenty-five acres of ground on the shore of Manistee lake and affords admirable facilities for handling lumber by rail and water. Besides the saw and shingle mill are a lath mill, machine shop and filing room, salt block, cooper's shop, three drill houses, barn, shingle sheds and office. The lumber mill has an output of 125,000 feet a day. The shingle mill has a capacity of 200,000 shingles a day. The stave mill turns out 25,000 staves and 1,000 sets of barrel headings daily. At the salt block 1,200 barrels of finished product are handled daily.

Storage room is provided on the docks for 5,000,000 feet of lumber and 6,000,000 shingles; the railroad yard is capable of storing 10,000,000 feet of lumber, and an enormous shingle shed provides shelter for 4,000,000 shingles. The tracks of two railroads—the Manistee & North-Eastern and the Manistee & Grand Rapids—enter the company's yard. In the mill and reserve booms the company is able to handle no less than 5,000,000 feet of logs at one time and there is plenty of water anywhere along the docks to permit of the loading of any lumber freighter.

The company owns enough timber tributary to Manistee to keep its mills busy for fifteen years or thereabouts. Its holdings now spread over Manistee, Lake, Mason, Wexford, Benzie, Leelanau and Kalkaska counties. The timber is mainly hemlock, cedar and hardwoods with some pine. A quantity of logs is still brought to Manistee every year by river, but greater amounts are shipped in over the Manistee & North-Eastern railroad. Mr. Blacker and Patrick Noud are the owners of most of the capital stock and the actual managers of the State Lumber Company.

Politically Mr. Blacker is a Democrat. The spring election of 1882 made him an alderman of the city of Manistee and six years later he was elected mayor. He continued to hold this office for four successive terms, an endorsement which the Salt City has seldom given any one. In 1882 he was elected to the state legislature as well as to the city council, and in 1884 was reëlected. In that year he was also a delegate to the Democratic national convention. He was an alternate at the convention of 1892 and delegate at large to the famous Chicago convention of 1896. December 24, 1891, he was appointed to the office of Secretary of State by Governor Winans, and he administered the affairs of the office most creditably.

Mr. Blacker's interests in Chicago as well as in Michigan are numerous and large. He is particularly careful to keep track of the industrial stocks and the various daily movements in finance and trade, and is one of the best posted men among outside investors in that class of securities. He uses the same care and foresight in such operations as he has always shown in his lumber business.

To Mr. Blacker belongs the credit of establishing a new philanthropy in Manistee, and one which promises to be very successful. He practically rebuilt a wing of Mercy Hospital, fitted it with all the requirements of a modern bath house and pumped brine into its reservoirs from the State Lumber Company's wells; giving the inmates the tonic benefit of salt water baths. Encouraged by Mr. Blacker's experiment, a public bath house has been completed in Manistee. It is possible that some of the credit for this innovation should be given to Mrs. Blacker, who has always taken a warm interest in the welfare of Mercy Hospital, or Mercy Sanitarium, as it is now called.

For several years Mr. Blacker has been a resident of Chicago, but during that time he has maintained his Manistee home, in which he spends the greater part of the summer. In 1903 Mr. Blacker, together with Mr. Noud and others, built the magnificent steel steamer Eastland, which is now running between Chicago and South Haven, Michigan. Mr. Blacker is a member of the Congregational Church and has a membership in the Manistee Olympian Club and in several clubs in Chicago.

Mr. Blacker has married twice but has no children. Some years after the death of his first wife he married Miss Nellie Canfield, daughter of the late John Canfield, of Manistee, a man of mark in the lumber history of the state.

JOHN CANFIELD

John Canfield

In the history of the lumber industry of Manistee, Michigan, the name of John Canfield will always be treasured, not only as a bit of vital history but also as a tender memory. He was born at Sandisfield, Massachusetts, in 1830, and attended the public school at that place and later at Homer, New York. In 1842 his father, Roswell Canfield, moved the family to Racine, Wisconsin, where the boy continued his education. When fourteen years of age he left school to become a clerk in a store at Racine. He was employed at this work for three years.

His father and his brother Edmund had formed a partnership known as R. Canfield & Son and had established a lumber yard at Racine. After quitting the store, John Canfield was employed in this lumber yard in piling and selling lumber.

In 1848, when he had attained the age of eighteen, he took charge of the firm's books. For a long time he was employed in the Racine yard and in superintending the firm's mills at Manistee. December 18, 1849, he moved to Manistee to reside permanently, the firm then becoming R. Canfield & Sons, John having been taken in as a partner.

His father had built mills at the mouth of the Manistee river and these the young man operated with success. The earliest constructed of these mills was torn down and rebuilt. The firm lost three mills by fire between 1864 and 1867. In 1860 the elder Canfield died and the firm became E. & J. Canfield. This firm erected a mill on Little lake, containing a mulay saw and a stock gang. At the close of the War of the Rebellion, in 1865, John Canfield and James Shrigley formed the firm of Shrigley & Canfield and erected a mill at the mouth of the Little Manistee river. This became famous as the "Shrigley mill." It contained two circulars and a gang edger of a new type. This mill was twice burned and rebuilt, and each time the most modern machinery was employed, until eventually it had a daily capacity of 100,000 feet of lumber and 100,000 shingles.

In 1887 Mr. Canfield bought an interest in the Stronach Lumber Company, which had a mill near the mouth of the Little Manistee river. He was made president of this company. The mill ended its operations in 1895 and the plant was sold to the Union Lumber Company.

Edmund Canfield died in 1868. In 1871 John Canfield took into partnership Edward D. Wheeler and the new firm of Canfield & Wheeler carried on the subsequent operations of the Canfield interests.

At one time, in addition to the large white pine and norway timber holdings of Mr. Canfield on the lower peninsula of Michigan, he owned 600,000,000 feet of standing pine in the Ashland district of Wisconsin. The forest fires of 1894 did an estimated damage of $175,000 to this timber. During the busiest period of his life Mr. Canfield is said to have handled 150,000,000 feet of lumber a year, and in the fifty years from 1849 until 1899 a total of 1,250,000,000 feet.

It is said that when Mr. Canfield came to Manistee the entire lumber production of the state of Michigan did not exceed 150,000,000 feet, yet he lived to compass an annual production of that size himself.

Mr. Canfield did his part in developing the famous salt industry of Manistee. The presence of salt was demonstrated by experiments which were made possible by popular subscriptions to which Mr. Canfield was a liberal contributor. It was found that the city was underlaid by a stratum of rock salt. In 1878 Canfield & Wheeler erected a salt block with a daily capacity of 500 barrels. This was operated in connection with their saw mill.

In 1854 Mr. Canfield married Miss Helen M. Beach, of Berkshire, Massachusetts, who died in 1860, leaving three daughters. In 1865 he married Miss Frances V. Wheeler, of Berkshire county, Massachusetts. Of the two sons born to them Charles J. is still living and has concluded the lumber operations of the estate in Michigan, and since has become prominent as a timber investor.

John Canfield died in 1898; Mrs. Canfield in 1904.

Mr. Canfield's influence for the benefit and education of his townspeople was powerful. To him Manistee owes its fine and imposing Congregational Church. He chose and secured the plans for this edifice and did not rest until it had taken shape and was completely finished and furnished, he himself bearing fully three-fourths of the expense. The great public hospital which embellishes the city was built by him in much the same way, the lesser contributors coöperating with him just enough to insure their interest and support. This was his wise way of giving.

Mr. Canfield strongly objected to being imposed upon in any direction and he invariably resisted what he considered an unjust claim against him to the limit of the court of last resort. He was simple in his manners, unostentatious to a degree, loyal to his friends and fair to his foes. The latter always found him fighting honestly in the open with no show of treachery or double dealing, and his opinions were always based upon the courage of his very decided convictions. He was a profound and discriminating reader of the best books; indeed, his extensive library contained no others.

The gentle side of his nature was manifest in his fondness for flowers and his enjoyment in giving them to others—one article of his creed being that flowers should be bestowed during one's lifetime rather than heaped upon the unknowing dead within the casket. One so quiet in manner could scarcely be called genial, but the unaffected and unvarying pleasure he displayed in the company of his friends endeared him to them, and his original ideas, the glints of irresistible humor and his many kindly acts have not failed to keep for him a tender place in their memories.

Henry W. Carey

When a man does many things well he is in the way of achieving particular distinction. Such a man is Henry Westonrae Carey, of Manistee, Michigan. He was born in the city of New York, September 21, 1850. His father was of English descent and was engaged in various manufacturing pursuits. His mother was a Ramsay, a lineal descendant of Allan Ramsay, the Scottish poet. Young Carey received his education in the public schools of the city of New York and the College of the City of New York, graduating from the latter institution about 1870. In his early life he was employed on 'Change in the metropolis, and for several years was in the publishing business.

In 1881 he left New York for the great West. He stopped at Manistee, Michigan, and fell under the notice of R. G. Peters. The young man from the East, with his polished manners, his business training and fine education, appealed to the sturdy lumberman. Mr. Carey entered the employ of Mr. Peters as private secretary and made rapid advancement. He became a general utility man about the Peters lumber institution. It was not long before he became a stockholder in the R. G. Peters Salt & Lumber Company and eventually secretary and treasurer of the company, an office he has retained ever since.

A few years ago the maple lumber industry of Michigan was apparently the victim of overproduction. The largest buyers of maple lumber were the flooring makers. They dictated their own prices and grades and their own terms of payment. The R. G. Peters Salt & Lumber Company was among the largest producers of this wood. Largely through the efforts of Mr. Carey the manufacturers of maple got together and carefully analyzed the situation. As a result there was organized a sales company—the Michigan Maple Company—of which Mr. Carey was made president, a position he still retains. This company takes the total output of maple lumber produced by a large proportion of the leading manufacturers of Michigan and sells the product to the trade of the country. Mr. Carey knows to a nicety every day in the year just how much maple lumber is in first hands. He knows the consuming requirements with exactness and keeps in touch with transportation features with equal accuracy. Through his own efforts he has succeeded in perfecting a system for an improvement in the quality of maple lumber production. He is able to direct how a log shall be sawed to the best advantage to meet the requirements of the market. The Michigan Maple Company has been eminently successful.

Furthermore, under Mr. Carey's direction the interests of consumers as well as producers have been kept in mind. While the primary object of the company is to benefit the producers, and that object has been attained, the power of the organization has been used with discretion. Mr. Carey has acted on the theory that a comparatively uniform price is better for both departments than quick and extreme fluctuations. Therefore the company has resisted the temptation to secure a temporary price advantage when it was within its power to do so, and, conversely, has not been obliged materially to reduce its price when trade conditions were unfavorable.

In 1903 the hemlock bark industry of Michigan degenerated into an unprofitable pursuit. The tannery people insisted upon a price for bark that left no profit to the stumpage owners. Mr. Carey came to the fore with a proposition to hemlock stumpage owners, of whom he was one, to organize the Hemlock Bark Company. Of this corporation he is president, and the history of the Michigan Maple Company is being repeated in the bark industry.

Mr. Carey is also president of the Lakewood Lumber Company, of Grand Rapids, Michigan; treasurer of the Gillette Roller Bearing Company, of Grand Rapids; secretary of the Manistee & Luther Railroad Company; secretary of the Batchelor Cypress Lumber Company, of Panasoffkee, Florida; vice president of the Peters Lumber & Shingle Company, of Benton Harbor, Michigan; president of the Wolverine Oil Company, of Manistee, and a director of the News Publishing Company, of Manistee. He is a member of the State Executive Committee of the Young Men's Christian Association and a diligent worker in the Congregational Church of his city, where he has become invaluable to both church and Sunday school.

In his youth Mr. Carey secured a soldier's discipline as a member of the Twenty-second Regiment, National Guard of New York, from which he retired with the rank of captain of the veteran corps of that regiment. In 1893 he was proffered a colonelcy by Governor Rich, of Michigan, and for four years served the state as paymaster general of the Michigan National Guard.

Mr. Carey's interest in educational matters found recognition in 1901, when he was elected regent of the University of Michigan, and he has been influential in having established courses whereby the students of that institution may be taught both the theory and practice of business.

For years Mr. Carey has been prominent in the councils of the Republican party and he is a recognized party leader. In 1888 he was made a member of the Republican State Central Committee and for fourteen years he has been a member of its executive committee, the longest term of service of any of its members. For a year he was chairman of the Manistee County Republican Committee and for a similar term served as secretary of the congressional committee of the ninth district of Michigan. At one time he was vice president of the National League of Republican Clubs. For twenty years he has been a member of the Manistee school board, on which he has done most effective service. In 1899 he became a Maccabee and his efforts for the betterment of that order soon won recognition from the Supreme Lodge.

He has administered the offices of supreme great lieutenant commander, great chapla master of the guard.

In 1879 Mr. Carey married Miss May M ter of Jonathan Ransom, of New York. tains three children—Mabel M., Archibald The son is a graduate of the University of

genius are legion. Special taste or in-
mental superiority; phenomenal capa-
physical power—these are a few of the
people the term
or fortunate cir-
principled shrewd-
applicable. Then, again, there is a
all of these. Genius untiring effort
of duty—the genius of hard work.
Buckley, a man who did
whose fame was not accidental;
cited no special
and place, starting out in life
without friends at court
them all—education, friends, money

, Michigan, was born in
August 8, 1842. In him
English yeomanry, and that he has lived
his services in the armies
The family crossed the Atlantic
Montreal. Here the father died
world alone save for two children,
years his junior. Mrs. Buckley,
to Toronto soon after the death of
remained there until 1855 and then
Wisconsin.
fifteen years old, and, three years later,
the family moved to Mil-
studying hard for some time, harder,
for the enjoyment of youth. While in

Edward Buckley

The definitions of genius are legion. Special taste or inclination; distinguished mental superiority; phenomenal capability; uncommon intellectual power — these are a few of the definitions found in the lexicon. By many people the term genius is applied where favored influence, or fortunate circumstances, or wealth, or sometimes even unprincipled shrewdness, would be more applicable. Then, again, there is a definition different from all of these: Genius; untiring effort and faithful performance of duty—the genius of hard work. This is the genius of Edward Buckley, a man who did not stumble into success; whose fame was not accidental; whose wealth came not by chance; who inherited no special opportunity; but who, unaided and alone, starting out in life handicapped by a meager education, without friends at court and without money, won them all—education, friends, money —by his own persistent efforts.

Edward Buckley, of Manistee, Michigan, was born in Bideford, Devonshire, England, August 8, 1842. In him is the blood of sturdy English yeomanry, and that he has lived up to the traditions of his ancestors his services in the armies of the United States testify. The family crossed the Atlantic ocean and made a home in Montreal. Here the father died and the mother faced the world alone save for two children, Edward and a sister two years his junior. Mrs. Buckley, with her children, moved to Toronto soon after the death of her husband. They remained there until 1855 and then moved to Sheboygan, Wisconsin.

The boy was then thirteen years old, and, three years later, to give him greater opportunities, the family moved to Milwaukee. He had been studying hard for some time, harder, perhaps, than is good for the enjoyment of youth. While in

Milwaukee he took a course in a commercial school, absorbing the A B C of business affairs with keen interest. Stirring days were near, however, and the fury of war roused the yeoman blood. He enlisted in the Twenty-fourth Wisconsin Infantry on August 5, 1862, when twenty years old. The regiment was hurried south to join Buell's Army of the Cumberland, and for three years the young fellow spent his best energies for the country of his adoption. He participated in the fighting at Perryville, Stone River, Chickamauga, Missionary Ridge and in the battles of the famous Atlanta campaign. He was discharged with honor in August, 1865, and thereupon returned to Milwaukee, his former home, where he remained for two years in the employ of the Chicago, Milwaukee & St. Paul Railway Company.

In the spring of 1867 he went to Manistee and accepted a situation with a hardware firm, little thinking that there was to be the scene of his most successful and durable achievements. In six months he was part owner of a hardware business, H. V. Marchant, of Milwaukee, being associated with him under the firm name of Edward Buckley & Co. In 1874 he closed out this business and for six years was associated with C. F. Ruggles in the pine land business.

In 1880, Edward Buckley and William Douglas formed a partnership for the purpose of carrying on a general logging and mill business, under the name of Buckley & Douglas. In 1886 the mill property and timber interests of Ruddock, Nuttall & Co. were purchased. The mill was situated on Manistee lake and the new owners immediately set to work to improve the property by the addition of machinery, buildings and boilers. The mill was practically rebuilt at an expenditure of about $115,000. By 1888 the mill had a cut of about 60,000,000 feet of logs annually. It was about this time that the Manistee & North-Eastern Railroad was organized, with Edward Buckley as president and general manager. This road now has a total of 175 miles and it also owns twelve locomotives, 532 freight cars, ten passenger and baggage cars, with two snow plows and a steam shovel, and is probably the only road in the country without a bond or mortgage upon it.

December 31, 1892, the Buckley & Douglas Lumber Company was organized, with Edward Buckley as president. In 1896-7 five salt wells were sunk and a salt block with a capacity of 2,500 barrels a day was built. The salt block now covers five acres and is probably the largest in the world. The company's buildings, yards and docks cover forty acres. Among the buildings are a double rotary mill, shingle mill, fuel storage holder, two brick engine houses, a salt block with five wells, a very extensive fire protection plant, machine shop, roundhouse, freight depot, electric light plant, several warehouses, office and general store. The plant is usually operated eleven months in the year. Brine is pumped by compressed air and both grainer and vacuum pan processes are used. There is a large cooperage shop fitted with the most approved machinery having a capacity of 3,000 barrels in ten hours. The supply of logs is largely brought over the company's railroad and dumped from the cars into booms capable of storing about 6,000,000 feet. The company also owns extensive docks.

Mr. Buckley has been twice married. His first wife was Miss Mary D. Ruggles, who became Mrs. Edward Buckley in 1869. Mrs. Buckley died, childless, in 1885, and nine years later, in 1894, Mr. Buckley married Miss Jonnie Sloan. They have one child, Virginia.

There is enough of the Anglo-Saxon in Mr. Buckley to make him somewhat reserved, and this may be one reason why he has never been conspicuous in politics. He is energetic and aggressive in all kinds of commercial enterprises, but the political limelight has no attraction for him. As a member of the Masonic order, in which he has taken all the degrees up to the thirty-second inclusive, he is well known and he has held nearly every office in the order to which he owes allegiance.

He is a quiet, rather uncommunicative and unassuming

man, who has achie
become a self edu
any aid except that

LIBRARY
OF THE
UNIVERSITY
OF
CALIFORNIA

CHARLES H. HACKLEY

Charles H. Hackley

The city of Muskegon, Michigan, enjoys lasting fame in the history of the lumber industry of the United States as the point of premier production in the early '80's. Linked indissolubly with the fame of Muskegon is the name of Charles H. Hackley. Her glory as a lumber city has departed, and in its place has come renown as a city of diversified industries, splendid institutions and public enterprise. Mr. Hackley contributed his share to the city's importance in the lumber world; and her later renown for more substantial things may be attributed almost entirely to his individual effort.

Charles H. Hackley, famed as a lumberman and as a philanthropist, was born at Michigan City, Indiana, January 3, 1837. His father, Joseph H. Hackley, was one of the early settlers at that end of Lake Michigan. The family moved to Southport, now Kenosha, Wisconsin, where the boy received such education as was obtainable in the public schools of that place at that time. When fifteen years of age he left school and began self support. In 1856 he worked his passage on a schooner across Lake Michigan, from Kenosha to Muskegon, and at noon on the day of his arrival, April 17, began work as a common laborer for Durkee, Truesdell & Co., lumber manufacturers. He rapidly rose in position, and in the fall was sent to the woods as log scaler. The following spring he was made outside foreman of the saw mill, having charge of sorting the lumber. At the suggestion of his employers, he returned to Kenosha in the fall of 1857 and spent the winter at a commercial college, training himself for business life. The following spring he returned to Muskegon as bookkeeper for Gideon Truesdell, successor to Durkee, Truesdell & Co.

By 1859 he had acquired sufficient experience to decide him to enter business for himself. His father had moved to

Muskegon in 1855, and the firm of J. H. Hackley & Co. was organized in 1859, purchasing a saw mill and adding another mill a year later. The first partners were J. H. Hackley, Charles H. Hackley and Gideon Truesdell. Later two brothers of Charles H. Hackley—Edwin and Porter—were associated with the concern. The father died in 1874 and was followed a few years later by Edwin Hackley and Porter Hackley. The firm of J. H. Hackley & Co. was succeeded by Hackley & Sons, and Hackley & Sons in turn by C. H. Hackley & Co. In 1866 Mr. Hackley and James McGordon, under the firm name of Hackley & McGordon, purchased the "Wing" mill which some years thereafter was burned.

In 1881 Thomas Hume purchased the McGordon interests in C. H. Hackley & Co. and Hackley & McGordon, on the death of James McGordon, and the firm of Hackley & Hume was founded, one destined to become historic in American lumber manufacture. Hackley & Hume continued operations on the Muskegon river until 1894, when their timber in that section became exhausted. They had foreseen this event and as early as 1886 had begun to buy timber lands in other states. Their early purchases were in Wisconsin, Minnesota and Louisiana, and later large bodies of land were acquired in Mississippi, South Carolina, Florida and British Columbia. Mr. Hackley continued to be interested in the manufacture of lumber after the shut-down and demolition of the Muskegon mill.

In 1892 Mr. Hackley and Mr. Hume bought the interest of S. B. Barker in the Itasca Lumber Company, of Minneapolis, which in 1903 bought the property and business of the H. C. Akeley Lumber Company, a concern that had been organized in 1889 by Hackley & Hume and H. C. Akeley and Freeman S. Farr, of Minneapolis.

Mr. Hackley was among the heaviest stockholders in the Itasca Lumber Company. An enumeration of his other interests would fill a page, for he was the mainstay of a number of Muskegon manufacturing enterprises. He was a member of the Gardner & Lacey Lumber Company, of Georgetown, South Carolina; of the J. S. Bennett Lumber Company, of Sandusky, Ohio, and of the Hackley & Hume Company, Limited.

The name of Charles H. Hackley is engraved forever on the hearts of the people of Muskegon because of his magnificent gifts to the city which saw his rise to fortune. They include one of the most beautiful soldiers' and sailors' monuments to be found in the United States; a public square embellished with the best work of American sculptors and landscape gardeners; a public library with a capacity of 100,000 volumes; a manual training school—the only one of its kind in the state; statues of Lincoln, Grant, W. T. Sherman, Farragut, Kearny and McKinley, the latter being the first statue of the martyred President to be erected in the United States, and a modern hospital. While the value of these things to Muskegon and to the future of her people far exceeds their cost, the following summary of Mr. Hackley's gifts during his lifetime will give an idea of the extent of his generosity.

Hackley Public Library (1888)	$155,000
Endowment (1891)	75,000
Hackley Manual Training School and Gymnasium (1895, 1900)	200,000
Endowment (1902)	400,000
Additional funds for the maintenance of the School from the opening in 1896	50,000
Hackley Park and Endowment (1890)	60,000
Soldiers' and Sailors' Monument (1889)	27,000
Statues of Abraham Lincoln, Ulysses S. Grant, William Tecumseh Sherman and David G. Farragut (1898)	26,000
Statue of Phil Kearny (1901)	5,000
Statue of Wm. McKinley (1902)	15,000
Home of the Friendless Endowment (1902)	25,000
Hackley Hospital and Endowment (1902)	340,000
Athletic Field for High School (1902)	5,000
First Congregational Church debt	6,525
	$1,389,525

Mr. Hackley was married in 1864 to Miss Julia E. Moore, of Centreville, New York. They had no children of their own but had two by adoption. Mr. Hackley was an active Republican and had several times been honored with office, somewhat against his wishes. In 1874 he was treasurer of Muskegon county. He served the city as alderman and member of the board of public works. For many years he was a member of the board of education and had been its president since 1892. He was a delegate to the Republican national convention at Minneapolis in 1892 and to the one at St. Louis in 1896. In 1894 he was elected a member of the Board of Regents of the University of Michigan, but resigned on the day on which his term of office began, on account of ill health.

Mr. Hackley died February 10, 1905, mourned by the entire city of Muskegon and honored throughout the state. Thousands of people who enjoy his benefactions participated in the final obsequies. He left an estate estimated at $9,000,000 and his will contained additional specific public bequests, amounting to $775,000, as follows.

Additional endowment for Hackley Manual Training School	$210,000
Additional endowment for Hackley Hospital	200,000
Additional endowment for Hackley Public Library	200,000
Fund for the purchase of pictures for Hackley Library	150,000
Bequest to Muskegon Humane Union	15,000

These bequests increased the total of Mr. Hackley's outright gifts to the people of Muskegon to $2,164,525. The residuary estate will amount to approximately $8,000,000, and of this amount one-quarter, or $2,000,000, shall, by the terms of the will, at the end of Mrs. Hackley's life become a trust fund, the income of which shall be applied perpetually to the maintenance and enlargement of the Hackley Public Library and the Hackley Manual Training School, and to such other charitable purposes as Mrs. Hackley may appoint. This means that eventually there will have been applied from the property of Charles H. Hackley to public and benevolent uses in Muskegon a total of at least $4,164,000.

THOMAS HUME

Thomas Hume

Opportunity has been described by a poet as the "master of human destinies." Yet opportunity in itself means very little. The real basis of success is the ability to recognize and the courage to embrace opportunity when it presents itself. Supplementing both opportunity and ability, and greater than either of them, is the activity of the man who is ambitious in the achievement of success.

A man whose present place in the lumber world may be attributed more to his untiring industry than to any other element of character, is Thomas Hume, of the lumber and timber firm of Hackley & Hume, of Muskegon, Michigan. He was born June 15, 1848, near Belfast, Ireland. He attended the national schools in the vicinity of his home until he had reached the age of nine years and then journeyed to Belfast, twelve miles away, where he was a student at the Belfast Royal Academical Institution until he was fourteen years of age.

At that time his experience in mercantile life began, for he was bound out to a storekeeper in Dungannon, county Tyrone. The term of his apprenticeship was to have been six years, but he served only four and one-half years, although he remained with this concern until he was twenty-two years of age, and in that time worked from the bottom to the top.

He sailed for America in May, 1870, and arrived at Muskegon May 31, of that year. He was able to begin work as a lumber tallyman soon after his arrival. During the summer he worked for George R. Selkirk and Montague & Hamilton, tallying lumber, and in the winter he scaled logs for O. P. Pillsbury & Co. and T. B. Wilcox & Co.

His connection with C. H. Hackley, which lasted until Mr. Hackley's death in February, 1905, began in November, 1872, when he became bookkeeper for C. H. Hackley and James

McGordon, composing the firm of Hackley & McGordon. His duties here were both complex and responsible, for two concerns conducted separate businesses in the one office—Hackley & McGordon, already mentioned, and Hackley & Sons, a firm composed of J. H. Hackley, the father, and Charles H., Edwin and Porter Hackley, the sons. The father died in 1874 and Mr. McGordon bought an interest in the firm, the name being changed to C. H. Hackley & Co. Mr. McGordon died in December, 1880, and in June, 1881, Thomas Hume bought his interest in the firms of Hackley & McGordon and C. H. Hackley & Co., and there was created to succeed Hackley & McGordon the new firm of Hackley & Hume, which has since continued. The concern of C. H. Hackley & Co. was continued until Porter Hackley's death and then its affairs were wound up, its mill and other property being acquired by Hackley & Hume. During all this time the two concerns had occupied the same office and Mr. Hume had had charge of their separate books, besides discharging other duties.

The mill of Hackley & McGordon had burned in 1874, but the mill originally built by Hackley & Sons and owned successively by C. H. Hackley & Co. and Hackley & Hume continued in operation until the timber on the Muskegon river belonging to Hackley & Hume was exhausted in 1894.

The members of the firm had foreseen that the end of the lumber industry on the Muskegon river must come eventually and they had also recognized the possibilities of the timber market. In 1886, eight years before they ceased mill operations at Muskegon, they began to buy timber lands in other states. Their first purchases outside of Michigan were in Wisconsin, Minnesota and Louisiana, but since that time they have increased their holdings by purchases in Mississippi, South Carolina, Florida and British Columbia, in all of which districts they still own large bodies of timber lands.

Mr. Hume's manufacturing interests by no means terminated with the demolition of the Hackley & Hume mill in

Muskegon. In 1886 occurred the organization of the Itasca Lumber Company which had its headquarters at Minneapolis and carried on extensive logging operations in northern Minnesota. In 1892 Mr. Hackley and Mr. Hume bought the interest in this company of S. B. Barker, and on February 1, 1903, the Itasca Lumber Company bought all the property and business of the H. C. Akeley Lumber Company, which had been organized in 1889 by Thomas Hume and Charles H. Hackley, of Muskegon, Michigan, and H. C. Akeley and Freeman S. Farr, of Minneapolis. Its timber and logging business aggregates 75,000,000 feet a year and its mill has been called the fastest in the world, cutting 90,000,000 to 110,000,000 feet a year in a season only seven months long. The great business of this company has been continued by the Itasca Lumber Company, in which concern Mr. Hume is a heavy stockholder.

Mr. Hume is interested in other important operating companies. He is a member of the Gardner & Lacey Lumber Company, of Georgetown, South Carolina, manufacturer of cypress lumber. He is also a heavy stockholder in the Jay S. Bennett Lumber Company, wholesale dealer in lumber at Sandusky, Ohio, and the Hackley & Hume Company, Limited, dealer in southern pine lands. Mr. Hume is president of the Citizens' Telephone Company, of Muskegon, and is interested in a large number of manufacturing enterprises in his home city. He is president of the Sargent Manufacturing Company; secretary and treasurer of the Amazon Knitting Company, operating the largest factory of its kind in this country; vice president of the Shaw Electric Crane Company, and a director and officer of the Alaska Refrigerator Company, the largest manufacturer of refrigerators in the world, of the Standard Malleable Iron Company and of the Chase-Hackley Piano Company. He is vice president of the National Lumberman's Bank and the Hackley National Bank.

In 1873 Mr. Hume married Margaret Annie Banks, daughter of Major B. Banks, of Marshall, Michigan. They

have a beautiful resid
sists of four daughters
A. Hume, is bookkee
ing in the footsteps of

Charles T. Hills

When Charles Turner Hills, of Muskegon, Michigan, passed away December 3, 1902, at the ripe age of eighty-one years, there departed a pioneer who left behind him material evidences of his energy, thrift and benevolence, the memory of a career worthy of emulation by posterity and a personal and business reputation that still lives and will continue to survive for many years. His name is so inseparably linked with the history of the white pine industry of Muskegon and of Michigan that the annals of the growth of that city and state would not be complete without a recital of his career.

Charles Turner Hills was the eldest of five children. He was born November 14, 1821, at Bennington, Vermont, where he obtained his early education in the public schools. At the age of thirteen he began his active career, going to Troy, New York, to take the position of clerk in a dry goods store. His father moved to Grand Rapids, Michigan, in January, 1838, and he followed in April of the same year. In the new state, which had but recently been admitted to the Union, his family experienced the trying hardships of an existence in its almost unbroken wilderness. Turner Hills, the father, died in 1842, and his mantle naturally fell upon the eldest son.

Looking for larger opportunities, Charles Turner Hills left home May 25, 1852, in company with a younger brother, and journeyed to Muskegon, reaching there after a two days' trip through leagues of unbroken timber. Although Muskegon at that time was nothing but a village, the young man recognized its great possibilities and the opportunities it afforded for making a fortune, to one who possessed the ability and—what was perhaps more necessary—the perseverance. With his brother he built a shanty on the banks of Black creek, four miles from the town, and there his connection with the lumber industry began with the shaving of shingles by hand. After two months of this work, he and his brother took up their habitation on the Muskegon river, four miles south of Sand Creek, and continued to work together until 1853, when Mr. Hills went to Muskegon and his brother returned to the family home in Kent county.

Mr. Hills' first business position in Muskegon was that of clerk for the lumber firm of Ryerson & Morris. His employment by this concern at that time did not seem a matter of any moment, but it was one of the most important steps in his career, for he was identified with the interests of this firm during the remainder of his active business life. His salary the first year was $350; the second year $450 with board. In 1859 he took charge of the firm's books and became more closely identified with the concern's interests. In 1865, when Mr. Ryerson bought out the interest of Mr. Morris in the saw mill, Mr. Hills was taken into partnership. The new firm, known as Ryerson, Hills & Co., was composed of Martin Ryerson, Charles T. Hills, H. H. Getty and Ezra Stevens. All of these, with the exception of Mr. Getty, are now deceased. Ryerson, Hills & Co. became one of the most important lumber firms on the Muskegon river. As Mr. Ryerson had moved to Chicago in 1851, the immediate management of the business devolved almost entirely upon Mr. Hills and Mr. Getty. Martin A. Ryerson became a member of the firm January 1, 1881, succeeding his father, Martin Ryerson, who had retired from active service and who died September 6, 1887.

Ryerson, Hills & Co. did a tremendous business in Michigan white pine. They made large investments on the Muskegon river. The manufacture of lumber and its marketing rendered them a large profit, which was augmented by the increase in the value of the lands. The output of the firm averaged 50,000,000 feet of white pine every year. It owned two saw mills and operated its own fleet of lumber-carrying vessels.

Although Ryerson, Hills & Co. was one of the most prominent of Muskegon's lumber manufacturing concerns, only one member of the firm continued to make Muskegon his home during the latter years of its operation and after it had ceased business. Mr. Hills invested money in local enterprises and closely identified himself with the material growth of the city. He was one of the prominent and potent factors in the upbuilding of Muskegon's present industrial greatness, which has succeeded her renown as a lumber producing point. In the latter years of his life he enjoyed some of the ease which he had so well earned by early hardship and untiring energy.

In the organization and in the administration of the affairs of the Muskegon Booming Company, Mr. Hills was one of the chief figures. He was the company's first president, and held that office at various periods for many terms. He possessed an expert knowledge of log running. He knew not only how to conduct the affairs of a great booming company, but also was familiar with the best methods employed in the woods and on the river.

Mr. Hills was an enthusiastic member of the Masonic fraternity. He was Eminent Commander of his commandery fifteen times. He was a thirty-third degree Mason and a charter member of Muskegon Chapter No. 47, Royal Arch, Muskegon Commandery No. 22, Knights Templar, and Dewitt Clinton Consistory. He held many offices in the Masonic bodies. He was two years District Deputy Grand Master. His Masonic history would fill a page. Its crowning event was the presentation by Mr. Hills to the Muskegon Masonic societies of a magnificent Masonic Temple. No building of its kind in the United States surpasses it in the artistic strength of its exterior or the beauty and utility of its interior arrangement. Mr. Hills spent $42,000 in erecting the building and $8,000 more was expended in furnishing it. It was completed in June, 1900, and dedicated September 12, of the same year, the event being marked by one of the greatest Masonic gatherings in the history of Michigan. Masons, disti both in the order and in public life, journeyed to from all over the country, and the entire Michiga Lodge attended. Mr. Hills lived to see the tem pleted and to have evidence of its appreciation by sonic bodies which used it. He died December The funeral services over the deceased lumberm among the most impressive in the history of the state conducted under the auspices of its most eminent officers.

time there, and on both
to the vast forests of
which up to that time h
the woodsman. His inhe

JAMES DIXON LACEY

James D. Lacey

The history of southern timber transactions for the last twenty years, and of the increase in the value of the property within a much shorter period, is an extremely interesting one. In the making of this history James Dixon Lacey played an important part. He has been closely identified with it—really a part of it all—since 1880.

Mr. Lacey was born on a farm in Wayne county, Pennsylvania, fifty-six years ago. As the northern tier of Pennsylvania counties was a heavily timbered region, his father, in addition to working his farm, ran an old fashioned sash saw mill and handle factory, which fact accounts for Mr. Lacey's earliest impressions being connected with the lumber and timber business.

When twelve years old he began life's struggle by securing employment in a drug store in the neighboring town of Honesdale, where he learned the profession of pharmacy. In 1866 he went to Grand Rapids, Michigan, and worked as a clerk in a drug store in that city until 1869. Then he went into the drug business for himself. In 1871 he sold his store and went on the road as a traveling salesman, visiting all the large cities, including those of Canada, east of the Rockies. In 1873, together with a partner, he reëntered the drug business in Grand Rapids, under the firm name of Mills & Lacey. He continued in the business there until 1879, when he went south for the purpose of introducing chemical preparations of his firm's manufacture.

He made two trips to the South, spending considerable time there, and on both occasions his attention was attracted to the vast forests of timber in that section of the country, which up to that time had remained practically untouched by the woodsman. His inherited aptitude for lumbering suggested to his mind the great possibilities that lay in these forests, waiting for recognition, and he decided to make his first venture in timber. Accordingly, in 1880, in association with Isaac Phelps and others, of Grand Rapids, he bought in southwestern Missouri the land which formed the basis of the present timber holdings of the Hersheys, of Muscatine, Iowa, now operating under the style of the Ozark Land & Lumber Company, and whose mills are at Winona, Missouri.

At this time Mr. Lacey decided to make the acquisition and handling of southern timber lands his vocation. He employed Michigan woodsmen of well known standing and started to work, learning the business in his usual practical and thorough manner. In January, 1881, he formed a copartnership with William M. Robinson, of Grand Rapids, and the firm of Robinson & Lacey was formed. It was one of the leading factors in the southern timber business until its dissolution in 1892, at which time Mr. Robinson retired. Mr. Lacey continued in the business alone until September, 1898, when he organized the firm of J. D. Lacey & Co., with Wood Beal, who had for years been in his employ, and his son-in-law, Victor Thrane, as partners. Their principal offices are in New Orleans, Louisiana; Chicago, Illinois; and Seattle, Washington.

Mr. Lacey's first operations in timber were in southern Missouri; later they were in Mississippi and Louisiana, and afterward extended to all parts of the South, his operations being confined mainly to pine and cypress. His first transaction of any magnitude in cypress was in 1889. Since that time Mr. Lacey has been acquiring and solidifying and placing on the market large tracts of cypress in Louisiana, Florida and the Carolinas. He is president of the Southern Cypress Company of Louisiana, vice president of the Gardner & Lacey Lumber Company, of Georgetown, South Carolina, and president of the Tensas Delta Land Company, Limited, of Louisiana.

Through his operations in timber lands in Alabama and

Georgia he became interested in iron and coal properties, and during the last six years has engaged largely in the production of iron ore. He is one of the principal owners of the Bluffton Iron Mines, of Bluffton, Alabama; of the Wilson Ridge Ore Company, of Randall, Alabama; of the Lacey-Buek Iron Company, of Birmingham, Alabama, which owns and operates a furnace at Trussville, Alabama; of coal mines at Birmingham, Alabama; of the Brown Ore Mines at Oremont, Georgia, and of large quarries at Birmingham, Alabama.

Mr. Lacey was one of the first lumbermen in Louisiana and Mississippi to realize the profits to be made in estimating, grouping and entering lands and reselling them in block to investors and operators. A conservative estimate of the transactions of this sort carried through by James D. Lacey and associates, since they began in 1880, places the total at an amount exceeding 5,000,000 acres; also during that time they have estimated fully double that amount of timber lands in the various southern states.

Individually and in association with others, Mr. Lacey is largely interested in timber holdings in Louisiana, Florida, Mississippi, the Carolinas, British Columbia and the Pacific Coast states. It is estimated that two-thirds of the large investments made by northern lumbermen in southern yellow pine and cypress timber have been made through Robinson & Lacey, James D. Lacey, or J. D. Lacey & Co.

Mr. Lacey has spent parts of three years in Honduras. He organized the Honduras Timber Company, which has large holdings of mahogany stumpage in that country.

Mr. Lacey does not force the attention of the world to himself by making a great outcry; on the contrary he is quiet in his manner and democratic in his ideas; but he possesses qualities which have enabled him to accomplish more in his chosen line of operation than perhaps any other half dozen men combined. He is a born timberman; he is by instinct a worker; his absolute honesty compels the acceptance at their face value of all his representations, and whoever once becomes his customer or associate remains so permanently. Thus his business influence and the volume of his transactions are growing constantly. He is also a man of wide information and one who is indefatigable in his labors. The technical training he received in his early profession; the knowledge gained by extensive travel; the careful study of trade conditions and requirements as applied to timber and lumber industries; his conservative judgment and intuitive knowledge of men and affairs—all qualify him preëminently for the business in which he is engaged, and make him a leader in his chosen occupation.

T. Stewart White

In the Grand river valley no name is more widely known or more highly respected than that of T. Stewart White, of Grand Rapids, Michigan, and Santa Barbara, California. Advancing years and the desire for the term of leisure which he so conscientiously and faithfully earned in a once great lumber district of Michigan, have caused Mr. White to spend many of his recent days in a sunnier clime; but, while his figure is less frequently seen upon the streets of Grand Rapids and his counsels perhaps less frequently heard in shaping its municipal affairs, he has by no means passed out of the life of that community.

For many years Mr. White made the Grand river valley the scene of his operations and he ranks as one of the pioneers of that section of Michigan. Although his residence is now chiefly in southern California, his business is still carried on in a lesser degree in Michigan. He has been forced by the exhaustion of Michigan timber into other scenes of action, but it is with Grand Rapids and the Grand river valley that the name of T. Stewart White is inseparably linked.

Mr. White was born at Grand Haven, Michigan, June 28, 1840. His father was Thomas W. White, of Ashfield, Massachusetts, who came to Michigan in 1836. The son acquired a common school education and intended to enter college, but was forced by financial considerations to give up the hope of a professional career for the imminent necessity of earning his daily bread. For three years he was employed in Ferry & Son's bank at Grand Haven. Banking, however, did not appeal to him and he took a position with Gray, Phelps & Co., wholesale grocers of Chicago. He stayed with them two years and then entered upon his first experience in lumbering. His father took up some swamp land at the head of

Spring lake, and T. Stewart White, then a lad of nineteen, undertook to job the timber on it. The enterprise, naturally, was not very successful in the hands of a boy who knew nothing whatever of the business, and Mr. White came out of it with much experience and a loss of $600.

In 1866, in partnership with one of the Ferrys, Mr. White bought a schooner doing a general freight business between Chicago and other ports and sold her at the end of the season. This venture resulted in a profit of about $2,000. In 1867 he went into the wrecking business with Heber Squier and was interested in it for ten years. The firm name was Squier & White. He also did contract work for railroads and the government, including dredging and harbor construction.

It was at this period that he became interested in a saw and planing mill business at Grand Rapids, Michigan. The business, which has continued until this time, was inaugurated in 1868, when, in partnership with Thomas Friant, he purchased a small quantity of timber. This was the beginning of a partnership which has existed in one form or another ever since. For twenty-one years the partners contracted for running, booming, sorting and delivering to mills at Grand Haven all of the logs on Grand river and the profits were put into timber holdings.

A new company, known as the White & Friant Lumber Company, in which John Rugee, of Milwaukee, Wisconsin, was a factor, was organized in 1878. It bought tracts on Flat river which contained 100,000,000 feet, and manufactured at Grand Haven. Its next purchase was of 75,000,000 feet on the Manistee river and two mills at Manistee with which to manufacture the timber. Afterward it bought large timber holdings on the Sturgeon river, a branch of the Menominee in the upper peninsula of Michigan, from which was cut and manufactured 100,000,000 feet of lumber.

In 1898 the F. & F. Lumber Company was organized in partnership with P. C. Fuller, of Grand Rapids, Michigan, and a mill was erected at Thompson in the upper peninsula of

Michigan. About 100,000,000 feet of standing timber in this section were bought, cut and manufactured. The company afterward owned and sold a large tract of pine in Minnesota, and it now owns 500,000,000 feet of cypress in Louisiana. In addition to this the concern possesses 700,000,000 feet of sugar pine in California.

During his career Mr. White has been interested in a large number of small ventures all over the United States. He is concerned in mining in Montana and in the manufacture of stoves in Grand Rapids, Michigan.

When asked for the cause of his success, Mr. White's reply was at once modest and humorous:

"Being in so many things," he said, "we couldn't bust them all at once."

Those who know T. Stewart White well, however, know that the characteristics that have won him success are tenacity of purpose, capacity for detail, trust in the good intentions of the other fellow, industrial courage and the ability to accept occasional absolute failure without losing nerve. Among his intimate friends he is known for his keen sense of humor, personal gentleness and kindliness. He is a member of the Peninsular Club and the Kent Country Club, of Grand Rapids, Michigan, and the Santa Barbara Country Club, of Santa Barbara, California, where he spends his winters. He is a Republican in politics. He has an active share in financial affairs as a director of the National City Bank, in the Michigan Trust Company and in the Kent County Savings Bank, all of Grand Rapids, Michigan.

Mr. White married Mary E. Daniell, of Milwaukee, April 20, 1870. A daughter died in infancy, but there are living five sons. The eldest is Stewart Edward, already famous as a writer. To him, perhaps, the forest has presented a side different from that which it turned to his father. He says in one of his books:

"How often have I ruminated the problem of the Forest. Subtle she is, and mysterious, and gifted with a charm that lures. Vast she is, and dreadful, so that man bows before her fiercer moods, a little thing. Gentle she is, and kindly, so that she denies nothing, whether of the material or spiritual, to those of her chosen who will seek. August she is, and yet of homely, sprightly gentleness. Variable she is in her many moods. Night, day, sun, cloud, rain, snow, wind, lend to her their best of warmth and cold, of comfort and awe, of peace and of many shoutings; and she accepts them, yet remains greater and more enduring than they. In her is all the sweetness of little things, murmurs of the waters and of the breeze, faint odors, wandering streams of tepid air, stray bird songs in fragments as when a door is opened and closed, the softness of moss, the coolness of shade, the glimpse of occult affairs in wood-life, accompany her as Titania her court."

Mr. White's other sons are T. Gilbert, aged twenty-six; Rugee, aged fifteen; Roderick, aged thirteen; and Harwood, aged eight.

LIBRARY
OF THE
UNIVERSITY
OF
CALIFORNIA

William W. Mitchell

Personal popularity may be due to any one of a thousand causes. It may be based upon trivial things—social standing, position in the business world, influence, family, wealth, or some pleasing trick of manner. When it depends upon any of these for its life it is of rapid growth and early decay, oftentimes being entombed with the lifeless clay it once invested with a fleeting glory. Or it may have its foundation in more solid qualities—kindliness, consideration for others, genuine good fellowship, honesty, integrity of purpose, or any of those elements which go to make up genuine character. Growing—slowly it may be—from any of these it reaches such magnitude and strength that the passing away of the one who possessed it only accentuates its value. Such popularity is lasting, oftentimes being recorded on history's pages. Held in such esteem by friends, business associates and acquaintances is W. W. Mitchell, of Cadillac, Michigan.

Mr. Mitchell was born at Hillsdale, Michigan, June 3, 1854. He was the son of Hon. C. T. Mitchell, one of the leading men of southern Michigan, who was prominent in both politics and business. In this frugal, prosperous little city, with its rich agricultural surroundings, he spent his boyhood and early youth, and there he attended the public schools. It was his father's wish that he should acquire a thorough education, including a college training, so that in time he might succeed to his father's old and solidly established banking business at Hillsdale. But young Mitchell preferred some other line of business to that of banking, which made no appeal to him.

At the age of nineteen, with no definite plan in his mind, he went to Clam Lake, now the city of Cadillac, Michigan, on a visit to his uncle, George A. Mitchell who was the real founder of Cadillac. After a short stay in Cadillac the boy became a tallyman in his uncle's saw mill; then he went into the woods and took practical lessons as a swamper, skidder and teamster. In the spring he returned to the mill and took up his every day task of hard work about the yard in piling, loading and inspecting lumber. His ambition to become a businessman on his own account led him soon after, in conjunction with his cousin, A. B. Mitchell, as a partner, to undertake a logging contract for his uncle. In this enterprise he accumulated several hundred dollars. Thus for four years he endured the rugged experiences of the life of a woodsman and millman and trained himself to perform his share of the duties that fall to the lot of a pioneer lumberman.

In 1877 he entered into partnership with Jonathan W. Cobbs and established the lumber firm of Cobbs & Mitchell, a firm whose history has become synonymous with the development and prosperity of that great section of lumbering country in Michigan of which Cadillac is the commercial center.

Mr. Cobbs died in 1898; and succeeding the firm of Cobbs & Mitchell came the corporation of Cobbs & Mitchell, Incorporated. Mr. Mitchell is the president and dominant factor in carrying on the immense lumber business of the house. So provident has been Mr. Mitchell's management of this great institution and so carefully planned and prudently executed has been his provision for a continued timber supply, that only now, after a progressive and successful history covering a quarter of a century, has the house arrived at the zenith of its career.

Cobbs & Mitchell and Cobbs & Mitchell, Incorporated, have produced of the splendid white pine growth of Michigan in the neighborhood of 500,000,000 feet of lumber. With the gradual exhaustion of white pine tributary to Cadillac they have become extensive producers of hemlock, hardwoods and maple flooring. The company operates two model double band mills within the city limits of Cadillac and has one of the largest and best equipped maple flooring factories in the country.

In addition to W. W. Mitchell's interest in Cobbs & Mitchell, Incorporated, he was, until the death of Austin W. Mitchell, a copartner of his brother under the firm name of Mitchell Brothers, a firm which had a history of twenty years. After the death of A. W. Mitchell the business was continued under the same name. This concern operates a triple saw mill plant at Jennings, twelve miles east of Cadillac, and an immense maple flooring plant also. It was originally a producer of white pine but, like the allied institution of Cobbs & Mitchell, has gradually drifted into the production of hemlock, hardwoods and maple flooring. This firm has produced more than 400,000,000 feet and operates over fifty miles of railroad in connection with its enterprise.

In 1876 Mr. Mitchell married Miss Ella Yost, of Hillsdale, who had been one of his school companions. They came at once to Cadillac to reside, occupying a very modest home. As time progressed and the once desolate hills overlooking Clam Lake gradually developed into a part of the city of Cadillac, Mr. Mitchell erected a more pretentious residence, which has been enlarged and improved from time to time until now it is thoroughly in keeping with both the wealth of its owner and the simple but artistic tastes of himself and family.

Contrary to the custom of many successful Michigan lumbermen Mr. Mitchell has not abandoned the lumber town where he made his fortune to make his home in a larger city. He has devoted much of his time, energy and money in helping build up a modern and model city of comfortable homes at Cadillac. And his efforts have been successful, as the city for which he is sponsor is one of the most homelike and comfortable places of residence in Michigan, a state famous for cities of beautiful homes.

Mr. Mitchell's family consists of a wife, a son, Charles T. Mitchell, now arrived at man's estate, and a daughter, Marie.

His son is following in his fath
engaged in the manufacture of
and promises to duplicate not on
well deserved popularity as well.

Samuel M. Stephenson

This bit of history is taken from the life of a man who began at the bottom of the ladder, working with his hands for meager wages; who has come to be a man of wealth; who is fortunate not only in the possession of money but also in the knowledge of how to use it to the best satisfaction of himself and to the happiness of others.

Samuel Merritt Stephenson, of Menominee, Michigan, was born in New Brunswick, just over the international boundary, in 1831, and when but six years of age was taken by his parents to Maine. Early in life he had to look out for himself, supporting himself when but seven years old and working in the woods of eastern Maine for $7 a month when only ten years of age. When fifteen years old he went to Delta county, Michigan, arriving there with just three ten-cent pieces in his pocket, and found work in a lumber camp. For a number of years he was engaged in lumbering upon streams tributary to the bays de Noquet and the northern end of Lake Michigan.

His first visit to Menominee was in 1853. He then took a logging job in Escanaba, during this time working with Isaac Stephenson, his brother, and William Holmes, later one of the most prominent loggers in the country, one of their chief contracts being the getting out of the square timbers for the Illinois Central breakwater then being built off the lake front at Chicago.

In 1858 he went to Menominee to reside permanently, and in company with Abner Kirby built a mill containing a single mulay saw and a so called siding machine. This was a circular saw arrangement that took cants from the mulay and, working automatically, sawed them into boards. This machine was a famous affair in its day; in fact, the entire mill was a remarkable one. The operation of this Stephenson & Kirby mill marked the beginning of the vast business later carried on under the name of the Kirby-Carpenter Company, which, until a few years ago, when it finally abandoned white pine manufacture, ranked as one of the leading manufacturing houses in the Northwest. Mr. Stephenson's connection with the business has been continuous from its beginning, but the connection of Augustus A. and William O. Carpenter dated from 1861.

The original mill had a capacity of about 3,000,000 feet a season, but enlarged facilities and improved saw mill machinery brought the output of the Kirby-Carpenter Company up to as high as 120,000,000 feet of lumber a year, with an extensive shingle and lath production and planing mills capable of dressing 250,000 a day.

For many years Mr. Stephenson was in practical charge of the logging and manufacturing departments of this great business. Upon the incorporation of the company in 1872 he was elected vice president, an office which he still holds, although the company has ceased white pine manufacture and gives its attention only to real estate and timber investments. Individually and in connection with others Mr. Stephenson has heavy timber holdings in the South and West. He is president of the First National Bank of Menominee, which was established in 1885. He is a stockholder in the Stephenson National Bank of Marinette, which was established by I. and S. M. Stephenson and A. Spies as a state bank. In furtherance of the welfare of Menominee he erected in 1881 the large hotel which bears his name.

Mr. Stephenson was the first supervisor of Menominee township after its organization, and was the first mayor of the city of Menominee. He was an early member of the county board of education and was for many years its chairman; in 1877-8 he represented his district in the lower house of the state legislature, and in 1879-80 and in 1885-6 he was elected a member of the state senate. A level headed businessman, but broader in his views than a majority, he was able to accomplish much, not only for his district but for the state of Michigan as a whole and for the Northern Peninsula in particular. He was a presidential elector in 1880 and a delegate to the Republican national conventions of 1884 and 1888.

During four successive terms he represented his district in Congress. Mr. Stephenson is not a man of one idea nor a man of one city or one state. It was natural, however, that he should give particular attention to the interests of the great lake region, with the needs of which he was so familiar. A member of the Committee on Rivers and Harbors, he was of great service in the improvement of lake navigation. He was an active and influential advocate of the building of the Hennepin canal, designed to connect the Great Lakes with the Mississippi river and the Gulf of Mexico.

He has always sought to promote the interests of the city in which he lives. If there is anything of a public nature to be done, a call is, as a matter of course, made upon Mr. Stephenson. It makes no difference whether it is a poor family that needs relief, a stray woodsman who needs hospital care, a school that wants a library, a church that wants an organ, or some hotel or theater to be built, Samuel M. Stephenson's money and personal interest can always be drawn upon.

It was formerly the opinion that pine stump lands were good for nothing, but Mr. Stephenson has demonstrated the reverse to be true. He began this demonstration many years ago when, adjoining his logging camps, he cleared lands on which to raise hay and potatoes. Since he has relieved himself of much of the active work of the lumber business, he has gone more extensively into these experiments.

At his Pine Hill farm he has a famous dairy barn which is said to have but one counterpart in the world. It is built of stone, a perfect circle in shape, 120 feet in diameter, with a silo in the center of thirty feet inside diameter and sixty feet height. On this farm are about 460 head of cattle, all thoroughbreds. There is also what is said to be the finest her Jerseys in the West. There is a model dairy heated by ste lighted by electricity and having its machinery driven steam power. The dairy business is carried on in the scientific fashion and Mr. Stephenson insists that it is pro ble. There is also the nine-mile farm, consisting of ab 1,400 acres, cleared and enclosed by a fence, on which more cattle, bringing the total number up to about 1,100.

In 1859 Mr. Stephenson married Miss Jane Harris, a tive of Wales. Of the nine children born to them only daughters survive.

ISAAC STEPHENSON

Isaac Stephenson

The lumber business on Lake Michigan dates back more than a hundred years, but it was not until the middle of the last century that the industry had fully begun the battle against the forests which only now is approaching its end. Among the leading spirits of those days was Isaac Stephenson, of Marinette, Wisconsin. He was born in York county, New Brunswick, near the city of Fredericton, June 18, 1829. His father, whose name also was Isaac, was of Scotch-Irish extraction, his mother, a native of London, England. Isaac Stephenson, senior, was a lumberman and farmer, and his son passed his early days on the farm, attending public school for a time when a boy but soon having to start out in the world for himself. When fourteen years old he went to Bangor, Maine, where he had his first experience in the woods. A year and a half later he accompanied Jefferson Sinclair to Milwaukee, Wisconsin. Here he had a winter term of schooling, but in April of the next year Mr. Sinclair located on a prairie farm near Janesville, Wisconsin, and during that spring and summer young Stephenson broke 130 acres of land and helped put in 400 acres of wheat.

Jefferson Sinclair became financially interested with Daniel Wells, junior, in northern Michigan lands around Escanaba, and Isaac Stephenson was transferred to that section, where as a boy he displayed such executive ability, sound judgment and honesty that in 1847 he was placed in charge of the lumber camps, continuing in this employment until he was of age. In the summer months during this period he sailed on Lake Michigan and before he was twenty-one years old owned a controlling interest in the schooner Cleopatra, which in 1853 was lost about a mile south of Chicago harbor. During the summer of 1848 he had attended an academy in Milwaukee.

His experience in the woods naturally made Mr. Stephenson an excellent judge of the value of timber lands and he explored large sections of the upper peninsula of Michigan, locating the more valuable tracts. The first land office in northern Michigan was opened in July, 1848, at Sault Ste. Marie. Mr. Stephenson, accompanied by Daniel Wells, junior, and Jefferson Sinclair, attended the sale and bought large tracts on the Escanaba, Ford and Sturgeon rivers and on Big Bay de Noquet. Among Mr. Stephenson's first ventures upon coming of age was the operation of a saw mill at Flat Rock, on Little Bay de Noquet, a short distance north of the present site of Escanaba. This mill was equipped with mulay saws and, with one other, made Flat Rock the largest lumber manufacturing point in the United States west of Albany at that time. During the four years beginning with 1852, Mr. Stephenson, in connection with N. Ludington & Co., cut and delivered timber that was used in constructing the first breakwater built in Chicago.

In 1858 Mr. Stephenson bought a quarter interest in the mill owned by N. Ludington & Co. In this business he at once became the controlling spirit and soon placed it upon a prosperous footing. By 1868 it was incorporated as the N. Ludington Company; its capital is now $700,000 and it is controlled by Mr. Stephenson. He was its vice president until 1883 and since then he has been its president.

In 1867 he acquired an interest in the Peshtigo Company and reorganized it as the Peshtigo Lumber Company with a capital of $1,500,000. Mr. Stephenson became vice president, but later was its president, which office he held until 1900. The mills of the company were at Peshtigo and it had a large yard in Chicago. In connection with this yard was erected what at that time was the largest woodenware factory in the world. The company was a heavy loser in the great fires of October, 1871, when its yards and plant in Chicago were destroyed and the whole village of Peshtigo wiped out. A loss of nearly $2,000,000 was entailed by this fire. However, the mill and village were immediately rebuilt.

Under Mr. Stephenson's direction the Peshtigo company operated the steamer Boscobel and six barges, although up to that time it was deemed impracticable to tow barges on Lake Michigan. He was instrumental in organizing the Sturgeon Bay Manufacturing Company, which was sold in 1900 to the N. Ludington Company.

Mr. Stephenson was the organizer of the Menominee River Boom Company, which in one year handled through its boom 675,000,000 feet of logs. He devised the plan for the main boom and superintended its construction. The company's capital is $1,250,000 and Mr. Stephenson is its president. He was intimately associated with river and lake interests, placing the first boats on the Menominee, taking the first steamboat into Cedar river, the first into the Whitefish and Ford rivers and the second into the Escanaba.

One of the most important companies in which Mr. Stephenson is interested is the I. Stephenson Company, of Escanaba, Michigan, with mills at Wells. It was organized in 1886 with a capital of $600,000. Up to 1899 it had an extensive yard in Chicago. Within the last few years the manufacturing business of this company has been greatly extended, a railroad—the Escanaba & Lake Superior—being built westward from Wells, tapping the Chicago, Milwaukee & St. Paul and traversing a country rich in hardwoods, cedar, etc. At Wells, Michigan, is a large mill equipped with two bands and a gang, a tie mill and lath and shingle machinery. In connection with it are a planing mill and a hardwood flooring factory which are among the largest in the country. In connection with this plant and tributary to the Escanaba & Lake Superior road, Mr. Stephenson and his associates own about 250,000 acres of land, which, with other tributary timber, assures a life for the Wells plant of at least thirty years. The railroad has about 100 miles of track, over which is transported to Little Bay de Noquet all the ore coming from the lines of the Chicago, Milwaukee & St. Paul.

In 1873 Mr. Stephenson organized the Stephenson Banking Company, which in 1888 became the Stephenson National Bank, with $100,000 capital. Of this he was president until 1900, when, retaining his financial interests, he resigned his office. He owns one-seventh interest in the Marinette & Menominee Paper Company, capitalized for $750,000. He was president of the Sturgeon Bay & Lake Michigan Ship Canal & Harbor Company, which constructed a canal from Sturgeon bay to Lake Michigan. With Jesse Spalding and William E. Strong, he supervised its construction. The canal was sold to the government and has been of much advantage to the Green Bay ports.

With his brother, Samuel M. Stephenson, and Henry Swartz he is joint owner of 800,000,000 feet of redwood in California. He also owns five-twelfths of the stock of the Calcasieu Pine Company, which owns 82,000 acres of Louisiana pine land. He has many side interests, one of which is farming. He has 900 acres near Kenosha, Wisconsin, devoted to stock and horses, and has a farm adjoining the city of Marinette.

He has served three terms in Congress, being first elected in 1882. Previous to that he served in the Wisconsin state legislature. While in Congress he served on the committees of agriculture, public lands, rivers and harbors and others. In 1880 he was a delegate to the Republican national convention which nominated Garfield; in 1892 he was a delegate at large to the Minneapolis convention and in 1900 chairman of the state delegation to the Philadelphia convention that nominated Harrison. Few men in the Northwest have so extensive an acquaintance with public affairs and public men as has Isaac Stephenson.

LIBRARY
OF THE
UNIVERSITY
OF
CALIFORNIA

with a splen

The nam
member wa
continued o
J. W. Coch

Joseph W. Cochran

There are men in the lumber trade whose training has been almost cosmopolitan. This article tells briefly the history of one of these men who, born in New Brunswick and receiving his early experience in Maine, laid the foundation of his fortune in Pennsylvania, later carried his enterprise to Wisconsin and is now interested in many states.

Joseph William Cochran was born in New Brunswick, just across the St. Croix river from Maine, August 3, 1842. His father was a lumberman, who, coming to New Brunswick as a young man, had most of his lumber experience there. When the boy was five years old the family moved to Calais, Maine, where he was brought up.

From the time that J. W. Cochran was fifteen years of age until he was twenty, he spent more or less time in the woods. In November, 1862, he went to Williamsport, Pennsylvania, then a comparatively new lumber town but rapidly growing in its timber and saw mill importance. There he went to work by the month, and in the third year of his residence took charge of the business of his employers. The next year he went into business for himself in company with his brother, James Henry Cochran, and J. M. Thompson. Their business was logging, which included not only woods work proper but river driving as well. Their operations were carried on in that section of Pennsylvania drained by the West Branch of the Susquehanna river, and were centered at Williamsport, Pennsylvania. At that time this region was heavily timbered with a splendid growth of white pine and hemlock.

The name of this first firm of which J. W. Cochran was a member was Thompson, Cochran & Co. The partnership continued one year and then the business was reorganized as J. W. Cochran & Bro., under which style it still exists. This business soon became the most extensive of its kind in the state. The partners were loggers both for themselves and others and gradually became heavy owners of timber lands. After some years the firm of Payne, Cochran & Co. was founded to engage in the manufacture of lumber. It purchased a mill and became a lumber producer, thus completing the chain of operations from ownership of the timber to the selling of the sawed product. Later the banking house of Cochran, Payne & McCormick, which has been a power in the Susquehanna valley, was established at Williamsport.

The Cochrans have been timber holders since early in their commercial history, and in the '80's were probably the heaviest in Pennsylvania; but since 1890 they have been lessening their holdings by selling and cutting. In 1902 they closed out one of their last large tracts to the Goodyears, of Buffalo, for upward of $1,000,000. It was bought about 1895 for a sum that was insignificant compared with the price at which it was sold.

In 1889 the Superior Lumber Company, of Ashland, Wisconsin, was purchased and the title at once changed to the Keystone Lumber Company, in honor of the state of which the Cochrans were residents, and J. W. Cochran moved to Ashland and took charge of operations. The chief owner and president of the Superior Lumber Company was Col. J. H. Knight, well known in northern Wisconsin as a lumberman and capitalist.

The purchase of the company carried with it the acquisition of a large saw mill, which had cut in some years approximately 25,000,000 feet, and about 300,000,000 feet of standing timber, which was augmented by later purchases. The Keystone Lumber Company has had an annual output of about 50,000,000 feet. Eventually the timber became nearly exhausted and in 1902 the remainder of the lumber owned by the company was sold to the Edward Hines Lumber Company, of Chicago. In the reorganization of the Hines company J. W. Cochran became a director.

As Mr. Cochran's Wisconsin operations drew to a close he began investing elsewhere, particularly on the Pacific Coast. In March, 1902, he bought about 500,000,000 feet of West Coast timber, chiefly fir, in Oregon. He is also interested in a company owning 550,000 acres of lands in Mexico, largely timbered.

Judge Cochran, though still in the prime of life, has been an observer of the development of the lumber business for a half century and has also been an active participant in this development. He recalls how when he was a boy in Calais there were several firms which cut from 3,000,000 to 6,000,000 feet of lumber a year each and were accounted among the big and wealthy lumber operators of the continent. Though their operations would now seem ridiculously small, they were extremely busy men. They had to oversee their woods work in the winter, their driving in the spring, the mills during the summer and then the shipments by water to Boston, New York, or across the Atlantic. Some of them owned their vessels. They were apparently busier than the ordinary lumberman of today who may manufacture 100,000,000 feet a year and be interested in a dozen states. Each of these men had a horse and buggy in which he would rush around from office to mill, and from mill to dock, and from dock to bank, and from bank to boom, some time during the day stopping at the postoffice for the infrequent mails of the time.

Judge Cochran was interested in the manufacture of lumber in the Lake Superior region when the industry of that section was in the height of its glory, and is now taking an active interest in newer enterprises whose greatest achievements are still in the future.

The honorary title of "Judge" is given to Mr. Cochran because it seems particularly suitable to one of his appearance and ability and also because he held at one time the office of associate judge—a position of honor and responsibility peculiar to the judicial system of Pennsylvania. While a man of personal dignity, Judge Cochran is nevertheless distinguished by many of the best qualities of the "good fellow," so called. He is companionable, democratic, charitable. He is a lover of sports, particularly hunting and fishing, and, by a judicious balance of work and play, by refreshing the mind, jaded by hard mental labor, by relaxation or activities of other sorts, he has preserved a sound mind in a sound body and bids fair to have before him many years of the mingled work and play which he so much enjoys.

Mr. Cochran was married in 1866 and again in 1901. He has four children, two sons and two daughters. The elder son is in the cattle business in Nebraska. The younger son is about twenty years of age. Judge Cochran's home is at Ashland, Wisconsin, and, although his residence there has not been a life long one, he is looked upon as one of the old inhabitants and as one of the most prominent citizens.

...kwell and
...den Hill.
... moved
the public
..., until
the year 1854,
..., where he
Baker, who
owned an old ... young
... working
hours a day ... Mr. Baker

he ... worked as
a carpenter. Wh... ...ication of
... became leader
... War he en-
listed ... the regi-
mental band of the ... York Infantry. In
capacity ... In 1863 he was
sent to a hospital at ... account of sickness contracted in the service, and after remaining there three months
returned to Boston.

In the fall of 1863 he ... more in the hope of
benefiting his health than for any business reason. In Chi-

HENRY HART ROCKWELL

Henry H. Rockwell

The name of Rockwell requires little introduction to the student of the history of the American lumber trade, or, more correctly, of that allied industry of the lumber trade, the sash and door interest. This name is indelibly stamped on that particular industry, with which Henry Hart Rockwell was so actively identified during his business life.

He was born February 11, 1838, at Leyden Hill, Lewis county, New York. His parents were James Rockwell and Adeline Hart Rockwell, of Glens Falls and Leyden Hill. Upon the death of his father, in 1846, Henry's mother moved to Turin, Lewis county. There the boy attended the public schools and supported himself by working for farmers, until he was sixteen years old. At that time, in the year 1854, young Rockwell went to Talcottville, New York, where he learned the carpenter's trade under Thomas Baker, who owned an old fashioned water power mill. There young Rockwell learned how to make handmade doors, working eighteen hours a day at his task and staying with Mr. Baker five years as an apprentice.

In 1859 he moved to Boonville, New York, and worked as a carpenter. While at that place he first gave indication of having a special love and talent for music, and became leader of a brass band. At the outbreak of the Civil War he enlisted in the army as a musician, being the leader of the regimental band of the Ninety-seventh New York Infantry. In this capacity he saw service for two years. In 1863 he was sent to a hospital at Washington on account of sickness contracted in the service, and after remaining there three months returned to Boonville.

In the fall of 1863 he moved west, more in the hope of benefiting his health than for any business reason. In Chicago he became foreman for Robert Wisdom & Co., who operated a general wood working factory, and ultimately became bookkeeper and superintendent.

In 1867 Mr. Rockwell went to Milwaukee and there became foreman for the firm of Judd & Hiles. He held this position for four years, until the factory was destroyed by a fire which occurred in 1870. In 1872 Mr. Rockwell and Charles H. Moss, of Milwaukee, formed a partnership with Mr. Hiles. The new firm of John A. Hiles & Co. built a factory at Park street and Sixth avenue, Milwaukee, which still forms a part of the present plant of the Rockwell Manufacturing Company. In 1873 Mr. Hiles died and then was formed the firm of Sanger, Rockwell & Co., composed of Casper Sanger, Charles H. Moss and H. H. Rockwell. This organization continued until 1893, when Mr. Sanger retired and a stock company was formed under the name of the Rockwell Manufacturing Company, with Henry Hart Rockwell as president and manager. Mr. Rockwell personally supervised the affairs of this company until within a short time of his death, when he was unable to do so on account of his health. His son, Fred W. Rockwell, assisted him for a number of years in the management of the business, relieving him of much responsibility, and finally succeeded him.

During his active life Mr. Rockwell was successful in the building up of a great business—establishing what was one of the largest institutions of its kind in this country, if not in the world. At the present time the Rockwell Manufacturing Company has a capacity of 700 doors, 1,000 windows and 150 pairs of blinds each day, and employs no less than three hundred and fifty men.

Mr. Rockwell did more to foster the invention of machinery, and devised more improved methods for the manufacture of dowel doors, than perhaps any other person; and his concern deserves especial credit for the encouragement it gave along this line. Under Mr. Rockwell's management this company may be credited with having originated and introduced dowel doors, which are now in use generally throughout the world. The company has in its possession many letters patent taken out both in this country and in England, covering machinery and methods of manufacture as well. The Rockwell Manufacturing Company still retains documents covering patents on dowel or dowel joint doors; on a boring machine; on dowel and joint; on a machine for making dowel pins; on an improvement in dowel pin joint (given by the government of Great Britain); on a boring machine, and a patent on cutoff and joining machine.

January 9, 1862, Mr. Rockwell was married to Eliza A. Ward, of Hillside, New York. Besides one son, Fred W. Rockwell, there were three daughters born to Mr. and Mrs. Rockwell, all of whom are living. The daughters are Mrs. James A. Cheyne, of Pittsburg, Pennsylvania, Mrs. Mary Rockwell Mahew, of Milwaukee, and Miss Adelina Rockwell, of Tucson, Arizona.

Mr. Rockwell stood high in the commercial world as a businessman of exceptional ability; but though well known in this capacity for a quarter of a century, it is doubtful if one out of a hundred of those who knew him so well ever saw the other side of his nature. They saw in him only the cool, calculating businessman—reserved, self contained, possessing in an unusual degree those qualities that go to make up the successful business character. The other Henry Hart Rockwell, so little known, was of an imaginative, artistic nature, possessing a strong love for music and for all that is beautiful or that appeals to man's higher nature. This was the man that was known in his home and to his comparatively small circle of intimates.

Mr. Rockwell was never a clubman in the sense that he enjoyed club life. He derived more satisfaction from his quiet home life. He was, however, a member of the Independent Order of Odd Fellows and stood high in the councils of Masonry, being a member of Ivanhoe Commandery, Knights Templar, of Milwaukee. He died at his home in

Milwaukee, after an
and his body was laid
city.

LIBRARY
OF THE
UNIVERSITY
OF
CALIFORNIA

Henry W. Wright

It is well that we do not always compute success in dollars and cents. The man of modest wealth who has conducted his affairs with consideration for the rights of others is in the best sense fully as successful as the man who has achieved greater fortunes by different methods. Stocks rise and fall, business interests fluctuate in value, but true character always stands at par. And such was the character of H. W. Wright.

Henry W. Wright, of Merrill, Wisconsin, who died May 23, 1901, was a native of Wisconsin. He was born at Racine March 10, 1844, and was the son of Thomas W. Wright, a wagon maker, who came from Manchester, England, and located at Racine in 1838. The elder Wright went to California in 1853 and died there, leaving his family in good circumstances; consequently Henry W. Wright had some educational advantages. He attended the ward schools and the high school at Racine, also studying bookkeeping.

He enlisted in the army when eighteen years of age. His uncle, Col. Albert Knowles, visited Racine and enlisted him as second lieutenant in the Second Missouri Cavalry, which was afterward consolidated with the Seventh Missouri. He was enrolled February 15, 1862, at Macon City, Missouri. February 11, 1863, he was made commissary sergeant of Company A of the Seventh Regiment of Missouri Volunteers. July 16, 1864, he was promoted to the office of sergeant major of the same regiment. March 22, 1865, he was made second lieutenant of Company H of the First Missouri Volunteers, to rank from February 22, 1865. He was honorably discharged May 30, 1865. He participated in fifty-two engagements of all kinds, most of them in the Southwestern Army under command of generals Steele, Canby and Powell Clayton. He was one of the detachment that pursued Quantrell's guerrilla band.

After the war he returned to Racine and was employed by various firms as bookkeeper and accountant, among them being the Western Union Railway Company and the J. I. Case Threshing Machine Company. After about eight years of this work he began business for himself as a manufacturer of sash, doors and blinds at Racine. He was a prominent citizen of that town, was supervisor and alderman, and in 1877 President Hayes appointed him postmaster, which position he held until he moved to Merrill, then called Jenny, in 1880. Here Mr. Wright formed a partnership in the saw mill business with M. H. McCord that lasted about a year, when the H. W. Wright Lumber Company was organized, of which Mr. Wright was president.

Mr. Wright was long a prominent factor in the sash and door and saw mill industries of the Northwest. For many years he was a producer of sash and doors but eventually he closed down the factory owing to changes in conditions in the trade and in his own circumstances, and it has not since been run as an entirety. A few years ago Mr. Wright cut out his timber holdings in the Wisconsin valley and after that he operated on more recently acquired tracts and purchased logs.

In Merrill he held various positions of trust and responsibility, serving as county supervisor and as mayor, being elected to the latter office the second time. He was intimately associated with school work, and was a public spirited and useful citizen generally. He was a delegate from the Ninth Congressional District of Wisconsin to the Republican national convention at St. Louis that nominated William McKinley for the presidency. At Merrill also he was postmaster for five years under Presidents Hayes and Garfield.

Mr. Wright was a Royal Arch Mason, a Knight Templar and a member of the Consistory. He was also a member of the Grand Army of the Republic, and a supporter, though not a member, of the West Side Presbyterian Church at Merrill. He was married at Union Grove, Wisconsin, November 1, 1872, to Miss Carrie Buchan, who, with their three children—James A., Alfred H. and Nettie—survived him.

Mr. Wright was of fine appearance, tall, erect and full of vigor. His death occurred very suddenly May 23, 1901, while he was on his way home from his logging camps. The funeral services were held at Merrill and were the largest attended of any ever held in that town. Showing the high esteem in which he was held, special trains were run from Stevens Point, Grand Rapids, Tomahawk and Wausau. Masonic bodies from these four cities, the G. A. R. post, Sons of Herman, the Druids, the city council, the board of education, firemen, policemen were in the funeral procession. Three thousand people paid their last tribute of respect to one whose loss they all felt so keenly.

Few men have commanded higher respect than Henry W. Wright. He had strong convictions and expressed them strongly, whether in politics, business or in other matters. He is said to have been naturally of extremely quick temper; but if so he learned the lesson of self control, which is one of the most valuable any man can learn. In all of his transactions he was the soul of honor. He had business reverses, but he never failed and always succeeded in paying every dollar he owed. He paid his debts in business, in politics and in friendship with scrupulous exactness and, more than that, he was a generous man.

A marked characteristic of Mr. Wright was his mental freshness and alertness. He was keenly interested in everything that was going on, whether in the large affairs of the world or nation, the smaller affairs of his city or state, or the individual concerns of himself and his friends. Lacking nothing of devotion to business, he yet had time and heart for everything and every one. Nothing seemed to please him better than to sit down with an acquaintance in his office, or outdoors in the shade of a building or tree, and question that acquaintance in regard to matters on which he was supposed to be informed. Mr. Wright was a good interviewer and his passion for information made him one of the best posted in regard to all current topics of his city or state. So 1 were his broad intelligence and his force of character re nized that he was often spoken of for high offices, but he no ambitions in that direction and the offices which he acce came to him practically unsought and were positions in w he could be of service to the community. The death of s a man is always felt as a bereavement, particularly whe comes in the prime of life before his work seems done. the old we can say that the time had come for rest, but f man like Mr. Wright there is the regret for what might been, as well as a feeling of immediate loss.

in Fulton county near North

occupation as farmer in addi... terial duties, which brought ... were the surroundings of ... youth. With the exceptio... Green Bay, he received his ... 1845 the family removed ... here Charles ... of most ...

It was in 185... manufacture of ... used to furnish ... business ... as ... be ...

With ... his partner ... taking their machinery and, after considering a number of locations ... Black river at a point where has since grown ... La Crosse. Here the manufacture of ...

CHARLES LANE COLMAN

Charles L. Colman

Prominent in the ranks of the pioneer lumbermen of Wisconsin was the late Charles Lane Colman, of La Crosse, Wisconsin. Mr. Colman was a native of the Empire State, having been born upon a farm in Fulton county, near Northampton, New York, February 23, 1826. His father was a farmer, afterward becoming a Methodist circuit rider and going to the then far West to take an appointment as missionary among the Oneida Indians west of Green Bay, Wisconsin. In 1840 he moved his family to that location, where he continued his occupation as farmer in addition to attending to his ministerial duties, which brought but small remuneration. Such were the surroundings of Charles L. Colman during his youth. With the exception of two winters' schooling at Green Bay, he received his education from his father. In 1845 the family removed to a location near Fond du Lac, Wisconsin, and here Charles for a number of years followed the occupation of most of the young men of his section—farming.

It was in 1853 that Mr. Colman was first interested in the manufacture of shingles by primitive machinery, horses being used to furnish the power. It was not long before the shingle business superseded farming entirely in Mr. Colman's career, as the price in those days of $5 a thousand paid a fair profit upon manufacture, and magnificent pine timber could then be had at hardly more than the price of cutting.

With the development of this business Mr. Colman and his partner at that time, a man named Noble, went inland, taking their machinery in a wagon drawn by their "power," and, after considering a number of locations, settled upon the Black river at a point where has since grown up the city of La Crosse. Here the manufacture of shingles by horse power was continued for two years, during which time Mr. Noble dropped out of the partnership. Mr. Colman persevered in the business alone. He had in the meantime saved enough from the enterprise to invest in a small steam engine, and with this very manifest improvement in the power and equipment of the plant his earnings correspondingly increased. In 1863 he purchased a mill which was then known as the Denton & Hurd saw mill, which gave him a total daily output of 350,000 shingles. Three years later he purchased another saw mill, with a daily capacity of 30,000 feet, which he used for the cutting of lumber, which then sold at $27 a thousand, log run. In 1868 his shingle mill burned and the following year the boilers of this mill were added to the saw mill, increasing its daily capacity to 50,000 feet.

In 1875 Mr. Colman lost his saw mill by fire. But men of his caliber are not discouraged by misfortune, and the next year he had a larger and more modern mill in operation. For eleven years this manufacturing plant was operated—until its destruction by fire in 1886, the last visitation Mr. Colman had from this devastating element. The following year a new mill was built on the same site, in which the circular saws were replaced by two band saws and other machinery very much like that in use today. This mill had an annual capacity of 40,000,000 feet of lumber, 16,000,000 shingles and 6,000,000 lath. This plant was closed down in 1903. It was a most excellent exemplification of modern saw mill methods, although its earliest predecessor was of the most primitive sort.

February 16, 1899, the C. L. Colman Lumber Company was incorporated with a capital stock of $1,000,000. C. L. Colman was president of the company, but the active management was left to the vice president, Lucius C. Colman, his eldest son, who had been his father's right hand man in business for several years. He was assisted by his brothers, Harry L. Colman, as secretary, and Edward L. Colman, as treasurer of the company. At this time the history of lumbering upon the Black river had nearly reached the end of its last chapter, but the C. L. Colman Lumber Company had a block of timber tributary to the Chippewa river of sufficient size to keep the mill in operation for a few years.

Mr. Colman was a public spirited citizen, though his labors for the upbuilding of the city were usually in an unofficial rather than an official capacity. However, he served the city for several terms as a member of the council and in 1869 took office for one term as mayor.

Mr. Colman was married in 1850 to Miss Laura A. Place, of Fond du Lac, who, with three sons and one daughter, survived him. With the growth of his lumbering business his sons became valuable aids to their father in his larger responsibilities. Mr. Colman still remained at the head of affairs after many of his employees had retired because of old age and had left their places in the mill to their sons. Other old men with greater vitality, or perhaps because of more urgent need for a continued daily wage, remained upon Mr. Colman's pay-roll. They were not pace makers in the amount of work they did; they belonged to the days of more primitive machinery, and could not readily in advanced years keep up with the new; they would doubtless have been rejected by the modern system which seeks to keep upon the pay-roll only men in their prime. Nevertheless Mr. Colman's loyalty to old associations and to old employees was doubtless more than compensated for by the enthusiasm and love of his employees. With more of such consideration on the part of employers there would be more efficient and faithful performance of duty, as well as longer terms of service on the part of employees.

Mr. Colman died July 1, 1901, having set all his affairs in order like one who prepares for a journey. Among his business competitors were none who could say that he had won his success by any unfair means or by endeavoring to keep another down that he might rise. Among his employees of so many years was none who did not hold his name in truly loving memory. Fame and fortune won by such methods constitute genuine success.

that the C. L. Colman Lumber Company had a block of timber tributary to the Chippewa river of sufficient size to keep the mill in operation for a few years.

Mr. Colman was a public spirited citizen, though his labors for the upbuilding of the city were usually in an unofficial rather than an official capacity. However, he served the city for several terms as a member of the council and in 1869 took office for one term as mayor.

Mr. Colman was married in 1850 to Miss Laura A. Hatch of [illegible], who, with three sons and one daughter, survive him. With the growth of his lumbering business his sons became valuable aids to their father in his larger responsibilities. Mr. Colman still [illegible] at the head of affairs [illegible] many of his employes who had retired because of old age had [illegible] their places in the mill to their sons. [illegible] with greater [illegible], or perhaps because of [illegible] for a [illegible] which remained [illegible] Mr. Colman's [illegible] pace makers in the amount of work [illegible] more [illegible] would not [illegible] in advanced years keep up with the new; they would doubtless have been rejected by the modern system which [illegible] to keep upon the pay-roll only men in their prime. Nevertheless Mr. Colman's loyalty to old associates and to old employes was doubtless more than compensated for by the [illegible] and love of his employes. With more of [illegible] consideration on the part of employers there would be [illegible] and [illegible] performance of duty and [illegible] of [illegible] on the part of employes.

Mr. Colman died July 1, 1905, leaving [illegible] all his affairs in order, like one who prepared for a journey. Among his business associates were none who could say that he had won his success by any unfair means or by endeavoring to keep another down that he might rise. Among his employes of so many years were [illegible] who did not hold his name in kindly loving memory. [illegible] and fortune won by such methods constitute [illegible]

mill which was pa
lived. Of Mr. F

shower mill," bec
on a mountain ri
only after a rain
doing was h dif-

of age. He
took the
first employme
to Charles R. T
G. C. Arnold, w
York the same ye
the following yea

NATHANIEL CALDWELL FOSTER

Nathaniel C. Foster

Some men owe their success in life to a fortunate start; some inherit another's success; some achieve it by taking advantage of an opportunity at a critical moment; some owe it to pure accident, and others win it by hard, unrelenting work and persistent, continued effort. To this last class belongs Nathaniel Caldwell Foster, of Fairchild, Wisconsin. The history of his life is that of a man who early realized the stern fact that for him, at least, there was no royal road to fortune, and that, if he attained it, it would be by his own hard efforts unaided by any fortunate circumstances. He worked hard for his share of prosperity and deserves all that has come to him.

Mr. Foster was born at Owego, Tioga county, New York, January 6, 1834. His father, Willard Foster, owned a saw mill which was part of the house in which he and his family lived. Of Mr. Foster it might be said that he was born in a saw mill. He gave it the appropriate name of a "thunder shower mill," because it was run by a water wheel and located on a mountain rivulet which furnished the necessary power only after a rain. The first work that Mr. Foster remembers doing was building fires in the school-house in the winter time. He carried live coals from his home in order to save matches.

Mr. Foster moved west in 1854, when he was twenty years of age. He reached Buffalo by way of the Erie road and took the steamer Michigan to Green Bay, Wisconsin. His first employment was at Fort Howard in a mill which belonged to Charles R. Tyler and of which Mr. Foster's brother-in-law, G. C. Arnold, was foreman. Mr. Foster went back to New York the same year but returned to Wisconsin in February of the following year. From Chicago to Fond du Lac he traveled by rail and then by stage to Green Bay. After his return to Wisconsin he worked for two years for C. R. Tyler, who owned a water mill on the Oneida reservation and a steam mill on Duck creek. Mr. Foster and Henry Lipscomb undertook the running of this steam mill on contract. In 1856 Mr. Foster bought interests in both mills. At first he held a half interest in the water mill on Duck creek but later acquired entire ownership of it. He owned this mill for two or three years and bought his trees of the Indians. That was in the days of abundance when a great portion of the tree which is now carefully husbanded was left in the woods. The Indians never cut more than two or three logs from the tree and they delivered these at the mill for from $2 to $2.50 a thousand feet.

These operations were interrupted by an altercation which resulted in a law suit. The mill men had trouble with the government concerning the purchase of logs from the Indians, and the government prosecuted the mill men, but N. C. Foster won his case. Mr. Foster traded his saw mill for a $6,000 brick house in Fort Howard which he afterward sold to L. M. Marshall. At about this time Schofield & Beard, a firm which afterward became Hoskinson & Beard, built a saw mill in Shawano county, Wisconsin, fourteen miles northwest of Green Bay. It was a steam mill equipped with a mulay saw and had a capacity of 5,000 feet of lumber a day. It had also a number of shingle machines. Mr. Foster came into possession of this plant in 1870, when it was considered a decided failure. He rebuilt the mill and ran it for six years, manufacturing both lumber and shingles, conveying the product to Green Bay on wagons and sleds. It proved to be one of the most profitable undertakings of his early life. In a period of six years he made a profit of approximately $100,000.

The mill was torn down in 1876 and 1877 and moved to Fairchild, Wisconsin, whither Mr. Foster's family followed him in 1878. Fairchild is situated thirteen miles northwest of Merrillan Junction and thirty-three miles from Eau Claire.

He purchased 4,300 acres of timber land from the West Wisconsin, now part of the Chicago, St. Paul, Minneapolis & Omaha railway. The first mill at Fairchild cut about 30,000 feet a day. At that point the N. C. Foster Lumber Company now has a saw mill consisting of two band mills and one gang, and is cutting 125,000 feet a day. This company was incorporated May, 18, 1891, with a paid up capital of $500,000. N. C. Foster, the father, is president, E. J. Foster, a son, vice president, and G. A. Foster, another son, secretary and treasurer. The company also operates the Fairchild & Northeastern railway, which is thirty-three miles in length, cost $400,000 and is estimated to be worth $1,000,000. It has four locomotives, forty or fifty cars and two passenger coaches and does a mail, express, freight and passenger business.

The N. C. Foster Lumber Company has many other interests. It owns an elevator and a buckwheat flour mill at Fairchild; a grist mill and custom mill at Greenwood, with an output of fifty barrels a day, and also an elevator that will hold 20,000 bushels of grain; a department store with sales of about $90,000 a year at Greenwood; and a store, 100 by 100 feet, with yearly gross sales of $250,000, at Fairchild.

During its career the company has cut over at least 40,000 acres of land and has three or four years' run ahead of it. It has 12,000 acres of hardwood land between Fairchild and Greenwood.

Mr. Foster's latest interests are in California, where his partners in the Del Norte Company are John S. Owen, Eugene Shaw, William Bigelow, H. H. Camp, John Paul, James Stout and Frank Stout. This company owns 30,000 acres, estimated to contain over 4,000,000,000 feet of standing redwood, fir, spruce and hemlock, the greater portion being redwood.

Mr. Foster was married June 6, 1858, to Esther M. Stearns, at Green Bay, Wisconsin.

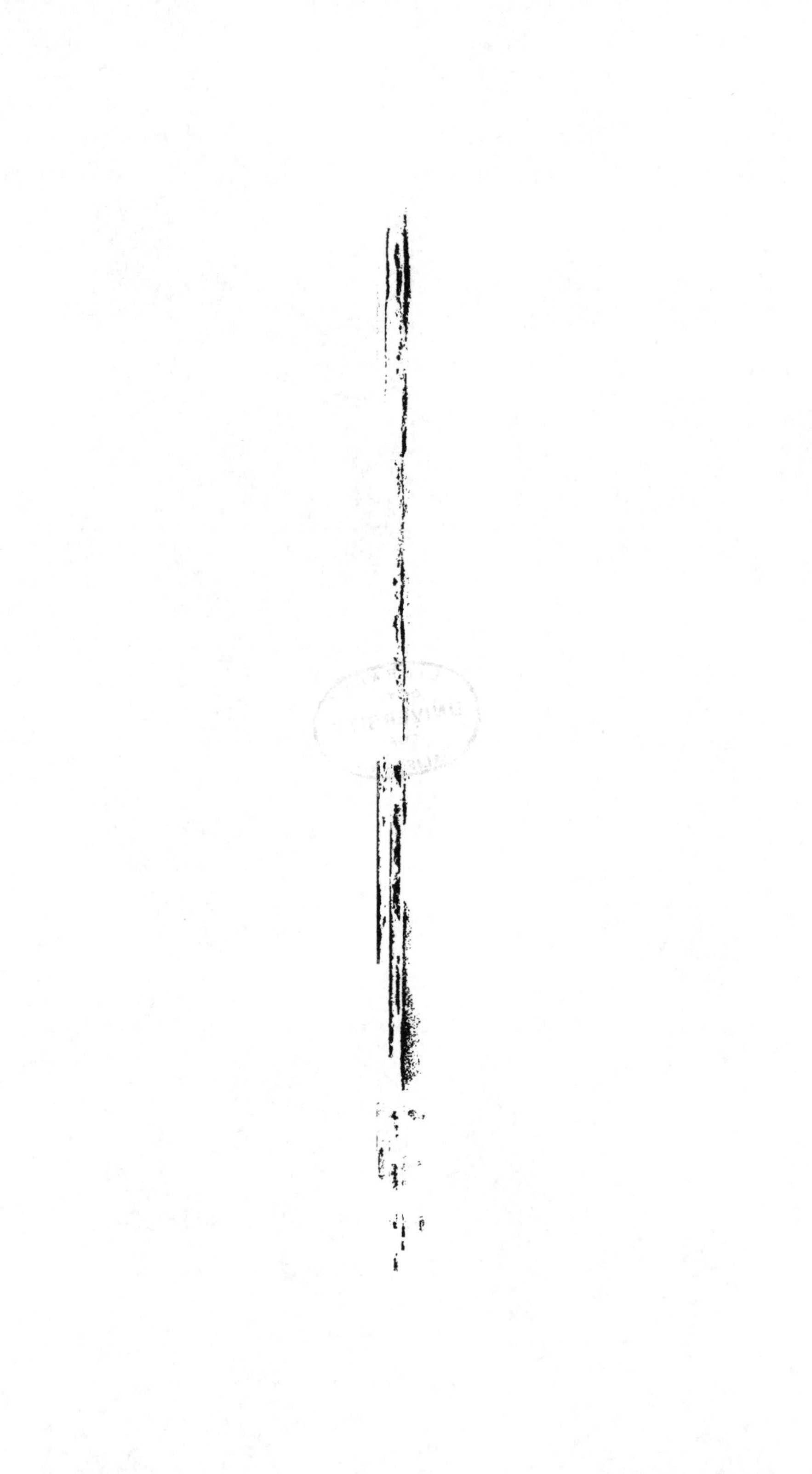

who was Sybil Storrs and whom he mar
county in June, 1854. They had th
whom are living. The son, George
business with his father. The daughter
Lopez, of Oshkosh.

Mr. Foster first stopped at Elgin, Ill
had worked for in the East had remove
building a flour mill there and offered
This was in September, 1855. From th
until April, 1856, he studied the advan
concluded he wished to settle there. H
that city and ever after made it his hom

He worked at his trade until the spr
March of that year he met Ira Griffin,
owned an old saw mill located on the
the [illegible] mill. This was an old fash
saw and a small circular and a total capa
a day. Mr. Griffin wished to sell Mr
notwithstanding his ability to get timbe
Mr. Foster rather doubted being able
money. However he at last accepted
notwithstanding the ridiculously low p
lumber, viewed from the standpoint of
his payments easily.

CARLTON FOSTER

Carlton Foster

Carlton Foster, of Oshkosh, Wisconsin, was born in Essex county, New York, August 20, 1826. The boy worked on a farm until about eighteen years of age and then started to learn the carpenter's trade with his father, but soon concluded that he preferred to learn the trade of a millwright. At this business he worked from the time he was twenty-one years old until he went west in 1855, taking with him his wife, who was Sybil Storrs and whom he married back in old Essex county in June, 1854. They had three children, two of whom are living. The son, George H. Foster, has been in business with his father. The daughter is Mrs. Anna Foster Loper, of Oshkosh.

Mr. Foster first stopped at Elgin, Illinois, but the firm he had worked for in the East had removed to Oshkosh and was building a flour mill there and offered Mr. Foster a position. This was in September, 1855. From the building of the mill until April, 1856, he studied the advantages of Oshkosh and concluded he wished to settle there. He brought his wife to that city and ever after made it his home.

He worked at his trade until the spring of 1859. During March of that year he met Ira Griffin, who with his brother owned an old saw mill located on the site of what was later the Conlee mill. This was an old fashioned plant with sash saw and a small circular and a total capacity of about 5,000 feet a day. Mr. Griffin wished to sell Mr. Foster the mill; but notwithstanding his ability to get timber with which to run it Mr. Foster rather doubted being able to get the necessary money. However, he at last accepted the proposition and, notwithstanding the ridiculously low prices received for his lumber, viewed from the standpoint of the present time, made his payments easily.

At the end of three years Mr. Foster had the mill clear from all incumbrance and had put in many improvements. He had installed a new boiler, a larger engine and a new circular, and was cutting from 15,000 to 20,000 feet of lumber a day. Across the street from Mr. Foster's mill was the little planing mill of P. Z. Wilson & Bro., who, in 1863, wished Mr. Foster to buy their "factory." Mr. Foster offered them $3,000—$1,000 down and the balance in a year—which terms they accepted. In 1865 Mr. Foster took in as partner in the planing mill venture J. V. Jones, and the business was run as Foster & Jones. Together they started the planing mill and began to make sash and doors. At that time if they made a hundred doors a day they thought they were doing remarkably well. Their machinery consisted of a planer, a planer and matcher, a rip saw, two stickers, a foot mortiser and a tenoner. The cross cutting of the lumber was all done with hand saws.

This "big" factory was altogether beyond the needs of the local trade and so outside markets were sought. The first carload was of 2-8 by 6-8 No. 2 doors, which were sold at $1 apiece to the father of R. B. Farson, of Chicago. U. N. Roberts, of Davenport, Iowa, was one of the first regular customers. It was a crude sort of business. All work was laid out with square and pencil, for the machinery of that time did not have guides and other arrangements for automatically regulating the work. This plant burned in the later '60's and was rebuilt on the corner of Oregon and Sixth streets, where the factory of The Morgan Company now stands.

This was one of the first real sash and door factories built in Oshkosh. In 1884 the saw mill was sold to Crane Brothers, and Mr. Foster thereafter devoted his attention exclusively to the sash and door business. The firm of Foster & Jones was dissolved by the retirement of J. V. Jones after many years of prosperity. Mr. Foster ran the factory alone for a time and then associated with himself Thomas R. Morgan, who had been bookkeeper in his office for a year and wished to purchase an interest. He secured a quarter interest in the business, and in 1884 the firm became Carlton Foster & Co.

In November, 1886, financial difficulties overtook Carlton Foster & Co., and it was not until March, 1889, that a final settlement was effected, although the factory was kept in operation. At that time The Morgan Company was organized, taking over the old establishment, while Mr. Foster temporarily retired from business and began to make arrangements for a reëntry into manufacture.

He had long had business relations with the Joseph Hafner Manufacturing Company, of St. Louis, and before Joseph Hafner's death he had an interest in that business. Upon the death of Mr. Hafner the old company was succeeded by the Hafner-Lothman Manufacturing Company and it seemed desirable to establish a northern manufacturing plant. The result was the erection in the winter of 1889-90 of what is known as the "Foster-Hafner Mills." This is really a nickname, adopted for business convenience, for it is the property of the Hafner-Lothman Manufacturing Company, of which Carlton Foster was, until his death, president; William Lothman, of St. Louis, vice president and treasurer, and T. B. Waters secretary.

These mills are located on the South Side in Oshkosh. The plant is one of the finest of its kind in arrangement and equipment in the country, and Mr. Foster believed it to be, though twelve years old, unexcelled by any of its size—and its size is not small by any means. Its capacity is about 1,000 doors, 1,000 to 1,200 windows and 200 pairs of blinds a day. This is exclusively a manufacturing business, for the product is all handled by two affiliated concerns—the Hafner-Lothman Manufacturing Company, before spoken of, and the Foster-Munger Company, of Chicago, of which also Mr. Foster was president until his death. The St. Louis house is the successor of an old institution, while the Foster-Munger Company is comparatively new, but has had a marked degree of success.

Mr. Foster was long an honored citizen of Oshkosh. He

served three terms as mayor—in 1865 an
again in 1886. He was a member of the
ture in 1873, 1874 and 1883. He was chair
of Trustees of the First Congregational Ch
secret society to which he owed allegiance was
Order of Odd Fellows. He died August 4,

LIBRARY
OF THE
UNIVERSITY
OF
CALIFORNIA

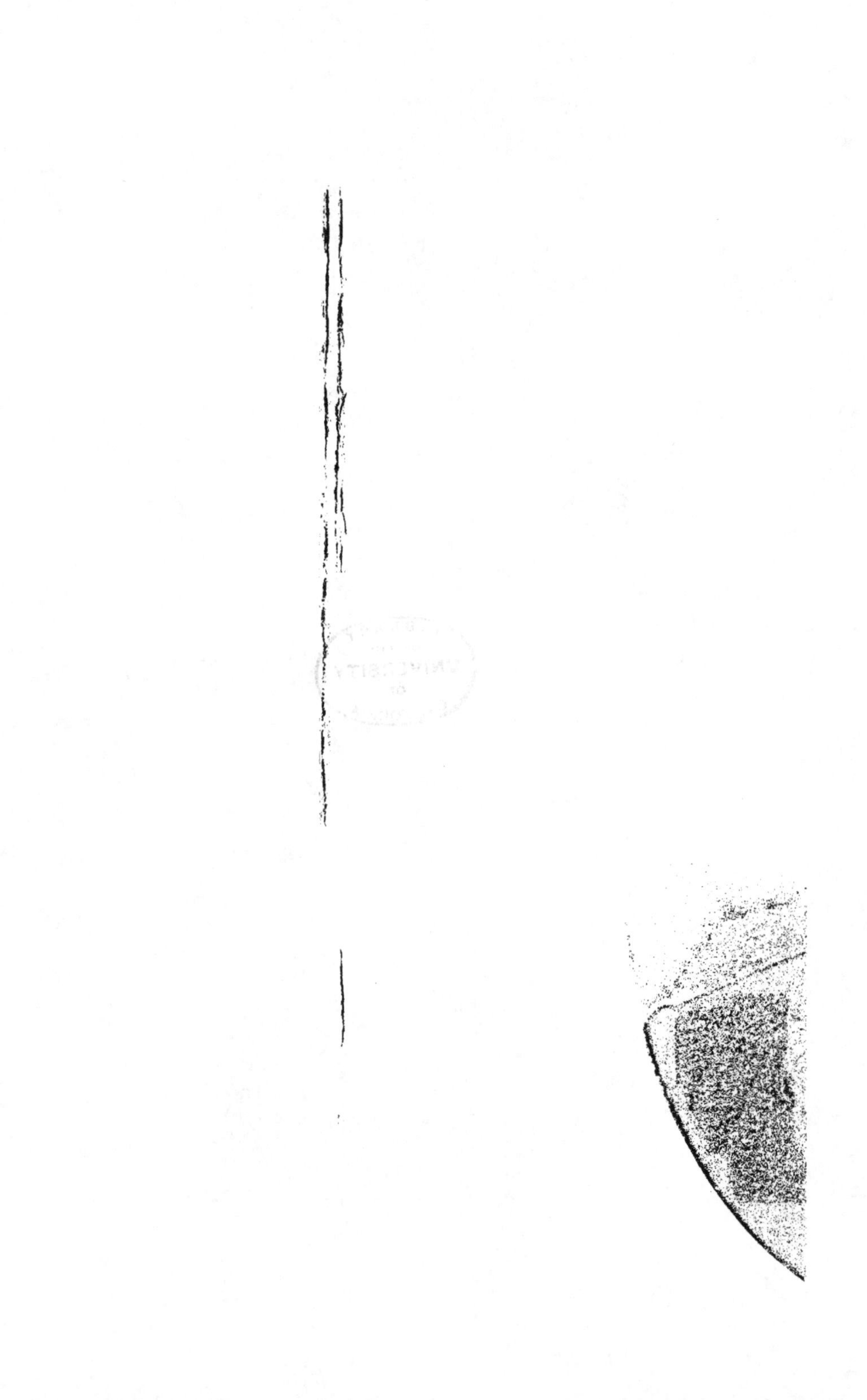

year a number of important chan
life of Mr. He returned to New Ham
married there, and in same year located at Oshkosh
[illegible], where he bought a half interest in the mill of
& Chase. Two years later he bought the remaining
of these gentlemen. Oshkosh at that time contained t
inhabitants, and Mr. Libbey not only witnessed
from that small beginning but assisted materially in br
about its industrial and mercantile prosperity. In r

DANIEL L. LIBBEY

Daniel L. Libbey

When Daniel L. Libbey, of Oshkosh, Wisconsin, died, December 25, 1894, there passed away one of the pioneer residents of that famous little lumber and sash and door city, and one of the most conspicuous and able lumbermen of the entire Northwest. He was born at Whitefield, New Hampshire, in 1823. His father was a lumberman and operated a small water mill. This mill played quite an important part in shaping the future destinies of the members of the family, for of the seven sons who were born to its owner, Nathaniel Libbey, all were lumbermen during the greater part of their lives.

In 1849—the year so famous in history for making or marring so many fortunes—Daniel L. Libbey joined the exodus from the East to the gold fields of California. It was his first business venture, for he bought the ship in which he and one hundred other gold seekers journeyed around the Horn to the Mecca of their dreams, and sold it upon arrival at their destination. The voyage consumed five months and the hazard proved a profitable one to Mr. Libbey. He spent three years in the gold regions and at the end of that time returned to New Hampshire on a short visit, afterward making another trip to California.

The year 1855 brought a number of important changes to the life of Mr. Libbey. He returned to New Hampshire, married there, and in the same year located at Oshkosh, Wisconsin, where he bought a half interest in the mill of Stilson & Chase. Two years later he bought the remaining interest of these gentlemen. Oshkosh at that time contained but 500 inhabitants, and Mr. Libbey not only witnessed its growth from that small beginning but assisted materially in bringing about its industrial and mercantile prosperity. In 1873 he sold his mill to Radford Brothers and bought an interest in the firm of Campbell Brothers & Cameron, in whose affairs he played an active part for a number of years. In 1879 he bought the old gang mill which had been built in 1850 by Knapp & Jenkins.

In the meantime the Williamson & Libbey Lumber Company had been organized and this mill was turned over to that company.

During this time there had been several important incidents in Mr. Libbey's career. In 1862 his mill and a large amount of lumber were destroyed by fire. It was not insured and this was a severe reverse. However, his nature was not one to be overcome by misfortune; he did not lose courage but set about the work of rebuilding his fortune. When the Union National Bank of Oshkosh was established, in 1871, Mr. Libbey was elected president, and he held this position until his death.

The Williamson & Libbey Lumber Company was established in 1875 under the name of Williamson, Libbey & Co. In January, 1884, it was incorporated as the Williamson & Libbey Lumber Company, with a capitalization of $200,000. It is a somewhat remarkable fact that all of the first officers—President Daniel L. Libbey, Vice President J. J. Cameron and Secretary and Treasurer G. M. Williamson—are now deceased. F. H. Libbey, a son of D. L. Libbey, is now president of the company and J. J. Stevenson is secretary and treasurer.

When the firm of Williamson, Libbey & Co. was formed it turned its attention to the manufacture of doors, sash, and blinds and their associated products. This business has steadily increased until now the plant uses 15,000,000 feet of purchased stock annually and manufactures 300,000 doors, 300,000 sash and 75,000 pairs of blinds, in addition to brackets, inside finishings, etc., every year. Much of the credit for the splendid equipment of the company and the successful operation of its business was due to Mr. Libbey's personal efforts.

Not only was Mr. Libbey conspicuous as a lumberman, but he was also prominent as a banker, and was interested in various manufacturing concerns. He was president of the Williamson & Libbey Lumber Company, treasurer of the Thompson Carriage Company, of Oshkosh, and also interested in the Fulton & Libbey Company, of Minneapolis. He was twice married and is survived by four children.

No man ever engaged in the lumber business in Oshkosh, or for that matter anywhere, who was better acquainted with the details of his occupation than was Mr. Libbey. He was an expert in the selection of timber lands, in the operation of a camp, in the driving of logs and in the manufacture and sale of lumber. He had a thorough knowledge of the business from its lowest to its highest forms. He was a man of tremendous energy and strength. He often walked from his home in Oshkosh to the pine woods in which he was interested—a distance of sixty miles. He enjoyed his work, with the consciousness of being physically and mentally adequate to it. He early learned to consider a subject thoroughly—to the bottom fact, before he put his ideas of it into active practice. He realized that deep conviction does not present itself suddenly; that one must work patiently for it and then watch the result of experience. When the time came for him to lay down the burdens of life, he received with his characteristic dignity the messenger that called him to everlasting rest.

LIBRARY
OF THE
UNIVERSITY
OF
CALIFORNIA

THOMAS R. MORGAN

Thomas R. Morgan

It seems almost as though the picturesque mountains and deep valleys of the little country of Wales give to its sons some of the sturdy characteristics for which they are famed. Certain it is that Thomas R. Morgan, who was born near the little village of Aberystwyth, in South Wales, June 28, 1856, possessed sturdiness of character, strength and ambition that won for him the high position he occupied in his community at the time of his death. His father, Thomas Morgan, was a farmer who tilled the soil on a small tract of land and operated a small flour mill, the power for which was derived from a mountain stream. As the country thereabouts did not yield sufficient grain to supply his mill, he bought American grain to grind and sold his flour in the mining district near by.

Young Thomas, when he became old enough, attended a private school and also a British school, acquiring in this way the English language when a mere child. He was twelve years of age when his parents came to this country, arriving at Oshkosh, Wisconsin, in October, 1868.

As a young man he was ambitious, and in 1872, when a lad of sixteen, he secured a position in the shingle mill of his uncles, members of the firm of Morgan Brothers, who were the first to begin the manufacture of sash and doors in Oshkosh. For several years Thomas worked in the shingle mill during the summers and pursued a course of study at the Oshkosh high school during the winters, afterward attending business college where he taught for a few months after he had completed his course.

Having acquired a good business education, in 1875 Mr. Morgan took charge of the bookkeeping and office work for Morgan Brothers, but in March, 1877, he left that firm to accept a similar position with Foster & Jones, who at that time were engaged in manufacturing sash and doors. This was the beginning of his career as a sash and door manufacturer, which afterward assumed an importance he little dreamed of at the time he entered upon it. Mr. Foster remained with Foster & Jones until 1881, when, desiring to get some experience in the selling end of the business, he traveled for the U. N. Roberts Company, of Davenport, Iowa, for a year as salesman and buyer.

At the beginning of the next year he returned to Oshkosh and took charge of the office of Carlton Foster & Co. Mr. Morgan remained with this concern continuously from 1882 until February 9, 1889, when The Morgan Company was organized by himself and his two cousins, J. Earl Morgan and the late Albert T. Morgan, and the factory, Chicago warehouse and entire business of Carlton Foster & Co. were purchased by the newly organized company. In 1902, after the death of Albert T. Morgan his interest was purchased jointly by Thomas R. and J. Earl Morgan.

The factory that The Morgan Company acquired in 1889 was not a large one, but the three enterprising young men who constituted this concern enlarged it from time to time and modernized it. It was entirely destroyed by fire September 18, 1895. Thirty days later the insurance was adjusted and the work of building a new plant was begun, and February 1, 1896, the new factory of The Morgan Company was in operation. The new plant is very much larger than the old one, entirely modern and up to date in every way. It has a stock capacity of 1,200 doors, 1,500 windows and 250 pairs of blinds daily, the remaining capacity being devoted to special work. The factory, which is of brick and is three stories high, has a floor space of 82,000 square feet. In addition there are extensive warehouses in Oshkosh and also a warehouse at West Twenty-second and Union streets, Chicago, 125 by 150 feet in size and five stories in height.

The credit for the organization of the extensive business of The Morgan Company cannot be said to be due to any one individual, but should be given to the united efforts of the three members of the company, each managing a particular department of the business, always united and pulling strongly together for the success of the enterprise. Thomas R. Morgan, however, from his years of experience in every detail of the sash and door industry, was particularly well qualified to direct the manufacturing and in a general way to oversee the business of the company.

While confining their attention almost entirely to the manufacture of sash and doors, the members of The Morgan Company are also largely interested in the Morgan Lumber & Cedar Company, which operates a saw mill at Foster City, Michigan.

Thomas R. Morgan devoted the best years of his life to the development of the extensive business of The Morgan Company, being an earnest and hard worker toward this end. He always took a great interest in association and other matters pertaining to the welfare of the sash and door business, and was a director of the Wholesale Sash, Door & Blind Manufacturers' Association of the Northwest for several years previous to his being elected president of the association in 1898, to which office he was twice reelected.

Mr. Morgan married in 1881 Miss Lydia Jones, of Oshkosh, and had two daughters. He was intensely fond of home life and spent with his family all the time he could spare from his business. He was a believer in the good of church work, and was the typical, conscientious and upright American man of affairs.

In the very zenith of his mental and physical powers Mr. Morgan fell a victim to the murderous assault of a drunken laborer, August 18, 1903. Mr. Morgan was walking in the company's yard at Oshkosh and was approached by the murderer, Frederick Hampel. No one was near enough to hear the brief conversation between them, but John Morgan, a foreman of The Morgan Company, saw Hampel draw a revolver and fire three shots at his employer, the distance between them being only three or four feet. Death was instantaneous, but occurred within an hour. Hampel, was believed to have been temporarily crazed by drink, c mitted suicide by hanging himself to the door of his shortly after his incarceration. The sad event cast a shadow over the city in which Thomas R. Morgan worked his way from a humble position to one of wealth influence, and which he was serving as an alderman at time of his death. His honorable and straightforward ness career had earned for him the respect of businessme all parts of the country, and in his social life he had w host of friends to whom his untimely end came as a g shock.

LIBRARY
OF THE
UNIVERSITY
OF
CALIFORNIA

born October 17,
New York. His
was a farmer,

father
his ... the

thirteen,
th of Stevens
Millan enga
, a tribu ... many

The output
mill was ... junc-
and on
Keokuk,
oper-
their

busi-
, decided
would be
mill at what
north of the present
there was not
The whole country
redwoods.

BENJAMIN FRANKLIN McMILLAN

Benjamin F. McMillan

The McMillans of Wisconsin, while not pioneer lumbermen of that state, are pioneers of the locality in which they operate. Benjamin Franklin McMillan was born October 17, 1845, at Fort Covington, Franklin county, New York. His father, David Stiles McMillan, in his early days was a farmer, and later engaged in the manufacture of woolen goods. When young Benjamin F. McMillan was six years old his father moved with his family to Malone, New York, where the senior McMillan founded the McMillan Woolen Mills, which are still running and bear the original name. In 1864 the family, consisting of the parents and six remaining children of a family of thirteen, moved to Wisconsin and located fourteen miles north of Stevens Point, on the Plover river, where the elder McMillan engaged in the manufacture of lumber.

The Plover, a tributary of the Wisconsin, was for many years an important lumbering stream and even to this day a few pine logs come down its waters every spring. The output of the McMillan mill was rafted down this stream to its junction with the Wisconsin and thence to the Mississippi and on to the lumbering markets of Dubuque, Davenport, Keokuk, St. Louis and other points. The McMillans themselves operated a large wholesale yard at Keokuk, Iowa, from which their lumber was shipped to the trade by rail.

In 1873 B. F. McMillan's father retired from active business, at which time he and his brother, Charles V., decided that a location farther west, in the then wilderness, would be desirable. In the spring of 1874 they built a saw mill at what is now McMillan, Wisconsin, five miles north of the present thriving city of Marshfield, though at that time there was not a house where Marshfield now stands. The whole country was one unbroken wilderness of timber—pine and hardwoods.

No corporation was formed—not even a partnership—but the two brothers called their business B. F. McMillan & Bro. and began sawing lumber in the summer of 1874, and are still sawing there.

Many important outgrowths have sprung from the McMillan business, some of them larger, in the amount of capital invested and in the value of the product, than the parent institution. Charles V. McMillan continued actively in the McMillan business until 1885, when he went to Ashland, Wisconsin, and ran a cold storage business as the McMillan Brothers Company, the ownership of which was identically the same as that of the McMillan interests at McMillan. This business was closed out in 1890 and the brothers then organized the Winnebago Furniture Company, buying the old C. J. L. Meyers sash and door plant at Fond du Lac, Wisconsin, and converting it into a furniture factory.

In 1899 the brothers built a mill at Ontonagon, Michigan, which was run under the name of C. V. McMillan & Bro., in order to distinguish it from the McMillan business, although its ownership is the same. The Ontonagon mill saws pine, hemlock and hardwoods. In 1894 the mill at McMillan exhausted its pine, which consisted largely of the finest to be found in Wisconsin, and has since sawed hemlock and hardwoods. The McMillans are also interested in a retail lumber yard at Fond du Lac, operated under the name of the Crofoot Lumber Company.

B. F. McMillan has always studied with particular care the subject of grading and the adaptation of lumber to use. He originated the percentage rule in hardwood which is used all over the United States. He also eliminated the word "cull" from hardwood rules, and his ideas as to hardwood grading are found in the rules of all the important hardwood lumber associations. He has always taken active interest in association work, was one of the organizers and prime movers in the Wisconsin Hardwood Lumbermen's Association and was one of the originators and was president for several years of the Wisconsin Hemlock Manufacturers' Association.

Mr. McMillan married on April 30, 1873, at Constable, Franklin county, New York, Miss Ada M. Beebee.

He has been a staunch Republican, taking much interest in the work of the party in his county and state and attending its conventions, although never seeking political honors. He has at McMillan a beautiful home which contains one of the finest libraries in central Wisconsin. It especially abounds in fine and limited editions of standard authors. The house is a product of Mr. McMillan's own plant, finished throughout in curly birch and showing to the best advantage the beauties of this native Wisconsin hardwood. Mr. McMillan has always taken a great interest in horses and a few years ago had in his stables at McMillan over one hundred specimens of the best trotting blood, but has gradually disposed of them.

The little village, which was incorporated twelve years ago, has the unique distinction of being the only incorporated village in the United States with neither a saloon nor a church within its limits. Every year a police justice is elected as a matter of form, but he never qualifies, and in the twelve years since its incorporation the village has never had a civil or criminal law suit. It is governed by a president and board of six trustees, and since its establishment Mr. McMillan has been its president. He has also been postmaster during the twenty-four years that the post office has been established there. When the village was incorporated a poor fund of $100 was raised, but it has not yet been expended, for there has never been a pauper within the limits of the village nor has it paid a cent of pauper tax.

No railroad reached McMillan when the mill was built and for many years the product was hauled by sleds or wagons to Mannville, a station on the Wisconsin Central railway not now in existence. Twelve years ago the Chicago & North-Western Railway Company built a line through McMillan from Wausau to Marshfield.

During the operation of their plant, the McMillans have owned many thousands of acres of land. They have made a practice of fitting this land for agricultural purposes and ing it on easy terms to good settlers, and in this manner been built up a rich agricultural district. The busine McMillan has never been a very large one, as such things but it has been uniformly successful. It was for many y chiefly employed in the manufacture of white pine and a ward hardwoods and hemlock. During all this develop B. F. McMillan has lived at the mill—the presiding geni the village and of the surrounding country—in almost fe fashion, for he is the father of all of his people, their gu counselor and friend, and yet he maintains a democratic plicity which makes his position more secure than could assumption of importance.

WILLIAM IRVINE

William Irvine

The Mississippi Valley Lumbermen's Association is acknowledged to be one of the most earnest and businesslike organizations of its character in the country. Much of its reputation is undoubtedly due to the services and policy of such members as William Irvine, one of the leading white pine lumbermen of the Northwest. He was born at Mount Carroll, Illinois, October 28, 1851. His father, John Irvine, senior, born in 1790 in Pennsylvania, was of Scotch-Irish descent, and served in the War of 1812. His mother was of New England ancestry and was born in New York.

Mount Carroll is ten miles east of Savanna, Illinois, a Mississippi river port. For a number of years prior to 1858 John Irvine, senior, operated a saw mill there. He sawed logs that came down the Mississippi river, his equipment being a rotary and a sash saw, the usual one in those days. He gave up the lumber business when William was but seven years old and thereafter carried on a merchandise business in Mount Carroll. William Irvine, therefore, cannot be said to have been born a lumberman; but, as will be seen, he was more or less directly connected with the lumber trade from the beginning of his own business experience.

A sister of William Irvine married Captain George Winans, who now runs a line of boats towing lumber and logs on the Mississippi river. At that time he was pilot of the steamer Union, engaged in towing lumber from Reed's Landing to St. Louis and other down river markets for Pound, Halbert & Co., at that time operating the Chippewa Falls mill. William Irvine attended school until he was sixteen years old, when he went to work for Captain Winans as watchman on the Union. This was in 1867. He worked as watchman on this and other boats engaged in towing lumber for the Chippewa Falls mill for two years and was then promoted to the position of clerk. He continued as such until 1875, when he accepted a position as lumber salesman for the Union Lumbering Company, at that time the owner of the Chippewa Falls plant.

He continued with the Union Lumbering Company and its successors until Mr. Weyerhaeuser and his associates bought the Chippewa Falls mill in the spring of 1881, when he became secretary of the Chippewa Lumber & Boom Company. E. W. Culver, now of Kansas City and a well known southwestern hardwood manufacturer, was the first manager of the company. In 1885 Mr. Culver resigned and Mr. Irvine was made manager as well as secretary.

Continuously since he was sixteen years old William Irvine has had something to do with the Chippewa Falls mill or its product. He first worked on the boats that towed its lumber to market, then sold its lumber and then managed the business. While serving as salesman he became familiar with grades and manufacturing methods, as he was about the mill more or less during all that period. Prior to that, during the winters of 1870, 1871 and 1872, while the boats were not running, he scaled logs in the woods for the people owning the mill, thus acquiring a knowledge of timber and logging.

William Irvine, in addition to his management of the Chippewa Lumber & Boom Company's affairs, is secretary of the Northern Lumber Company, of Cloquet, Minnesota, and secretary and general manager of the Chippewa River & Menominee Railway Company.

His connection with one of the greatest lumbering plants in the country has long made Mr. Irvine's name a familiar one to the white pine trade, but he is also and more widely known in the lumber industry of the United States by virtue of his connection with what is probably the greatest and most successful lumber organization in the country—the Mississippi Valley Lumbermen's Association. This is an organization which embraces within its own membership or that of its affiliated bodies probably nine-tenths of the output of all the white pine lumber manufactured in Wisconsin and Minnesota outside of the mills on lakes Superior and Michigan. The output of its mills includes more than half of the white pine production of the United States and probably 90 percent of the interior product of the two states in which it operates.

Mr. Irvine has been actively identified with the association since its organization, September 1, 1891. At that time B. F. Nelson, of Minneapolis, was elected president and served in that capacity until February 28, 1893, when W. H. Laird, of the Laird, Norton Company, of Winona, succeeded him and served five annual terms. Mr. Irvine was made vice president in 1896, serving through that year and 1897, and on March 1, 1898, was elected to succeed Mr. Laird. He served three years as president. He takes a deep interest in the welfare of this association and keeps closely in touch with the details of its several departments. As a parliamentarian he has few equals and when he is in the chair business is transacted with dispatch and accuracy.

Mr. Irvine has great faith in the value of association effort and gives much of his time to the affairs of the organization. He is particularly interested in the work being done by the bureau of uniform grades and considers this department of inestimable value to the manufacturers. Mr. Irvine is entitled to much of the credit for the leading position which the Mississippi Valley Lumbermen's Association today occupies among the lumbermen's organizations of the country. Conservative, always mindful of the best interests of the members and striving to accomplish the greatest good for the greatest number, Mr. Irvine made an ideal executive for an up-to-date organization of energetic businessmen.

Mr. Irvine is of medium height, of compact frame, and in prime physical condition. He is clear eyed, alert, quick in his movements, but with every movement intelligently directed. His mental processes are rapid and exact. He is democratic in his manner, unaffected and companionable.

He is a man whom it i
whose assistance and
highest value.

LIBRARY
OF THE
UNIVERSITY
OF
CALIFORNIA

There is undoubtedly much in heredity. The ancestors of Robert Laird McCormick, of Tacoma, Washington, were of good stock. His great-grandfather, John McCormick, was born in Ireland, but came to this country at an early age and joined the revolutionary army from Pennsylvania, becoming an ensign, or third lieutenant. Both of his grandfathers were in the War of 1812, and Colonel Hugh White, famous in that war, was a relative. His mother's father was a Laird, of Scotch descent, but a Pennsylvania Quaker. His father, Alexander McCormick, resided on a farm near Lock Haven, Pennsylvania, where Robert Laird McCormick was born October 29, 1847.

When a lad Mr. McCormick attended Saunders Institute, a Presbyterian military academy in Philadelphia, and after two years there spent a year at the Tuscarora Academy at Mifflin, Pennsylvania. Not having any particular liking for school he left the academy before graduating and entered the employ of the Erie railway. When the war broke out he was a youth of but thirteen years, yet he wanted to enlist, and ran away from home, staying several days at Camp Curtin, at Harrisburg, in the hope that he would be able to join a regiment going to the front; but his parents took him home.

For several years after leaving the employ of the railroad company Mr. McCormick worked at various occupations, among others office work, in which he became proficient; and in [illegible] he went west to Winona, Minnesota, to take charge of the office of Laird, Norton & Co. W. H. Laird, of this company, was a maternal uncle of Mr. McCormick.

In the fall of 1874 he conceived the idea of buying a retail lumber yard at Waseca, Minnesota, with the aid of Laird, Norton & Co. This yard he ran until 188[illegible]. He also acted

ROBERT LAIRD McCORMICK

Robert L. McCormick

There is undoubtedly much in heredity. The ancestors of Robert Laird McCormick, of Tacoma, Washington, were of good stock. His great-grandfather, John McCormick, was born in Ireland, but came to this country at an early age and joined the revolutionary army from Pennsylvania, becoming an ensign, or third lieutenant. Both of his grandfathers were in the War of 1812, and Colonel Hugh White, famous in that war, was a relative. His mother's father was a Laird, of Scotch descent, but a Pennsylvania Quaker. His father, Alexander McCormick, resided on a farm near Lock Haven, Pennsylvania, where Robert Laird McCormick was born October 29, 1847.

When a lad Mr. McCormick attended Saunders Institute, a Presbyterian military academy in Philadelphia, and after two years there spent a year at the Tuscarora Academy at Mifflin, Pennsylvania. Not having any particular liking for school he left the academy before graduating and entered the employ of the Erie railway. When the war broke out he was a youth of but thirteen years, yet he wanted to enlist, and ran away from home, staying several days at Camp Curtin, at Harrisburg, in the hope that he would be able to join a regiment going to the front; but his parents took him home.

For several years after leaving the employ of the railroad company Mr. McCormick worked at various occupations, among others office work, in which he became proficient; and in 1868 he went west to Winona, Minnesota, to take charge of the office of Laird, Norton & Co. W. H. Laird, of this company, was a maternal uncle of Mr. McCormick.

In the fall of 1874 he conceived the idea of buying a retail lumber yard at Waseca, Minnesota, with the aid of Laird, Norton & Co. This yard he ran until 1881. He also acted as auditor for Laird, Norton & Co., visiting their various yards in southern Minnesota. As the railroads were extended through that region and into South Dakota, he located new yards, in some of which he was personally interested with the firm. He was also interested in the large stone quarries of W. B. Craig & Co., at Mankato, Minnesota.

In Mr. McCormick the people of Waseca recognized an able and public spirited citizen, and during all the time he resided there, except the first year, he was mayor of the city. Personally possessing those characteristics that made him popular with the people—although never a politician as the term is commonly understood—it was but natural that Mr. McCormick should have been elected to the state senate of Minnesota in 1880, where he served through two regular and two extra sessions with credit to himself and satisfaction to his constituents. He was a delegate from Wisconsin to the Republican national convention at Philadelphia in 1900 which renominated William McKinley for President.

In October, 1881, the North Wisconsin Lumber Company was incorporated and fifteen townships, heavily timbered, in the vicinity of Hayward were purchased by the company from the Omaha railway. The company's mill was completed and began sawing early in 1883, and since then it has manufactured over 700,000,000 feet of lumber. During all this time, up to 1903, Mr. McCormick was the active manager of its affairs. In 1903 the stock of this company was acquired by Edward Hines, of Chicago, and his associates.

Frederick Weyerhaeuser early recognized the fact that Mr. McCormick possessed great technical and executive ability and since the founding of the North Wisconsin Lumber Company, he has been associated with him in many large business enterprises. Together they established the Sawyer County Bank at Hayward, of which Mr. McCormick was made president. Until he resigned at the beginning of 1905, because of his removal to the Pacific Coast, he was president of the Mississippi & Rum River Boom Company, of Minneapolis, also of the Northern Boom Company, of Brainerd, Minnesota; vice president of the St. Paul Boom Company, of St. Paul, and the Flambeau Land Company, of Chippewa Falls, Wisconsin, and secretary and treasurer of the Mississippi River Lumber Company, of Clinton, Iowa.

Mr. McCormick was largely instrumental in bringing about the purchase of an immense tract of timber in the state of Washington by Mr. Weyerhaeuser and his associates and the formation of the Weyerhaeuser Timber Company, with headquarters at Tacoma, Washington. Of this company Mr. McCormick is secretary.

Besides being a lumberman and banker, Mr. McCormick is extensively engaged in the grain trade. The Northern Grain Company is a corporation of which he is secretary and treasurer and in which Mr. Weyerhaeuser also is interested. It has elevators and warehouses in Wisconsin, Minnesota, Iowa, Nebraska and the Dakotas, with headquarters and general offices in Chicago. He is treasurer of the New Richmond Mill Company, which has flour mills at New Richmond, Wisconsin. He is also president of the Duluth Universal Flour Mill Company, of Duluth, Minnesota.

Mr. McCormick moved from Hayward, Wisconsin, to Tacoma, Washington, in July, 1903. In addition to being secretary of the Weyerhaeuser Timber Company, he is officially connected with a number of companies subsidiary to that company and is also president of the Lumbermen's National Bank of Tacoma.

With all his many business interests Mr. McCormick is a student. He is fond of history and has devoted much time to research into the early history of exploration and discovery in this country, particularly in the Lake Superior region. A few years ago, at the request of the State Historical Society of Wisconsin, of which he was president, he prepared and published a history of the press of Sawyer county, which is written in the terse and clear style characteristic of the man. His "Evolution of Indian Education" has attracted the attention of the friends of the Indians throughout the United States.

Mr. McCormick is trustee of the State Historical Society of Washington and of the Ferry Museum of Tacoma, and a director of the Tacoma Chamber of Commerce. He is interested also in educational matters, having been president of the school board of Hayward, Wisconsin, of the Hayward Library Association and of the Ashland Academy at Ashland, Wisconsin. He is a thirty-second degree Mason and, while living in Minnesota, was at one time grand commander of the Minnesota Knights Templar. He is a member of the order of the Mystic Shrine and also of the Sons of Veterans. His love for things historical, together with his descent from a fighting ancestry, has led him to join the Society of the War of 1812, with membership in the Chicago chapter. He is also a member of the Minnesota society of the Sons of the American Revolution.

During 1866 and 1867 Mr. McCormick lived in Ohio and there married Anna E. Goodman. They have two sons—William Laird, twenty-nine years old, and Robert Allen, twenty years of age. The elder son was elected in 1900 to the Wisconsin legislature.

LIBRARY
OF THE
UNIVERSITY
OF
CALIFORNIA

A [illegible] lumberman who has spent a half century in Wausau, who, like so many others, is a product of the West, is Sumner Thomas McKnight, of Minneapolis, Minnesota, president of the North Western Lumber Company. He was born at [illegible], Cortland county, New York, in 1836, [illegible] from a distinguished colonial family of New Jersey. When but sixteen years of age, after having received an education in the common schools near his home, he went west to Ripon, Wisconsin, where he became a clerk in a general store. Two years later, at Wausau, Wisconsin, in a similar capacity, he entered the employ of George N. Lyman, who operated a saw mill there.

This was in 1854, when Wausau was just beginning to attract attention as a lumber manufacturing point and establishing a prestige which it has well maintained for a half century. Two years after Mr. McKnight entered the Lyman store he became general manager of Mr. Lyman's entire mercantile, logging and lumbering business. He continued in this responsible position until 1859, when Mr. Lyman disposed of his interests in Wausau. The experience gained while holding this position gave Mr. McKnight the thorough knowledge of the details of the lumber business which was the foundation for his subsequent career.

From 1859 to 1862 Mr. McKnight operated a general store at Blue Earth City, Minnesota. However, his predilection was for the lumber business, and in 1862, with J. B. [illegible], he entered into a partnership for the operation of a wholesale and retail lumber yard at Hannibal, Missouri. This partnership lasted six years. In 1870 Mr. McKnight became associated with Porter, Moon & Co., manufacturers of lumber

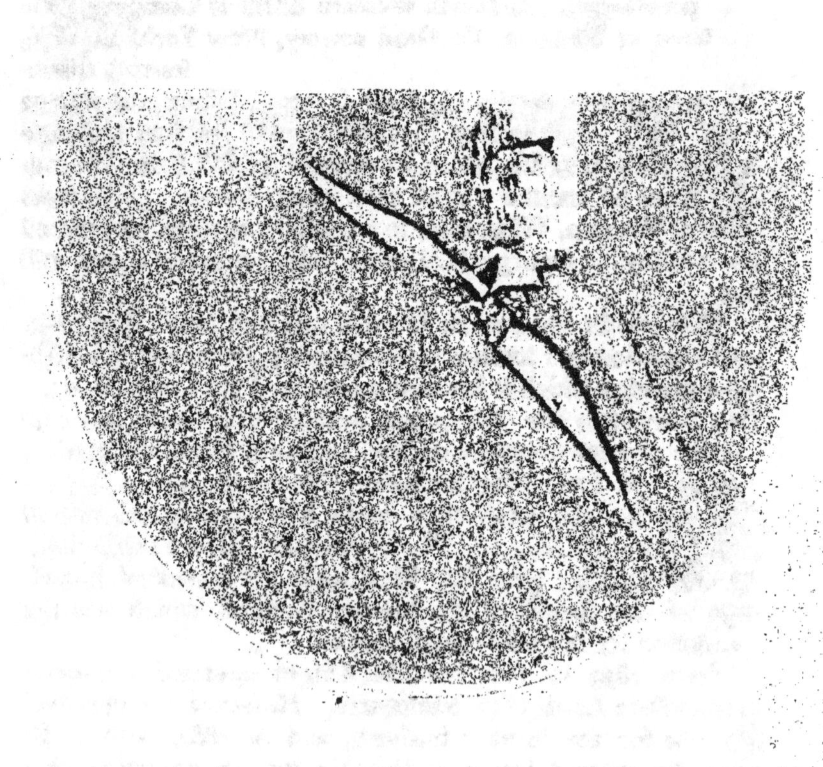

Sumner T. McKnight

A northwestern lumberman who has spent a half century in the West but who, like so many others, is a product of the East, is Sumner Thomas McKnight, of Minneapolis, Minnesota, president of the North Western Lumber Company. He was born at Truxton, Cortland county, New York, in 1836, the son of a merchant who was descended from a distinguished colonial family of New Jersey. When but sixteen years of age, after having received an education in the common schools near his home, he went west to Ripon, Wisconsin, where he became a clerk in a general store. Two years later, at Wausau, Wisconsin, in a similar capacity, he entered the employ of George N. Lyman, who operated a saw mill also.

This was in 1854, when Wausau was just beginning to attract attention as a lumber manufacturing point and establishing a prestige which it has well maintained for a half century. Two years after Mr. McKnight entered the Lyman store he became general manager of Mr. Lyman's entire mercantile, logging and lumbering business. He continued in this responsible position until 1859, when Mr. Lyman disposed of his interests in Wausau. The experience gained while holding this position gave Mr. McKnight the thorough knowledge of the details of the lumber business which was the foundation for his subsequent career.

From 1859 to 1862 Mr. McKnight operated a general store at Blue Earth City, Minnesota. However, his predilection was for the lumber business, and in 1862, with J. B. Price, he entered into a partnership for the operation of a wholesale and retail lumber yard at Hannibal, Missouri. This partnership lasted six years. In 1870 Mr. McKnight became associated with Porter, Moon & Co., manufacturers of lumber at Eau Claire, Wisconsin. The lumber of this firm was rafted down the Chippewa and Mississippi rivers and distributed from Hannibal by a separate concern known as S. T. McKnight & Co. From that time until 1902 Mr. McKnight was intimately associated with the interests headed by the North Western Lumber Company, and was similarly connected with D. R. Moon during that well known lumberman's lifetime.

Mr. Moon had, in 1867, in partnership with Gilbert E. Porter, begun the operation of a saw mill at Porter's Mills, four miles below Eau Claire, on the Chippewa river. When the North Western Lumber Company was incorporated, in 1873, Mr. McKnight was made its secretary and treasurer, Mr. Porter being the president and Mr. Moon the vice president. Mr. McKnight continued in this double capacity until the death of D. R. Moon, in 1898, when the latter's son, Sumner G. Moon, was made secretary and treasurer and Mr. McKnight was advanced to the presidency. The North Western Lumber Company at this time manufactured annually 100,000,000 feet of lumber, of which more than three-quarters was white pine and the remainder hemlock and hardwoods. It has steadily grown from one saw mill at Porter's Mills to its present large capacity. Its second mill was built in 1880 at Porter's Mills. In 1886 a third mill was purchased at Sterling, Wisconsin, together with a block of timber which was manufactured there, the work being completed in 1892.

In 1890 the company purchased the controlling interest in the Montreal River Lumber Company at Gile, Wisconsin, which is still operated under that name, with Sumner T. McKnight as president. In 1892, in order to increase its output, the North Western Lumber Company bought the Eau Claire Lumber Company's plant at Eau Claire, the purchase including the saw mill, water power, yards, office and other buildings and the timber. In the same year, at Stanley, Wisconsin, on the Wisconsin Central railway, the company erected a double band and gang mill and operated a logging railway in connection with it.

Mr. McKnight has had other business connections. He was one of the organizers, in the early '80's, of both the Shell Lake and Barronett lumber companies. He was president of the Mississippi Valley Lumbermen's Association, served it many years as vice president, and was one of its active members from its organization in 1889. He has been for years and is still connected with several banks as director or vice president.

In June, 1902, Mr. McKnight sold his interest in the North Western Lumber Company and the Montreal River Lumber Company, of each of which he was president, and also withdrew from the Mississippi Valley Lumbermen's Association, declining a reëlection as president. Although he has retired from an active part in the lumber business he is still interested in several lumber companies and largely so in Washington timber. He spent the winter of 1903-4 in Egypt.

His home since 1887 has been in Minneapolis, where he has a beautiful residence on Park avenue. Previous to that, after leaving Hannibal, he resided in Milwaukee, Wisconsin.

Mr. McKnight has played an important part in the history of American lumber, not only because of his prominence as a manufacturer but because of the active interest he has taken in lumber legislation. During the great tariff campaign of 1897 he frequently sacrificed his personal business and comfort to journey to Washington, or Quebec, or anywhere else he was needed, to look after the interests of the lumbermen at the time when they were trying to obtain for lumber the same recognition and consideration as were afforded other American industrial products. It is probable that no lumberman in the United States took a greater personal interest or devoted more earnest effort to this work than did Mr. McKnight. He was an aggressive and able representative of the lumbermen before the Joint High Commission and has in many ways helped to shape the history of the lumber industry in this country.

Mr. McKnight is a man of great force of character but is

unostentatious and simple in his manner. Although conversationalist, he is not a public speaker. His infl doubtless due to his personality and to those qual means of which he is able to carry his plans to a su issue in the face of adverse circumstances. He is ent more fame than his modesty will allow him to seek; c is that the lumber manufacturing industry of the States owes him a debt of gratitude for what he has plished by his untiring efforts in its behalf.

DELOS R. MOON

Delos R. Moon

It has been properly said that truth is stranger than fiction, and biography, in many instances, carries an interest that any supposititious career of a fictitious hero fails utterly to arouse. Among biographies of lumbermen none offers a story of more interest than that of the active and highly successful career of Delos R. Moon.

Delos R. Moon, of Eau Claire, Wisconsin, was born in Chenango county, New York, August 29, 1835. When very young he was left fatherless, but happily in the care of a wise and tender mother. With her he moved to Kendall county, Illinois, in 1843, where they resided for two years, at the end of which time they established themselves in Aurora, Illinois. Mr. Moon's boyhood was uneventful and spent like that of other youths of the time.

At the age of nineteen he made his first serious business engagement, entering the bank of Hall Brothers, of Aurora, as bookkeeper, where he remained until 1857. In that same year he was sent by Hall Brothers to take charge of their bank at Eau Claire, Wisconsin. This bank was closed in 1861 by the state comptroller, its securities in Missouri state bonds depreciating to such an extent that they became practically worthless. During the next six years Mr. Moon engaged in buying and selling timber lands, logs, lumber and general merchandise. By the exercise of intelligence, good judgment and great industry, he accumulated some money so that in 1867 he formed a partnership with Gilbert E. Porter to enter the manufacture of lumber at Porter's Mills, on the Chippewa river, about four miles below Eau Claire. From this point the firm rafted its product down the Mississippi river and conducted the whole venture in such a progressive and profitable manner, that the increase of business warranted a still further widening of its sphere of activity. As an immediate result, in 1869 the firm established a wholesale lumber yard at Hannibal, Missouri, where the distribution of lumber continued until 1882. In that year also it began the distribution of lumber by rail from Eau Claire.

In 1870 Messrs. Porter and Moon consolidated their interests at Hannibal with those of S. T. McKnight and the firm name there became S. T. McKnight & Co., although the manufacturing business at Eau Claire was continued under the title of Porter, Moon & Co. In 1873 the two firms were merged into the North Western Lumber Company, of Eau Claire and Stanley, Wisconsin, with Mr. Porter president, Mr. Moon vice president and Mr. McKnight secretary and treasurer. After the death of Mr. Porter, in 1880, Mr. Moon was elected president and had the general management of the company's affairs until his death.

The enormous increase in the business of the company is strikingly illustrated by the fact that at its inception in 1873 there were in the employ of the concern seventy-eight men, whose compensation amounted to $26,676. In 1897 it had in its employ 1,282 men, with a yearly pay-roll of over $373,000. In 1867 the capacity of the saw mill was, in round numbers, 5,000,000 feet; in 1877 it was 7,000,000 feet; in 1887, 41,000,000 feet, and in 1897 the product was 108,000,000 feet.

In all these large operations Mr. Moon was the controlling spirit. His marked executive ability, supplemented by other unusual business qualities, made the conduct of enterprises of this character, in his particular case, a comparatively easy task. His entire career was marked by an honesty and integrity that brought their just recognition in life and at his death, which occurred on November 5, 1898, made doubly prominent the place left vacant in the ranks of the pioneer lumbermen of the Northwest which had been filled by him so ably and so long.

Mr. Moon was married October 12, 1858, to Miss Sallie Gilman, of Harrison, Ohio, who, with seven children, survived him. The eldest son, Lawrence G. Moon, resides at Spokane, Washington; Frank H. lives at San Jose, California; Angeline is the wife of Joseph G. Dudley, a lawyer, of Buffalo, New York; Sumner G. is vice president and treasurer of the North Western Lumber Company, at Eau Claire, Wisconsin; Chester D. is secretary of the same company; Pauline is the wife of Otto F. Haueisen, a banker of Indianapolis, Indiana, and Delos R. is president of the Linderman Box & Veneer Company, at Eau Claire, Wisconsin.

In character Mr. Moon was a man plain of speech, quick of decision and prompt of action, but above all he was eminently just and was singularly considerate of others. His busy life was warmed and lighted by a genial sense of humor as pleasant to himself as it was to others. Though necessarily immersed in work and often troubled by the worries incident to such a business as he conducted, he never lost his bright and cheerful spirits. Full of courage and a just faith in his own tried ability he dared much before which many lesser men would have fallen back appalled. As a consequence, by the sheer force of his own bravery and determination, he compassed his ends and brought to a successful termination the most daring of business ventures.

One of Mr. Moon's most marked characteristics was his warm affection for his wife. In his numerous business and pleasure trips Mrs. Moon was almost invariably his companion. They each retained for the other, through advancing years, the youthful charm and mutual appreciation which makes beautiful the marriage bond.

Mr. Moon had a strong hold upon the men who were in his employ. He was brought much in contact with them, and by his universal consideration as much as by his other staunch traits of character, he won and retained their respect and confidence. His death was mourned by scores of men who had been in his service for many years. Striking evidence of this fact was shown at his funeral. The active pallbearers were employees who had been associated with Mr.

Moon for periods of twenty years and upward. The e ployees from Stanley, to the number of two hundred, were attendance at the funeral, and nearly an hour and a half consumed in affording these men and women who had kno and loved Mr. Moon for years an opportunity to look up his face for the last time. Touching incidents of the occasi proved how near he had been to the men who had been cc nected with the North Western Lumber Company at the s eral points where it had representatives.

The funeral was one of the largest ever held in E Claire. The attendance included many from distant citi hundreds of employees from the various industries with whi the deceased had been connected and a large concourse sorrowing neighbors and friends. The Rev. Joseph Mor rector of Christ Episcopal Church, Eau Claire, conducted t services. The honorary pallbearers were Frederick Wey haeuser, J. T. Barber, S. T. McKnight, William Irvi Smith Robertson, I. K. Kerr, N. C. Wilcox and Hon. Griffin.

JAMES TILLY BARBER

James T. Barber

Wherever work is to be done, wherever wise counsel is needed, wherever quick wit and instantaneous decision are wanted, there James Tilly Barber, of Eau Claire, Wisconsin, is at home. James T. Barber was born at Ashfield, Franklin county, Massachusetts, January 25, 1847. His father was William Henry Barber, whose occupation was that of mechanic. His father's father came from England to New England about 1790. His mother was a daughter of Stephen Hayward, a member of a Massachusetts family prominent in the early part of the nineteenth century. Stephen Hayward had several brothers, among them James and Tilly, for whom the subject of this sketch was named. His mother's grandfather, named Brown, was one of the minute men in the Lexington affair. Among other trophies of those days in possession of the family, Col. J. T. Barber remembers an old British musket that his Great-grandfather Brown took from an English sergeant whom he killed in that battle.

While Colonel Barber was a lad his parents moved to Greenfield, the county seat of Franklin county, where he attended a common school until he was about fourteen years old. The Civil War broke out at this time and the family moved to Windsor, Vermont, where young Barber's father secured work making muskets for a concern which was under contract to do such work for the government.

In 1863 young Barber went to Springfield, Massachusetts, and secured a job as printer's devil in the job office of the Springfield Republican, then one of the most influential papers in the United States and edited by the elder Samuel Bowles, who was a friend of Greeley, Tilden and many other great men of the time, and who was a leader in the political world as well as in the newspaper world. In this character-forming atmosphere young Barber spent six years as office boy, compositor, proofreader and then manager of the mailing department.

In 1869 J. T. Barber, in partnership with his brothers, became interested in a small hemlock saw mill at Colerain, Massachusetts, in connection with which he gained his first lumber experience. In 1870, a young man of twenty-three years, he accepted an invitation from an uncle named Hayward to come to Hannibal, Missouri. There he connected himself with the wholesale grocery and produce commission house of Hayward & Loomis. In 1873 he entered the employ of the lumber firm of Davis, Bockee & Garth, with which he stayed until it retired from business.

July 1, 1875, Colonel Barber entered into a mercantile relation which proved to be the foundation of all his after business career. On that date he entered the employ of the North Western Lumber Company, at Hannibal, as bookkeeper. From that office he rose steadily through the intervening years to his present important position. Today he is president and general manager of the enlarged operations of that same company, which grew proportionately with the years, until it took rank as one of the leading operating lumber organizations of the country.

In 1883 he was elected assistant treasurer of the company. In 1884 he was made vice president, and in 1902 was promoted to the presidency, which office he still holds. In 1886 the distributing yards and office in Hannibal were closed, and December 1 of the same year Colonel Barber moved to Eau Claire, where he has since resided. In 1890 the members of the North Western Lumber Company bought a controlling interest in the Montreal River Lumber Company at Gile, Wisconsin, and Mr. Barber was made secretary of that company. After the death of D. R. Moon he was elected vice president of the Chippewa Logging Company.

Mr. Barber is also president of the Barber Lumber Company, of Boise, Idaho, a Wisconsin corporation organized to operate in the West and which owns large tracts of pine timber lands in Idaho. This property is being rapidly developed. Large saw mills, a box factory and a planing mill have been erected at Boise and it promises to become one of the largest and most complete lumber manufacturing plants in that region.

Reference has been made to J. T. Barber as "Colonel" Barber. This comes from his connection with the Missouri militia, which he entered as a lieutenant, rising eventually to the rank of colonel.

Mr. Barber has always been a strong Republican and a man of influence in his party, but he has never accepted political preferment except of an honorary sort, beyond doing "day's work" as an alderman for several terms in Hannibal. He was a delegate to the Republican national convention of 1884, at which James G. Blaine was nominated, and in 1900 was a delegate from Wisconsin to the convention at Philadelphia. He was at one time a member of the Republican State Central Committee of Wisconsin.

Mr. Barber has been one of the most prominent supporters of the bureau of uniform grades of the Mississippi Valley Lumbermen's Association and, in fact, brought it to a successful fruition by agitation and example. Another illustration of his talent for organization is seen in the Lumbermen's Lloyds. In 1893 a number of large white pine lumber companies, most of them connected with the Weyerhaeuser interests, banded together for the purpose of mutually insuring one another. No company was formed, but one man was given power of attorney for all, on the Lloyds' plan. There are twenty-two lumber companies in this arrangement, each of which has a policy of $25,000 on its plant issued on this mutual plan. Mr. Barber is treasurer of this aggregation, having now in his charge about $200,000. In addition to his other association affiliations, Colonel Barber has been president of the Northwestern Hemlock Manufacturers' Associa-

tion, which embraces w
the leading hemlock pr
peninsula of Michigan.

LIBRARY
OF THE
UNIVERSITY
OF
CALIFORNIA

One of the surest ways to win success is to make the most
at hand, whether they are many or few.
have attained an enviable position by keep-
constantly in mind, Charles Horton, of
a conspicuous place. Like
many other prominent men of today, Charles Horton, as a
farm work and learned what he could
Yet this hard life seems to have been
as in numerous others, in developing
have, under his severe discipline, re-

Mr. Horton was born March 31, 1836, at Niles, Cayuga county, New York, where he secured his education at the district school during the winter months and worked on his father's farm during the summer. When he was sixteen years of age he started out in the world on his own account, and his connection with the lumber business dates from that time. He went to Athens, Pennsylvania, and secured work in the lumber woods. For four years he was engaged in that vicinity in all branches of the business, from logging in the woods to manufacturing lumber and rafting it down the Susquehanna river to Columbia. The lumber was cross-piled together into cribs; these were made into rafts and steered down the Susquehanna. Columbia was the transfer point where the lumber was taken from the water and put upon canal boats destined for Philadelphia and Baltimore.

In the autumn of 1856, Mr. Horton moved west, attracted by the business outlook in that section, and found employment with Porter & Garlock at Winona, Minnesota. Winona was then in its infancy as a lumber manufacturing center—in fact, the first saw mill had been erected only the year previous

CHARLES HORTON

Charles Horton

One of the surest ways to win success is to make the most of the advantages at hand, whether they are many or few. Among those who have attained an enviable position by keeping this thought constantly in mind, Charles Horton, of Winona, Minnesota, occupies a conspicuous place. Like many other prominent men of today, Charles Horton, as a boy, did his portion of farm work and learned what he could at the district school. Yet this hard life seems to have been efficacious in his case, as in numerous others, in developing faculties that might have, under less severe discipline, remained dormant.

Mr. Horton was born March 31, 1836, at Niles, Cayuga county, New York, where he secured his education at the district school during the winter months and worked on his father's farm during the summer. When he was sixteen years of age he started out in the world on his own account, and his connection with the lumber business dates from that time. He went to Athens, Pennsylvania, and secured work in the lumber woods. For four years he was engaged in that vicinity in all branches of the business, from logging in the woods to manufacturing lumber and rafting it down the Susquehanna river to Columbia. The lumber was cross-piled together into cribs; these were made into rafts and steered down the Susquehanna. Columbia was the transfer point where the lumber was taken from the water and put upon canal boats destined for Philadelphia and Baltimore.

In the autumn of 1856, Mr. Horton moved west, attracted by the business outlook in that section, and found employment with Porter & Garlock at Winona, Minnesota. Winona was then in its infancy as a lumber manufacturing center—in fact, the first saw mill had been erected only the year previous by Highland & Wycoff. This mill had been purchased by Porter & Garlock, with whom young Horton secured employment. The mill was equipped with mulay and circular saws and manufactured from 25,000 to 30,000 feet of lumber a day, or about 4,500,000 feet every season. These figures form a striking contrast to those representing the output of the present plant of the Empire Lumber Company, which is the outgrowth of this first mill at Winona, and in which Mr. Horton is now actively interested. The present company's mill cuts 30,000,000 feet of lumber and 20,000,000 shingles each year.

When not employed in Winona's first mill Mr. Horton went into the woods for the winter. His first season's logging experience in Minnesota was in the camp of William Duckendorf. The following summer he returned to the mill for employment. The winter of 1858-9 found him employed on Hay creek, a tributary of the Menominee, by C. C. Washburn, and he worked during the two subsequent summers for this gentleman in his mill at Waubeck, Wisconsin. The financial panic of 1857, preceding the Civil War, proved disastrous to many northwestern lumbermen and affected all of them more or less.

At the end of the season's work in 1860, Mr. Horton was compelled to take in payment for his labors a raft of ten cribs of lumber and shingles. It is an ill wind that blows nobody good; it is also true that apparent misfortune is often good fortune in disguise, as it proved to be in this instance. Mr. Horton ran his raft down the Chippewa river to Winona and sold it. This was the starting point of his own lumbering operations which afterward became so extensive. He suddenly found himself in possession of considerable ready cash by the sale of his raft, and he immediately determined to associate himself with some one having a similar capital and engage in the manufacturing business. He entered into partnership with L. C. Porter, of Porter & Garlock, his former employers, and Andrew Hamilton. The name of the new concern was Porter, Horton & Hamilton. It purchased the lumber yard of Mr. Garlock, whose mill had been destroyed by fire, and began a general lumber business, including logging and rafting. This continued until 1866, when Mr. Porter retired, and the firm became Horton & Hamilton.

In 1880 Mr. Horton bought out Mr. Hamilton's interest. In the meantime Mr. Horton had associated himself with Ingram, Kennedy & Co., of Eau Claire, Wisconsin, and the C. Horton Lumber Company, of Winona, was organized. A year later it was merged into the Empire Lumber Company. In the fall of 1886 the Empire Lumber Company erected a large mill of 200,000 feet daily capacity. The plant was equipped with two band saws, two gangs and all the other machinery necessary in a complete and modern mill. A logging railroad was constructed extending from Dedham, Wisconsin, thirty miles to the upper waters of the St. Croix river in Douglas county, Wisconsin. The equipment of the plant of the company has kept pace with the progress of the years, and it is today recognized as one of the most complete and up-to-date plants to be found in the white pine territory. Mr. Horton's interests and activities have centered in this company, of which in 1899 he was made president.

Mr. Horton is connected with other large and important enterprises. He is interested in the Interstate Elevator Company and what was formerly the Western Grain Company but is now known as the Western Elevator Company, both of which companies were organized by him. The Western Elevator Company operates two hundred country elevators in southern Minnesota, Iowa and South Dakota on the Illinois Central and the Chicago, Milwaukee & St. Paul railroads. The Standard Lumber Company, in which Mr. Horton is the chief factor, operates a line of retail yards in southern Minnesota. He is vice president and a director of the First National Bank of Winona, president of the Woodlawn Cemetery Association, has been a member of the school board for a number of years and is senior warden of St. Paul's Episcopal Church of Winona.

He was married in 1864 to Miss Alice M. Rogers, hamton, New York, and one son and four daught been born to them.

Although still retaining his interests in the vario prises with which he is connected, Mr. Horton is re much responsibility by his son, Frank Horton, his so Robert E. Tearse, and his nephew, Roscoe Horton. zen of Winona is more honored or more highly e than Charles Horton, a man who occupies his high more by virtue of his superior qualities of character his financial success or social relations.

LIBRARY
OF THE
UNIVERSITY
OF
CALIFORNIA

STIMSON B. GARDINER

Stimson B. Gardiner

What men consider bad luck but serves, if rightly met, to strengthen character and stimulate ambition. In considering the life histories of lumbermen there are numerous examples of those who finally achieved success and wealth despite many early misfortunes—ill health, accident, business failure and disaster of one sort and another. These misfortunes often are, as far as our study of them can determine, entirely beyond the power of those concerned to avoid or mitigate. The most carefully laid plans may come to naught from causes beyond control and outside the sphere of prevision. But it is seldom that a man whose courage remains undaunted and whose ambition continues regnant fails to find some time, early or late, a turn in this lane of apparent defeat. The example of such a man is stimulating. He of whom this article is written had perhaps no exceptional amount of misfortune, but he was forty-seven years old before the turn in his fortunes came. The man of whom we speak is Stimson B. Gardiner, of Clinton, Iowa.

Mr. Gardiner was born at Wayne, Steuben county, New York, August 28, 1819. He was of distinguished American ancestry. His father, Lyon Gardiner, was a member of the sixth generation of his family born in this country. His most remote American ancestor, Lion Gardiner, landed at Boston on November 28, 1635. He had a son David who was the first child born in Connecticut of English parents. This ancestor was by profession a military engineer. He completed Fort Hill, Boston, Massachusetts, and built Fort Saybrooke, at the mouth of the Connecticut river, commanding it throughout the Piquot Indian war. He bought from the Indians an island east of Long Island, now known as Gardiner's Island, which is still owned and occupied by descendants of Lion Gardiner.

Down through all the history of this country, in colonial days and under the Republic, the Gardiner family has furnished men of character, ability and prominence in affairs. Stimson B. Gardiner has upheld the traditions of the family, but his work has not been the making of history of colonization or of politics, but of the lumber industry. As a boy Mr. Gardiner felt the press of poverty, though of him, as of others, it perhaps might be said that he was "blessed with poverty." He worked as a farm hand among the farms of Steuben county, New York, and attended the country schools when opportunity offered until fifteen years of age. His first introduction to the lumber business in any form was when he engaged his services to Richard L. Chapman, who did an extensive business near Penn Yan, New York. Here he met Chancy Lamb, with whom was begun a friendship which lasted almost continuously until the death of Mr. Lamb. Mr. Gardiner's interests in the West for a number of years were identified with those of Mr. Lamb, who was successively Mr. Gardiner's employer and partner as well as friend.

Mr. Gardiner was married to Miss Nancy Bonney on May 2, 1844. Three children were born to them—Silas W., in 1846; Sarah Elizabeth, in 1848, and George S., in 1854. In the same year as their marriage the newly wedded couple, with Mr. and Mrs. Lamb and their child, went west and settled near Mount Carroll, Illinois. In 1847, however, Mr. Gardiner returned to Penn Yan to take charge of the Chapman mill. In 1851 he erected a large gang saw mill at Tioga, Pennsylvania, for Mr. Chapman, who failed, bringing down in the crash those associated with him.

In 1854 Mr. Gardiner formed a partnership with B. W. Franklin for the manufacture of lumber and land plaster at Penn Yan. For ten years his business and personal history was uneventful, but in 1864-5 the oil excitement of that period attracted Mr. Gardiner, who invested his savings in oil and lost them all in the general decline of speculative values. Facing the necessity of making a fresh start in life, Mr.

Gardiner decided to make the attempt in the West and in 1866 went to Chicago. The following year, 1867, he moved to Clinton, Iowa, and with his sons entered the employ of C. Lamb & Sons.

This proved the turning point in his fortunes. In 1869 he bought a small interest in one of their mills, known as the Lamb-Byng Company. The Wheeler & Warner mill was soon purchased and added to the business. In 1877 Mr. Gardiner sold his interest to C. Lamb & Sons. In 1877, following the sale of his interest to C. Lamb & Sons, he and his sons purchased L. B. Wadleigh's interest in the saw mill of Wadleigh, Welles & Co., at Lyons. This business was operated successfully and in 1891 it was incorporated as Gardiner, Batchelder & Welles, with Stimson B. Gardiner as president and Silas W. Gardiner as secretary and treasurer.* The corporation operated two mills until 1894 with an annual production of 40,000,000 feet.

In the latter years of his life Mr. Gardiner's principal interest was in the business of Eastman, Gardiner & Co., of Laurel, Mississippi. He took an active part in locating this enterprise. After one of his sons and his son-in-law, Lawrence C. Eastman, had made a tour of inspection, investigating the opportunities offered in the state of Mississippi, Stimson B. Gardiner, with George S. Gardiner, looked over the properties along the Illinois Central and the New Orleans & Northeastern railways. While investigating the situation along the latter road they met John Kamper, who told them that he had for sale some valuable timber land at or near Laurel and invited them to look it over. Mr. Gardiner was immediately impressed with the value of the property and also with the favorable opportunity presented to acquire a large quantity of yellow pine timber in addition to that owned by Mr. Kamper. He advised the purchase of a tract of timber large enough to sustain a yellow pine manufacturing business of sufficient magnitude to unite the interests and employ the capital of the several members of the family, and large enough to maintain such a business for at least a generation.

The history of the business of Eastman, Gardiner & Co. shows that this advice was accepted and the results growing out of it proved that it was the advice of a man who could see well into the future growth and development of the country, for the business of Eastman, Gardiner & Co. has been no ephemeral affair. It was not organized to buy a tract of timber that would be cut out in five or ten years, but rather was to make such an investment and so to operate that the business could be conducted practically in perpetuity.

In May, 1899, Mr. Gardiner lost the helpmate of a long life. In the death of Mrs. Gardiner the family and all who knew her were saddened, and doubtless this loss hastened the death of Stimson B. Gardiner, who passed away November 12, 1903, at the ripe age of eighty-four years.

It is a favorite theory of some that it is the young who plan and dare and do while the old counsel and conserve, but it is worth noting that Mr. Gardiner had passed what many consider the prime of life before he began that part of his career which led to success and wealth. Before that time his reverses had been severe and his progress apparently slow, yet when the end of his life came he had overcome all obstacles, had provided for his family and left his children not only a heritage of wealth, but a name and reputation of which they are justly proud.

UNIVERSITY
OF
CALIFORNIA

and attended schools in the

In 1847 his connection
when he started to work
Pharaoh, New York, receiving
winter and $13 a month
summer. Soon he had
quently he accepted a
tendent for Fox & Anglin,
building a mill on the
did not agree with him
where he superintended
Two years later his former
had watched his work closely,
breaking mill for them at

The young man had now
man and Gilmour & Co., of
operators in the world,
year with free house rent ... accepted
this offer, remodeled several ... complete
charge of their manufacturing ... superintending the
work from the felling of the ... of the finished lumber.

During this period Mr. ... gang edger,

ORRIN H. INGRAM

Orrin H. Ingram

One of the pioneers of the northwestern white pine industry is Orrin H. Ingram, of Eau Claire, Wisconsin, his operations in the Chippewa valley extending back to 1857. He was born May 12, 1830, at Southwick, Massachusetts. His parents, David A. and Fannie Ingram, moved to Saratoga, New York, when he was a child. The father died in 1841, leaving the boy of eleven years to depend upon his own resources. He worked on farms for his board and clothing and attended schools in the winter.

In 1847 his connection with the lumber industry began when he started to work for Harris & Bronson, near Lake Pharaoh, New York, receiving $12 a month in the woods in winter and $13 a month when employed in the mill in the summer. Soon he had entire charge of this mill. Subsequently he accepted a position as logging and mill superintendent for Fox & Anglin, Kingston, Canada, who were building a mill on the Rideau canal. The climate, however, did not agree with him and he moved to Belleville, Ontario, where he superintended the building of several gang mills. Two years later his former employers, Harris & Bronson, who had watched his work closely, engaged him to build a record-breaking mill for them at Ottawa.

The young man had now attained a reputation as a saw mill man and Gilmour & Co., of Ottawa, then the largest lumber operators in the world, tendered him a position at $4,000 a year with free house rent and other perquisites. He accepted this offer, remodeled several of their mills and took complete charge of their manufacturing operations, superintending the work from the felling of the tree to the production of the finished lumber.

During this period Mr. Ingram invented the gang edger,

now an indispensable part of every mill, and made it a gift to the lumber industry, which incident alone certainly entitles him to a place in lumber history far beyond that which he could attain by his own business operations. There is an unwritten law in the medical profession that all discoveries in the science are for the good of all—not one. In business, however, each man reaps the profits of his own knowledge, unless, like Mr. Ingram, he thinks more of improving methods and benefiting the trade than he does of harvesting great results for himself alone. That all are not so unselfish in these matters is illustrated by the fact that another man tried to patent Mr. Ingram's invention; but he defended his gift by proving that it was the result of his own inventive skill, and the gang edger remained free to the lumbering world.

When his agreement with Gilmour & Co. had expired they offered him $6,000 a year to renew it; but, having saved some money, he desired to go into business for himself. He went west in 1857 and located at Eau Claire, Wisconsin, one hundred and fifty miles from a railroad. A. M. Dole and Donald Kennedy went west with him and together they formed the lumber firm of Dole, Ingram & Kennedy. They purchased a portable mill at Eau Claire and sawed the timber for their new mill and for that of the Daniel Shaw Lumber Company. The firm had the first gang saw mill of modern type in the West. It rafted lumber down the Chippewa and Mississippi rivers and established yards at Wabasha, Minnesota, and Dubuque, Iowa. At Dubuque a mill was erected. In October, 1860, the Eau Claire mill burned. It was uninsured, but a new one was soon erected in its place.

As a step toward the storing and handling of logs, the Daniel Shaw Company, Mr. Ingram's firm and a company operating at Chippewa Falls built a dam and boom at Eagle Rapids, which was a preliminary to the construction of the dam at Eau Claire that made lumbering at that point really safe and profitable.

Mr. Dole retired from the firm in 1862 and two years later,

when an interest in the business was given to two of the employees, it became Ingram, Kennedy & Co. In 1865 the firm built the steamer Silas Wright and did the greater part of the freight business between Reed's Landing and Eau Claire.

In 1880 Mr. Ingram organized the Charles Horton Lumber Company, of Winona, Minnesota. In 1881 Mr. Kennedy sold his interests to Messrs. Dulaney and McVeigh, who, with Mr. Ingram, organized the Empire Lumber Company, capitalized at $800,000. This company absorbed Ingram & Kennedy in Dubuque, Iowa, but the business was kept separate and incorporated as the Standard Lumber Company. Mr. Ingram took stock in the Chippewa Logging Company when it was organized and has been one of its directors since its inception. He has been vice president of the Chippewa Lumber & Boom Company, of Chippewa Falls, one of the largest handlers of white pine in the Northwest, since its organization. He has been president of the Rice Lake Lumber Company, capitalized at $600,000, since he organized it in 1883. He is president of the Empire Lumber Company, of Eau Claire, Wisconsin; the principal stockholder in the new Empire Lumber Company of Minnesota, and vice president of the Standard Lumber Company, of Dubuque, Iowa. He is a heavy investor in Pacific Coast timber, being a stockholder in the Weyerhaeuser Timber Company, and also interested with Major W. H. Day, of Dubuque, Iowa. Mr. Ingram is president of the Eau Claire National Bank and of the Eau Claire Water Works Company, a director and treasurer of the Canadian Anthracite Coal Company and an officer in many other large enterprises. He has a small interest in mines in Arizona and Nevada.

His large business ventures have not kept Mr. Ingram from enjoying life as he went along. He has a beautiful country home near Eau Claire, a cottage on Long lake and also one six miles above the head of Long lake, on Lake Sissabagama, at all of which he is a frequent and ideal host. He is a member of the Congregational Church and of its American Board of Commissioners for Foreign Missions. He was a warm admirer of Dwight L. Moody, the famous evangelist, and he and Mrs. Ingram regularly contribute to the support of students at the Moody Bible Institute in Chicago. He is also a trustee of Ripon College, at Ripon, Wisconsin, and an active and valued supporter of the Young Men's Christian Association. Among his many public benefactions are a free public library at Eau Claire and the Ingram Science Hall at Ripon College.

Mr. Ingram married in 1851 Miss Cornelia E. Pierce, of Lake George, New York. They have three living children—Charles H., Erskine B. and Marion P. Hayes, wife of Doctor Hayes, a prominent physician of Eau Claire.

Like all other successful men, Mr. Ingram thinks more of his work than the monetary advantages it brings him. His ambition is not to pile up the little silver disks we call dollars so high that he can see nothing beyond them, but to know the truth and bring it within the reach of those about him.

thrift and determination [illegible] its prosperity. In the long list of men who have won success and reputation [illegible] be found who has made for himself a [illegible] regard of its people than has Charles A[illegible] apolis, one of the leading lumbermen of [illegible]

Mr. Smith was born in Sweden, December 11, 1852. When [illegible] with his father and sister he left the [illegible] United States.

During 1868 and 1869 he attended the [illegible] and in 1872 and 1873, the state univers[illegible] the university he lived with Governor [illegible] ing for him all his spare time during [illegible] ployed in the governor's hardware [illegible] Illness made it impossible for him [illegible] and he reluctantly abandoned his amb[illegible] ity education and entered the gov[illegible] where he worked until 1878.

In that year he went to Herman[illegible] town on the Great Northern railway [illegible] Pillsbury he built an elevator and [illegible] and a lumber yard. Here he did [illegible] C. A. Smith & Co., he and Mr. Pill[illegible] ners. During this time he found [illegible] business, and, taking as a partner [illegible] retail yards at Evansville, Bran[illegible]

CHARLES ALTON SMITH

Charles A. Smith

The state of Minnesota has undoubtedly been the scene of greater business achievement by men of Swedish birth than has any other state in the Union. For some reason that locality has appealed particularly to the Swedish immigrant, and to his sturdiness, thrift and determination the state owes much of its prosperity. In the long list of men of Swedish nativity who have won success and reputation in Minnesota, none can be found who has made for himself a higher position in the regard of its people than has Charles Alton Smith, of Minneapolis, one of the leading lumbermen of the Northwest.

Mr. Smith was born in the province of Ostergötland, Sweden, December 11, 1852. When fourteen years of age, with his father and sister he left the land of his birth for the United States.

During 1868 and 1869 he attended the Minneapolis schools and in 1872 and 1873, the state university. While a student at the university he lived with Governor John S. Pillsbury, working for him all his spare time during winter and being employed in the governor's hardware store during vacations. Illness made it impossible for him to continue in this way, and he reluctantly abandoned his ambition to secure a university education and entered the governor's hardware store, where he worked until 1878.

In that year he went to Herman, Minnesota, then a new town on the Great Northern railway. With the help of Mr. Pillsbury he built an elevator and opened an implement store and a lumber yard. Here he did business for six years as C. A. Smith & Co., he and Mr. Pillsbury being equal partners. During this time he found opportunity to extend his business, and, taking as a partner C. J. Johnson, he opened retail yards at Evansville, Brandon and Ashby, Minnesota.

During these six years Mr. Smith was remarkably successful, having cleared in his Herman business for his firm $50,000, and in his other ventures $40,000, a half of each being his individual profits.

Being then thirty-one years of age, reasonably successful and ambitious, he was ready for an offer that came from Mr. Pillsbury in 1884. The governor had loaned some loggers about $30,000 and, as they had logs but were without the money with which to pay their debt, he suggested that Mr. Smith help him buy the logs and manufacture them into lumber. This Mr. Smith agreed to do, and at that time the lumber manufacturing concern of C. A. Smith & Co. was formed. In this purchase C. J. Johnson had an interest and he and Mr. Smith and Mr. Pillsbury made up the partnership in the manufacturing enterprise. This first purchase of logs was sawed at custom mills in Minneapolis, as were all the firm's logs up to 1887, when was bought the mill of the John Martin Lumber Company, one of a group of five mills utilizing the water power at Minneapolis.

On a Saturday night, sixty days after the purchase of the mill, fire started in the mill settlement and entirely wiped out the five plants. In 1890 C. A. Smith & Co. bought the Clough brothers' interest in the mill of Clough Bros. & Kilgore and ran this mill during 1890 and 1891 and then sold it to Nelson, Tenney & Co., who sawed for C. A. Smith & Co. in 1892. During the time from 1884 to 1892 the firm had increased its cut to about 25,000,000 feet annually.

In 1893 the business was incorporated as the C. A. Smith Lumber Company and began its career by building the largest, most expensive and most complete mill up to that time erected in Minneapolis. This is the mill that broke all Minneapolis records by sawing in eleven hours, with three band saws and a gang, 599,627 feet of lumber, turning out also 71,500 lath and 130,000 shingles.

It is thought by many who are competent to judge that this mill saws lumber at less cost than any other mill in Minneapolis. No trouble or expense has been spared to save labor and avoid waste. In the lumber yards are thirty-five miles of steel tramways, over which five horses do the work of one hundred and twenty wagons. No load of lumber is ever dumped. The waste fuel from the mill is sold to the city pumping station near by, thus saving to the city $40 a day on its fuel bill the year around. The waste edgings are utilized by the Northwestern Compo-Board Company, an institution that belongs to the C. A. Smith Lumber Company and whose factory forms a part of the company's mill settlement north of the city. The saw mill has been increasing its cut steadily since 1893, the cut of 1898 being 87,000,000 feet of lumber, 36,000,000 shingles and 9,000,000 lath. In 1899 the cut was 108,000,000 feet and in 1901 it reached 112,000,000 feet. Mr. Smith is now the chief owner of the company's property. Associated with him in the ownership and management of the business are C. J. Johnson, vice president; Edgar Dalzell, secretary; and Enoch Oren, treasurer. The handling of the timber and logging interests of the concern is looked after by the C. A. Smith Timber Company, of which Mr. Smith is president and C. L. Trabert secretary. In addition to the splendid mill properties of the company, it owns standing timber sufficient to stock the mill for six or seven years to come.

In addition to his interests in Minnesota Mr. Smith is one of the largest individual holders of Pacific Coast timber, if not the largest.

As a lumberman he has always been particularly prominent in the higher councils of the trade. He is vice president of the National Lumber Manufacturers' Association and treasurer of the Mississippi Valley Lumbermen's Association. During the tariff campaign of 1897 he was a leader in directing thought and effort. In 1896 he was the presidential elector chosen to carry to Washington the vote of the state for McKinley and Hobart, which fact indicates his political affiliations, and in 1900 he served as a delegate to the convention which nominated McKinley and Roosevelt.

Mr. Smith has been signally honored by the king of Sweden in recognition of his service to the subjects of that country both in America and in the fatherland, by being created a Commander of the First Degree, Order of Vasa. Mr. Smith is well known to all Scandinavians in the middle West for his generosity to numerous churches and schools, and for the prominent part he took in raising funds for the relief of the famine sufferers in Finland, giving liberally to that cause himself.

Mr. Smith's domestic relations are happy. In his home are five children—three daughters, the eldest of whom is twenty-five years of age, and two sons, the youngest being eleven years old. He still keeps before him on his office desk a reminder of his eldest son, who died when a young man of seventeen years, with whom he had planned some day to share the responsibility of his large and rapidly increasing business.

LIBRARY
OF THE
UNIVERSITY
OF
CALIFORNIA

Thomas H. Shevlin

A lumberman can have no better credentials than the fact that he received his business education in the pine districts of Michigan. The great lumber producing section around Minneapolis owes much to the Michigan men who, looking for newer and larger fields, went to Minneapolis in the early '80's to develop the timber resources of the upper Mississippi river country. Among the [illegible] Thomas Henry Shevlin.

He was born January [illegible] mother's maiden name was M[illegible] parents were of Irish descent [illegible] of Albany until he was [illegible] entered the employ of John [illegible] of that city. He began there [illegible] authority today on the manu[illegible] also on all questions appertaining [illegible] remained ten years in the emp[illegible] of important interests at Alban[illegible]

In 1879 he severed his busi[illegible] firm and went to Chicago. [illegible] Harvey to look after his [illegible] A year later Mr. Shevlin became [illegible] Hall, of Muskegon, and be[illegible] of logs, timber and timbe[illegible] treasurer and general manage[illegible] ber Company, of Muskego[illegible] that Mr. Shevlin began making [illegible] company in the white pine woods of Minnesota [illegible] he organized a branch company in Minneapolis [illegible] manufacture of lumber. This was known as the North Star Lumber Company.

THOMAS HENRY SHEVLIN

Thomas H. Shevlin

A lumberman can have no better credentials than the fact that he received his business education in the pine districts of Michigan. The great lumber producing section around Minneapolis owes much to the Michigan men who, looking for newer and larger fields, went to Minneapolis in the early '80's to develop the timber resources of the upper Mississippi river country. Among the most prominent of these is Thomas Henry Shevlin.

He was born January 3, 1852, at Albany, New York. His mother's maiden name was Matilda Leonard. Both of his parents were of Irish descent. Thomas attended the public schools of Albany until he was fifteen years old, and then he entered the employ of John McGraw & Co., a lumber firm of that city. He began there the education that makes him an authority today on the manufacture and sale of lumber and also on all questions appertaining to the lumber industry. He remained ten years in the employ of this firm, taking charge of important interests at Albany, Tonawanda and Bay City.

In 1879 he severed his business relations with the McGraw firm and went to Chicago. There he was employed by T. W. Harvey to look after his interests at Muskegon, Michigan. A year later Mr. Shevlin became associated with Stephen C. Hall, of Muskegon, and began, as a side issue, the purchase of logs, timber and timber lands. In 1882 he was appointed treasurer and general manager of the Stephen C. Hall Lumber Company, of Muskegon. It was at this time that Mr. Shevlin began making timber investments for his company in the white pine woods of Minnesota. In 1884 he organized a branch company in Minneapolis for the manufacture of lumber. This was known as the North Star Lumber Company.

Mr. Shevlin went to Minneapolis to reside in 1886, and assisted in organizing the Hall & Ducey Lumber Company, composed of Mr. Shevlin, P. A. Ducey and S. C. Hall. In 1887 Mr. Ducey sold his interests and the concern became the Hall & Shevlin Lumber Company. This company built the Minneapolis mill now owned by the Shevlin-Carpenter Company. Mr. Hall died in 1889. In 1892 Elbert L. Carpenter, a member of the lumber firm of Carpenter Brothers, bought an interest in the business, forming, with the varied lumber interests with which Mr. Shevlin was identified, the Shevlin-Carpenter Company, with Mr. Shevlin as its president. This company still continues to transact a thriving and steadily growing business.

Mr. Shevlin has not confined his energies to this one company, however. In 1895 he formed a partnership with J. Neils, of Sauk Rapids, Minnesota, this firm being known as the J. Neils Lumber Company, its Sauk Rapids mill sawing 15,000,000 feet of lumber annually. In 1900 the J. Neils Lumber Company built a band and band resaw mill at Cass Lake, Minnesota, which has since been enlarged by the addition of a gang saw, increasing the annual output of the plant to 50,000,000 feet a year.

Impressed with the advantage of manufacturing near the stump as well as near the consuming territory, Mr. Shevlin, in company with Frank P. Hixon, of La Crosse, Wisconsin, in 1896 bought a large amount of timber on the Red Lake Indian Reservation, tributary to Clearwater river, and organized the St. Hilaire Lumber Company, which built a saw mill with a capacity of 40,000,000 feet a year. A year later the members of the St. Hilaire Lumber Company bought the saw mill and logs of the Red River Lumber Company at Crookston, Minnesota, and all its tributary timber holdings, and organized the Crookston Lumber Company, with Mr. Shevlin as its president. Hovey C. Clarke is a member and the treasurer of this company. The Crookston plant has a capacity of 40,000,000 feet a year. In the winter of 1902-3 the Crookston Lumber Company and the St. Hilaire Lumber Company, having previously been consolidated under the name of the Crookston Lumber Company with Mr. Shevlin as president, built a large mill at Bemidji, containing two bands and a gang, with an annual capacity of 70,000,000 feet. To supply this mill with logs a logging spur twelve miles in length was built, penetrating the timber to the east of Red lake and connecting with the Minnesota & International railway at Hovey Junction, thus giving direct transportation by rail from the timber to the mill and making available a large body of timber which had hitherto been difficult of access. In January, 1904, the general offices of the Crookston Lumber Company were removed from Crookston to Bemidji. The Crookston Lumber Company owns tributary to its various plants approximately 400,000,000 feet of stumpage, which insures its operation for many years.

In connection with these manufacturing plants a number of retail yards are now operated under the name of the St. Hilaire Retail Lumber Company, and additional yards are established from time to time, completing the chain of lumber handling, from the tree to the consumer.

An investigation of the timber and lumber business in the South led to the purchase by the Crookston Lumber Company of a large interest in the Winn Parish Lumber Company, which owns approximately 1,000,000,000 feet of virgin pine in Louisiana and is engaged in the manufacture of this timber at Pyburn, that state. A similar examination of the Pacific Coast territory led to the purchase by Mr. Shevlin personally of large holdings in British Columbia.

In the fall of 1903 Mr. Shevlin and his associates organized the Shevlin-Clarke Company, Limited, in Ontario, and purchased a number of timber berths from the Canadian government, aggregating 225,000,000 feet of pine stumpage. In the same year the Rainy River Lumber Company, Limited, was organized by Mr. Shevlin, with E. L. Carpenter, of the Shevlin-Carpenter Company, and E. W. Backus and W. F. Brooks, of the Backus-Brooks Company, as principal stockholders. This company purchased a large amount of timber from the Canadian government and in the winter of 1903-4 erected at Rainy River, Ontario, one of the most complete saw mill plants in the world, with a capacity of 70,000,000 feet a year. This mill began sawing lumber in the spring of 1904 and carries in its yards a large stock of lumber which the company is marketing in Winnipeg and elsewhere in Manitoba and in the territories to the west. The various lumber companies in which Mr. Shevlin is interested as chief or half owner now have an annual output exceeding 300,000,000 feet.

Mr. Shevlin is an active Republican and was the Minnesota member of the Republican National Committee for the four years preceding 1904, and during the campaign of 1900 rendered most valuable assistance to his party. He is a member of the Union League clubs of New York and Chicago, the Minneapolis Club, the Minnesota Club, the Manitoba Club and various minor clubs throughout the country. He is a heavy stockholder and a director in the Security Bank of Minnesota and is president of the Iron Range Electric Telephone Company, besides being interested in many other important business enterprises. Mr. Shevlin was married February 8, 1882, to Alice A. Hall. They have three children —Thomas Leonard, Florence and Helen.

UNIVERSITY
OF
CALIFORNIA

The qualities that go to make up a str[illegible] character were possessed by the successful lumber pioneers of the middle West. What a man does is the real test of what he is. Jerman S. Keator, one of the best known among the pioneer lumbermen of the upper Mississippi valley, possessed these qualities in a marked degree

He was born at Hancock, Delaware county, New York, November 1, 1822, of Dutch ancestry. He secured a rudimentary education in the common schools. At the age of twelve years he became clerk in a store, [illegible] getting this business training during the near [illegible] schooling. When he was [illegible] steady employment at Honesdale, Wayne county, Pennsylvania, with Bassett & Hornbeck, who conducted a combined lumbering and mercantile busi[illegible] $150 a year and remained with [illegible] majority, by which time he had saved from his [illegible] earnings $300. He was then offered an interest in the business and the firm of Hornbeck & [illegible] tinued successfully for twelve yea[illegible]

In 1855 Mr. Keator visited Chicago, from thence proceeded into the Northwest as far as St. Cloud, Minnesota, and from there down the Mississippi river to Moline, Illinois, where he found for sale the saw mill of [illegible] Ruggles & Hartzell. In 1856 in connection with [illegible] Skinner, he purchased this property. The year following occurred one of the memorable financial panics of the country. The price of lumber dropped from $20 to $6 a thousand and demand was reduced almost to the zero mark. The firm of Keator & Skinner, however, struggled bravely against all discouragements and the manufacture of lumber was carried on without

JERMAN S. KEATOR

Jerman S. Keator

The qualities that go to make up strong character were possessed by the successful lumber pioneers of the middle West. What a man does is the real test of what he is. Jerman S. Keator, one of the best known among the pioneer lumbermen of the upper Mississippi valley, possessed these qualities in a marked degree.

He was born at Hancock, Delaware county, New York, November 1, 1822, of Dutch ancestry. He secured a rudimentary education in the common schools. At the age of twelve years he became clerk in a store, interspersing this business training during the next two years with some additional schooling. When he was fourteen years old he secured steady employment at Honesdale, Wayne county, Pennsylvania, with Bassett & Hornbeck, who conducted a combined lumbering and mercantile business. He started at a salary of $150 a year and remained with this firm until he reached his majority, by which time he had saved from his meager earnings $300. He was then offered an interest in the business and the firm of Hornbeck & Keator was organized and continued successfully for twelve years.

In 1855 Mr. Keator visited Chicago, from thence proceeded into the Northwest as far as St. Cloud, Minnesota, and from there down the Mississippi river to Moline, Illinois, where he found for sale the saw mill of Stevens, Ruggles & Hartzell. In 1856 in connection with Porter Skinner, he purchased this property. The year following occurred one of the memorable financial panics of the century. The price of lumber dropped from $20 to $6 a thousand and demand was reduced almost to the zero mark. The firm of Keator & Skinner, however, struggled bravely against all discouragements and the manufacture of lumber was carried on without interruption. Eventually, in 1861, Mr. Keator bought out his discouraged partner and from that time business conditions began to improve.

The faith of Jerman S. Keator in the value of timber land investments was well illustrated during the panic of 1857 and 1858. A firm at Elgin, Illinois, had entered about 8,000 acres of pine land containing some of the choicest timber along the Black river in Wisconsin, but because of the stringency of the money market some members of this concern were forced to sell and Mr. Keator purchased a one-third interest for $8,000. Later he purchased another third for about the same amount. He also bought government timber lands at $1.25 an acre and from private parties purchased additional blocks, sometimes paying as high as $5 an acre. His purchases were so large for that period that they caused general comment, and he was called an "Illinois fool," not only because he bought large quantities but because much of the land that he had purchased was from three to five miles back from waterways. He also began buying along the Chippewa, adjacent to the river, and at one time his holdings amounted to more than 30,000 acres.

The firm of Keator & Skinner operated a sash, door and blind factory as well as a planing mill at Moline; the factory was destroyed by fire in June, 1861, with a loss of $25,000. In 1869 Mr. Keator built a saw mill at Rock Island, Illinois, under the firm name of Keator & Co., in which his son, Samuel J. Keator, was a partner. This was combined later with the firm of Annawalt & Denkmann, and then was formed the Rock Island Lumber & Manufacturing Company, of which Jerman S. Keator was a director and his son, Samuel J. Keator, the secretary and treasurer.

In 1870 Mr. Keator encountered a second misfortune in the destruction by fire of his plant at Moline. This was at once replaced by a large mill having a capacity of 150,000 feet in eleven hours. This mill was operated with great success until August 18, 1883, when it was destroyed by fire, entailing a loss of $350,000 with but $90,000 insurance. In 1872 the Moline firm was changed to J. S. Keator & Son, the second son, Ben C. Keator, being admitted to partnership. This firm continued until 1880, when the business was incorporated as the J. S. Keator Lumber Company with a capital stock of $200,000, and in this company were associated Samuel J. Keator, the eldest son; Ben C. Keator, the second son, and Edward B. Keator, the youngest son. This business continued uninterruptedly until 1893, when it was closed out. With the destruction of the saw mill in 1883 Mr. Keator lost the greater part of his fortune and was compelled to sell considerable standing timber in order to rebuild the mill, which, however, he did not operate.

During the period of his operations on the Black, Chippewa and St. Croix rivers Mr. Keator was known as one of the heaviest loggers in that district, his brand, "Diamond K," being one of the best known log marks in the northern Mississippi country. So familiar was it to the lumbermen of that region that Mr. Keator himself was popularly known among many of his acquaintances as "Diamond K." With such extensive interests in logging as those which he controlled, it was a natural sequence that he should have joined with others in the great corporation organized by down-river lumbermen for the purpose of rafting logs from the headquarters of the Mississippi river. The Mississippi River Logging Company was organized January 12, 1871, and of this great enterprise he was a director.

Mr. Keator took an active part in the organization of the First National Bank of Moline and was its first president. He also assisted in organizing the first street railway company in Moline and was its president for three years. He was one of the incorporators and the president of the Mississippi Valley Insurance Company. He erected several business buildings in Moline and was active in numerous other enterprises that contributed to the commercial growth of the city. For eight years he served as a member of the common council and for twenty years as a member of the school board.

Mr. Keator married July, 1847, Miss Mary Baldwin, of Durham, New York. Four sons were born to them—Samuel J., of Castlewood, South Dakota; Ben C., of Fair & Keator, wholesale lumber dealers of Pittsburg, Pennsylvania; Frederick W., bishop of the Protestant Episcopal Church at Olympia, Washington, and Edward B., of Moline, Illinois. Mr. Keator's first wife died in 1857 and three years later he married Miss Sarah Yelverton, of Fayetteville, New York, and to them were born a son and a daughter, the latter dying in 1890.

As a young man Mr. Keator ardently espoused the cause of John C. Fremont upon the organization of the Republican party and aided materially in the formation of that great political body. He was a consistent advocate of its principles and continuously voted its ticket from its inception.

For many seasons before his death, it was Mr. Keator's custom to go every summer to a large ranch in South Dakota. This ranch comprised over 6,000 acres and was managed by two of his sons, Samuel J. and Edward B. He died at Castlewood, South Dakota, in October, 1904, at the ripe age of eighty-two.

In America so many men have accumulated wealth on a basis of no other capital than character, that a recital of their histories would seem like repetition, yet certain of these are more vital than others. In some cases these fortune builders resent the bite of early adverse circumstances. Others of sterner mould rejoice in it. Of the latter is Peter Musser, of Muscatine, Iowa. He considers the condition so in the lives of so many men as an advantage above price. "I am thankful I was born poor," he asserts. And indeed he may well be, for among the other things taught by the hard master, "straightened circumstances," were habits of industry, rigid economy and persistent, studious effort, all of which combined to lay the foundation of a life now rich in experience as well as in the goods of this world.

Mr. Musser is a native of Lancaster county, Pennsylvania, and was born at Adamstown, February 22, 1826. His parents were Peter and Elizabeth Adams Musser. Both were natives of Pennsylvania. The father, who was born in Berks county, was of Swiss descent, while the mother, who was born in Lancaster county, came of Scotch and English people. Young Musser was reared in his native state and on attaining manhood engaged in the tanning and leather business in Schuylkill county in company with his brother Richard. He continued in this line of business for six years. In 1851 he was married to Miss Tamson Rhodes at Pine Grove, Schuylkill county. His wife died June 21, 1896, leaving the following children: Mrs. C. H. Huttig, of St. Louis, Missouri; R. D. Musser, now of Little Falls, Minnesota, and Mrs. E. L. McColm, of Muscatine, Iowa.

In October, 1854, Mr. Musser went west and located at Iowa City, Iowa. The following year, in company with his

PETER MUSSER

Peter Musser

In America so many men have accumulated wealth on a basis of no other capital than character, that a recital of their histories would seem like repetition, yet certain of these are more vital than others. In some cases these fortune builders resent the bite of early adverse circumstances. Others of sterner mould rejoice in it. Of the latter is Peter Musser, of Muscatine, Iowa. He considers this condition in the lives of so many men as an advantage above price. "I am thankful I was born poor," he asserts. And indeed he may well be, for among the other things taught by the hard master, "straightened circumstances," were habits of industry, rigid economy and persistent, studious effort, all of which combined to lay the foundation of a life now rich in experience as well as in the goods of this world.

Mr. Musser is a native of Lancaster county, Pennsylvania, and was born at Adamstown, February 22, 1826. His parents were Peter and Elizabeth Adams Musser. Both were natives of Pennsylvania. The father, who was born in Berks county, was of Swiss descent, while the mother, who was born in Lancaster county, came of Scotch and English people. Young Musser was reared in his native state and on attaining manhood engaged in the tanning and leather business in Schuylkill county in company with his brother Richard. He continued in this line of business for six years. In 1851 he was married to Miss Tamson Rhodes at Pine Grove, Schuylkill county. His wife died June 21, 1896, leaving the following children: Mrs. C. H. Huttig, of St. Louis, Missouri; R. D. Musser, now of Little Falls, Minnesota, and Mrs. E. L. McColm, of Muscatine, Iowa.

In October, 1854, Mr. Musser went west and located at Iowa City, Iowa. The following year, in company with his brother Richard, and Edward Hoch, he opened a lumber yard at Muscatine under the firm name of Hoch & Musser. One year later the firm established a branch yard at Iowa City, of which Peter Musser had the management until 1864. In that year, complying with his physician's directions, he went to California in search of health, crossing the plains with teams and meeting the hardships and dangers incident to the time when hostile Indians were lords of the western prairies and of the mountains beyond them. Notwithstanding attacks by the red men, Mr. Musser reached his destination safely, and in October, 1869, he returned to Iowa by way of the Isthmus of Panama.

In 1870 he joined his brother, his nephew, P. M. Musser, and C. R. Fox in the organization of the Musser Lumber Company, at Muscatine, Iowa. They began sawing lumber in 1871 and from that time on the mill was in constant operation up to the close of 1904. In December of that year the company discontinued cutting at that point, owing to the natural and inevitable result of mill operations long continued at any given location—namely, the utter exhaustion of the virgin forests which had so long supplied the necessary timber.

During the first ten years of the company's existence it averaged a product of 13,000,000 feet a year, but after increasing the capacity it cut as high as 45,000,000 feet in a single season, and during the thirty-four years of the Musser company's operations it has sawed and marketed over 1,000,000,000 feet of lumber, and paid out over $2,500,000 in wages.

In February, 1872, Mr. Musser became a member of the Mississippi River Logging Company, organized the year previous by Mississippi river lumbermen. From that time on Mr. Musser steadily enlarged his field of operations in the Mississippi river district, finally becoming identified with the Weyerhaeuser interests, Mr. Weyerhaeuser being the executive head of the Mississippi River Logging Company. In 1884-5 Mr. Musser invested largely in timber lands in Minnesota and Wisconsin for the purpose both of manufacture and investment. In 1886 the Musser-Sauntry Land, Logging & Manufacturing Company, of which Mr. Musser was president, was organized to utilize the timber in the vicinity of the St. Croix river. In the same year the Musser, Weyerhaeuser, Denkmann, Laird and Norton interests came together for the purpose of organizing the Pine Tree Lumber Company, at Little Falls, Minnesota. In 1890 certain steps were taken toward the perfection of this organization, and Peter Musser was elected president of the new company, Frederick Weyerhaeuser vice president, Richard D. Musser secretary and treasurer and Charles A. Weyerhaeuser general manager. It was not, however, until 1891 or 1892 that this company reached complete organization. Since that time the company's operations have grown to mammoth proportions. It is now manufacturing 80,000,000 to 90,000,000 feet of lumber annually and still has many years of operation before it.

Mr. Musser is president of the Musser Lumber Company, the Musser-Sauntry Land, Logging & Manufacturing Company and the Pine Tree Lumber Company, and a stockholder in the following other concerns: P. & P. M. Musser Securities Company; Louisiana & Texas Lumber Company; Weyerhaeuser Timber Company; Lumbermen's National Bank, Tacoma, Washington; Payette Lumber & Manufacturing Company, Idaho; Potlatch Lumber Company, Idaho; Third National Bank, St. Louis, Missouri; Manchester Bank, St. Louis, Missouri; New England National Bank, Kansas City, Missouri, and the Interstate Trust & Banking Company, New Orleans, Louisiana.

Mr. Musser's whole career has been one of unwearied activity. Like most successful men of this age, the amount of work he has accomplished is almost incredible, but along with his ability to work are coupled those other gifts so necessary to the rapid upward movement in business or in any other sphere in life, namely, the gifts of seeing clearly into the needs of the future and of acting with aggressive intelligence and determination when the moment of moments arrives. Even at this late time of his life Mr. M several hours each day to business pertaining t which extend from the Mississippi river to the and from the British possessions to the shores of Mexico.

Though so far advanced in years Mr. Musser ually good health, and is a fine example of the a frugal, temperate and well regulated youth about a ripe and well rounded old age.

OF THE
UNIVERSITY
OF
CALIFORNIA

, at White Hall, now Reinholds Station, Lancaster Pennsylvania. His father was a lumber merchant early was the lad pressed into service as a clerk in a store that he knew little of the joys that make boyhood Of so few years and so diminutive size was he when he entered upon his [illegible] [illegible] weigh sugar and deal it out with [illegible] compelled to stand on a [illegible] behind [illegible]

But young Musser, [illegible] American, felt that the [illegible] to make himself its master. [illegible] demonstrated to him that [illegible] equal, it is only the brains [illegible] are on the heavy side of the [illegible] man is within himself a [illegible] [illegible] of this conviction, young Musser [illegible] been named after his grandfather [illegible] the spring of 1863, when he journeyed [illegible] Richard Musser. They located at M[illegible] Peter Musser, who had charge [illegible] at Iowa City, sold his interest [illegible] to Iowa City to manage the [illegible] owned by R. Musser & Co. Here he [illegible] followed the steps of his uncle, Peter Musser [illegible] the selling of $143,000 worth of lumber in one year on the wagon trade alone, notwithstanding the fact that there were five yards in the town. This business continued in operation from 1864 until 1873. In this interim Mr Musser married, December 19, 1865, Miss Julia Hutchinson, daughter of Robert and Julia Hutchinson. They had four children One daughter, Laura,

PETER MILLER MUSSER

Peter M. Musser

Peter Miller Musser, of Muscatine, Iowa, was born April 3, 1841, at White Hall, now Reinholds Station, Lancaster county, Pennsylvania. His father was a lumber merchant and so early was the lad pressed into service as a clerk in a general store that he knew little of the joys that make boyhood sweet. Of so few years and so diminutive size was he when he entered upon his mercantile life that in order to weigh sugar and deal it out with dignity befitting his position he was compelled to stand on a stool behind the counter.

But young Musser, like many another working young American, felt that the world was before him and he set out to make himself its master. As the years went on it was demonstrated to him that in this country where every one is equal, it is only the brains that are unequal, and where they are on the heavy side of the balance as in his own case, each man is within himself a potential millionaire. Possessed of this conviction, young Musser went to Adamstown, which had been named after his grandfather, and stayed there until the spring of 1863, when he journeyed west with his uncle Richard Musser. They located at Muscatine, Iowa. A year later Peter Musser, who had charge of the Hoch & Musser yard at Iowa City, sold his interest in it, and P. M. Musser moved to Iowa City to manage the business which was then owned by R. Musser & Co. Here he met with such success as followed the steps of his uncle, Peter Musser—namely, the selling of $143,000 worth of lumber in one year to the wagon trade alone, notwithstanding the fact that there were five yards in the town. This business continued in operation from 1864 until 1873. In this interim Mr. Musser married, December 19, 1865, Miss Julia Hutchinson, daughter of Robert and Julia Hutchinson. They had four children. One daughter, Laura, died in infancy; John and Helen died of diphtheria in February, 1888, and one son, Clifton R. Musser, survives.

In April, 1873, the yard of R. Musser & Co., at Iowa City was sold to Musser & Porter and Mr. Musser returned to Muscatine eventually to buy the interests of R. Musser, and the P. M. Musser Company was organized. This business was later taken over by the Musser Lumber Company, organized in 1870. The officers of the Musser Lumber Company were P. Musser president; R. Musser vice president, and P. M. Musser secretary and treasurer.

From 1871 to the present time the Mussers have been actively engaged in the manufacture of lumber at Muscatine and since 1885 have produced from 35,000,000 to 45,000,000 feet annually.

Mr. Musser has been secretary and treasurer of the Musser Lumber Company since its organization. He is now president of Cook, Musser & Co., of the State Bank & Trust Company and of the P. & P. M. Musser Securities Company; director of the Pine Tree Lumber Company, Cook's Hereford Cattle Company, Keystone Land & Cattle Company, Mississippi River Logging Company, Chippewa Lumber & Boom Company, Musser-Sauntry Land, Logging & Manufacturing Company and of the Weyerhaeuser Timber Company.

Mr. Musser is a great traveler. Between the years 1885 and 1895 he twice toured the republic of Mexico, and as if to emphasize by the most violent of contrasts the impressions received in semi-tropical Mexico, he directed his itinerary to the icy North, and by dog team skimmed his way over snowy Alaska as Peter Musser had, by ox team, opened a trail across the plains thirty years before. His taste for travel still unsated, Mr. Musser in 1890 sailed for South America, and in 1899 visited Denmark, Russia, Norway and Sweden. In 1903 he spent several weeks in the Hawaiian Islands. In addition to his foreign travels, Mr. Musser has visited almost every state in the Union.

Mr. Musser has the public spirit expected of, but not always possessed by men of his position, but he has none of the pride of achievement which might so naturally accompany assured accomplishment. Indeed one of his most pronounced characteristics is modesty, and he impresses those about him with the belief that he would do much more for the city in which he resides if he could but hide the hand of the giver. As it is, his interest in the welfare of the town has been of the most practical sort, and his crowning gift is of a nature to give lasting pleasure and benefit to the citizens of Muscatine. This is the P. M. Musser Public Library, containing 8,000 volumes, and which was dedicated December 20, 1901. Mr. Musser gave the ground and erected the building on the condition that the people of the city would support a free library. The condition was gladly accepted with the above happy results, but so opposed is Mr. Musser to taking to himself either due or undue praise that he positively declined to have his name inscribed over the doorway of the building, even at the most urgent request of the public.

Hon. G. M. Titus, president of the Muscatine Library Board, when asked for an estimate of Mr. Musser's character, said:

"The best estimate of Mr. Musser's character can be formed by a study of the regard his fellow citizens in Muscatine have for him. No man ever lived in this thriving city who was more highly esteemed. The word 'esteemed' does not express it; he is in fact loved by all who know him intimately. Scores of Muscatine men have him to thank very largely for their commercial success. He is never happier than when assisting some struggling but deserving friend to get on in the world. What he does in this direction is not with blast of trumpet or with public parade of his generosity, but always with the admonition that 'nothing be said about this.'"

His friends, fully appreciating his business acumen, are eager to secure and act upon his advice. Mr. Musser is very careful in his expressions concerning business matters, even where his own affairs or those of others justify it; still his knowledge is ever at the command of his friends, and when the opinion does come it is doubly valuable, framed as it were in the light of his broad experience and superior judgment. Knowing this his friends and intimates consult him with the utmost freedom, safe in the conviction that once Mr. Musser takes the helm in a business enterprise even in the matter of advice, the other participants are pretty sure to be steered clear of the shoals of commercial disaster.

There may be some who envy him the possession of wealth, the result of his own keen business foresight, but to those who have carefully studied his position in his home community a far greater cause for emulation exists in his universal popularity and the genuine affection for him of all classes in Muscatine where he is considered the "ideal citizen."

LIBRARY
OF THE
UNIVERSITY
OF
CALIFORNIA

In the business world the ... ...ful man usually
is the patient, steady work... ...his business by
progressive steps, is con... ...himself by a
wise prevision which looks ... months or even
years for profits which are ... men are the
builders of commercial ... another kind
of busin... ...make
fortunes

It is
have to
was one of the most pro...
the upper Mississippi valley ...
time when people struggled ...
...ttle of its good things
eagerly sought—an exponent ...
the present, when children ...
education with ease and ...
ciousness; a time and a life ...
for those sturdy, brave hea...
with such tenacity.

Of such, none has shown ... he
was made than the subject ...
deed from his position as a ...
that of the presidency of ... number
companies in the West. ...
accomplishment.

Mr. Shaw was born ...
April 14, 1824. In his ...
only three years' schooling ...
ter seasons. The inter... been
the twentieth century ... clearing

GEORGE STEARNS SHAW

George S. Shaw

In the business world the dominant, successful man usually is the patient, steady worker who builds up his business by progressive steps, is conservative, and restrains himself by a wise prevision which looks ahead and can wait months or even years for profits which are sure to come. Such men are the builders of commercial empire. There is also another kind of businessmen, the brilliant Napoleons of finance who make fortunes in a day, a year, and mayhap lose them in an hour.

It is with one of the stable, dependable first class that we have to do—with George Stearns Shaw, who for thirty years was one of the most prominent figures in lumber circles in the upper Mississippi valley. This man was an exponent of a time when people struggled for the bare necessities of life and knew little of its good things; when schools were few and eagerly sought—an exponent of a time in strong contrast with the present, when children of even the poorest acquire an education with ease and luxury, and frequently with ungraciousness; a time and a life which arouses only admiration for those sturdy, brave hearted pioneers who fought upward with such tenacity.

Of such, none has shown more plainly of what stuff he was made than the subject of this sketch. It was a far cry indeed from his position as a little New England farmer boy to that of the presidency of one of the largest operating lumber companies in the West. Yet that leap was the measure of his accomplishment.

Mr. Shaw was born at Chelsea, Orange county, Vermont, April 14, 1824. In his boyhood he received the benefit of only three years' schooling and that in the depths of the winter seasons. The intervening time, which would have been the twentieth century boy's vacation, was spent in clearing his father's farm of the abounding rocks. From 1834 to 1839 he worked as a farm laborer with no other remuneration for the first two years than the privilege of attending the district school. His next move was to apprentice himself to a house carpenter and millwright. After completing his service with this employer he sought Boston as a broader field of action. Needing his little store of money for possible emergencies, he walked the entire distance, one hundred and fifty-five miles, to save stage fare. On reaching Boston he worked for a while as a journeyman, but soon began contracting on his own account, with such success that he broadened out his business as the years went by.

In the midst of his busy early life, in 1846, he was married to Miss Mary Ross, of Bakersfield, Vermont, who, with the six children, three sons and three daughters, that came to enlarge the family circle, made home for George Shaw wherever he chose to pitch his tent. Four of the children, with their mother, survived him.

In the meantime Mr. Shaw had removed to Chelsea, Massachusetts, near Boston, and continued to prosecute his business with much good fortune. The founding and building of the town of Winthrop was largely due to his efforts. He was perhaps one of the first men in the country to recognize the advantage of buying unimproved lands adjacent to a thriving city and erecting dwellings for rental and sale. He continued this work until 1865, when failing health made it necessary for him to seek another climate.

Upon the advice of his physician, he moved to Davenport, Iowa, and for ten years—until 1875—conducted his building and real estate business with his usual energy and judgment. He purchased land in close proximity to the city and built subdivisions, selling the houses in most instances to laborers on easy payments. Up to this time he had been connected with the lumber business in only an indirect manner, but he now became, and continued to be through life, one of the most active members of the great throng of northern lumbermen.

In 1875, Mr. Shaw, William Renwick and E. S. Crossett, formed a partnership for the manufacture of lumber. The mill then owned by Mr. Renwick was leased and a contract was made with Wisconsin lumbermen to furnish logs for the mill. The plant was operated until 1883, when the increasing cost of logs made it necessary to establish a mill nearer the forests. Up to that time the business had been conducted upon a partnership basis. In November, 1883, however, Mr. Shaw bought the plant of the Knife Falls Lumber Company, at Cloquet, Minnesota, and February 4, 1884, secured incorporation papers for the Renwick, Shaw & Crossett Lumber Company, of Davenport, Iowa, with a capital stock of $300,000. A part of the purchase price of the Knife Falls Lumber Company was paid with the capital of the new organization.

The mill was equipped with two circular saws, a gang saw and a small planing mill for finishing lumber. During the first year of its operation the company cut 17,426,000 feet of lumber.

In 1885, having purchased the stock formerly held by Messrs. Renwick and Crossett, Mr. Shaw moved to Cloquet and took the active management of the plant. The name of the corporation was changed to the Cloquet Lumber Company in 1886. Plans for alterations and extensions, which included the addition of a band mill and increased shipping facilities, were matured and put into operation almost immediately.

During the few years in which Mr. Shaw was engaged in the manufacture of lumber the remunerative possibilities lying in the accumulation of white pine timber had been brought very forcibly to his mind. Upon assuming control of operations at Cloquet, he made heavy investments in timber lands, the resulting profits in which justified in every way his early anticipations. The profits on the sale of lumber he reinvested in stumpage. Not satisfied with the progress he was making, although additions to his plant had increased the capacity to 60,200,000 feet in 1892, he made application for and received permission to increase the capital stock of the company to $1,000,000, fully paid up.

It was during the crisis of 1893 that his generalship displayed itself most clearly. He adopted a policy of retrenchment, cutting only from 40,000,000 to 45,000,000 feet until, for the year 1898, he had arranged to have 50,000,000 feet of logs put in for the season's cut.

Mr. Shaw was not a politician in the accepted meaning of that word, but close observation of current events made him a valuable man when it became necessary to foster some movement for the welfare of the state or nation. His familiarity with the lumber business and its needs fitted him specially for work in its behalf. He visited Washington many times in the interests of the lumbermen and placed existing conditions before the congressional committees in such a clear and forcible manner, that the securing of tariff legislation to their advantage may be said to be largely due to his persistent and intelligent efforts.

George Stearns Shaw began the voyage of life, in truth, against both wind and tide, but he steered his bark so well and carefully that he entered the harbor under full sail and in the pleasant glow of assured prosperity. When his life's journey ended, at Cloquet, Minnesota, November 5, 1897, George S. Shaw's accounts were all straight. He had done his best, and that best was worthy of enduring record.

JOHN B. PHELPS

John B. Phelps

One evening at the close of the day's business John B. Phelps, of Davenport, Iowa, drove quietly home and expired as he was about to step from his carriage. This sudden and tragic occurrence brought to an end a career of marked activity and terminated the life of a man who had been of great value to his city and an ideal character in his home.

Mr. Phelps was born May 10, 1840, in Schroon, Essex county, New York. His father had settled in the lumber district of this section in 1816, and the boy early secured a lumber training. There was an old fashioned sash mill on the farm, operated by a flutter wheel and supplied with power by the Schroon river, one of the branches of the Hudson.

The lumber industry became extinct in that section in the '50's, and in 1862 Mr. Phelps went west to Davenport, Iowa, and entered into partnership with his brother-in-law, James E. Lindsay, also a native of Essex county. In 1866 they erected a small mill. It was equipped with a circular saw, but in 1867 a gang saw was put in, the first of its kind in that part of the country. A band mill was installed in 1880, which, with the various improvements made from time to time, kept the plant up to date in its equipment. Its capacity eventually reached 25,000,000 feet of lumber, 5,000,000 shingles and 4,000,000 lath a season. In 1890 the Lindsay & Phelps Company was incorporated.

Mr. Phelps took an active part in the business and other interests of the city of Davenport, and in the lumber development of the Northwest. At the time of his death he held the following offices: Vice president and a director of the Cloquet Lumber Company; vice president and a director of the Hayward Timber Company; secretary and treasurer and a director of the Lindsay Land & Timber Company; director of the Richardson Land & Timber Company; director of the Sound Timber Company; director of the Riverside Milling Company; vice president and a director of the Security Fire Insurance Company; director of the Davenport National Bank; director of the Scott County Savings Bank; director of the Bettendorf Axle Company; director of the Tri-City Packing Company; trustee of the Cook Home for the Friendless; trustee and member of the Finance Committee of the Academy of Sciences; trustee of the Central Methodist Church, and chairman of the building committee of the Young Men's Christian Association.

These offices represent a number and a diversity of interests which only a man of Mr. Phelps' capacity could handle with success. He organized a number of the companies here mentioned and was their actual promoter as well. His commercial ventures were not by any means confined to Davenport. The Cloquet Lumber Company brought Minnesota within the field of his operations. His part in the Lindsay-Hayward-Richardson companies made him a factor in the Arkansas forests, and the stock he held in the Sound company brought the distant states of Washington and Oregon within the scope of his lumber manipulations.

Not all of his talents were utilized in lumber manufacture. He had been an important factor in the local banks for many years. He not only gave freely of his means to the Central Methodist Church, Young Men's Christian Association and other organizations working for the betterment of the condition of mankind, but he also gave the benefit of his valuable experience and his keen business intelligence. His personality was one to command admiration.

Mr. Phelps was married May 20, 1869, to Cornelia R. Woodward. One of the most beautiful features of their home life was the friendship of Mr. and Mrs. Phelps for Mrs. Elizabeth Woodward Atkinson, of Davenport, who was Mrs. Phelps' sister. Mrs. Atkinson came to them as a little girl and remained with them through her life up to her marriage with Doctor Atkinson. Mr. Phelps built for her across the way from his own home at the corner of Mississippi and Fourth avenues, a magnificent residence and presented it to her as a wedding gift. She was the companion of her sister, Mrs. Phelps, and of her brother-in-law, Mr. Phelps, from 1879 to 1897, the year of her marriage.

Mr. Phelps was a great story teller, his stories always being apropos, and he never repeated himself. In this respect he was likened to Abraham Lincoln by many who knew them both. Mr. Phelps was also a great traveler. His journeys were not undertaken in a haphazard manner but his plans were carefully laid and as carefully carried out. This methodical trait was displayed quite as much in his business life as in his traveling.

A comparatively small incident which showed his kindliness of heart occurred each Christmas. There were a number of people in Davenport from the Lake Champlain region —the Lindsays, the Phelps and the Haywards. These families were accustomed to gather annually at Christmastide, and on these occasions Mr. Phelps always played the part of Santa Claus. Every gift which he delivered was accompanied by an appropriate remark or witticism that made the occurrence doubly delightful.

Mr. Phelps went out of the world with the harness of life about him on the evening of July 16, 1900. He was busy in his office all the day and had been intensely interested in the news concerning the frightful siege of Pekin. His sister-in-law, Mrs. Morgan S. Woodward, was the guest of Minister Conger and was shut up in what seemed at that time the doomed city. On that day he received many letters. He also received and sent several cablegrams, and consequently was a little late in going home. Doctor and Mrs. Atkinson saw him drive through the twilight up the long Mississippi avenue hill, from the river to the top of the slope, and as he went by he waved his hand in his usual salute, bidding them good even-

ing. In the light of the sad event following this circums
peculiarly fitting to it seem the lines

> "Say not good night,
> But in some brighter clime
> Bid me good morning."

Five minutes later a servant ran to the Atkinson resi
announcing that Mr. Phelps was very ill. He had drive
his yard, thrown the reins aside, leaned forward in the ca
with his head upon his breast, and died.

He is buried in Oakdale cemetery, Davenport. The
is marked by a beautiful and massive gray monument, b
real monument is erected in the hearts of those who
him best while living, and is made up of loving memo
a well spent life.

OF TH
UNIVERSITY
OF
CALIFORNIA

No amount of work seems able to wear out some men—to the contrary, their very activity seems to bring to them a hale, hearty old age as its especial reward. For fifty years James Edwin Lindsay, of Davenport, Iowa, has been actively engaged in the lumber business and now at the age of nearly four score years still retains active control of large interests. He was born at Schroon, Essex county, New York, April 12, 1826. His schooling terminated with one year's training in engineering at Norwich, Vermont. His father was a hotel keeper, farmer and lumber manufacturer combined.

Young Lindsay worked at measuring and hauling logs at his father's mill, a water power affair propelled by the old style flutter wheel. This saw mill was facetiously called the "thunder shower mill" on account of its utter inability to operate unless a copious rain would kindly fill the small creek dam from which it derived its power. Young Lindsay lived in an atmosphere that tended to make him a lumberman, and included among his neighbors Israel Johnson, the inventor of the much used "muley" saw, and Philetus Sawyer, the long-time prominent lumberman who was for many years United States senator from Wisconsin.

Before his twenty-first birthday Mr. Lindsay had gained some experience in the logging business in partnership with his brother-in-law, John Tompkins. The firm was known as Lindsay & Tompkins and existed for four years. In the fall of 1856, the year he was thirty years old, Mr. Lindsay went west, and with his own savings and some money that had been entrusted to him, secured through land warrants about $7,000 worth of lands in the Black River Falls (Wisconsin) country.

In March, 1861, Mr. Lindsay located at Davenport, Iowa, and his Black river timber was logged and rafted to Daven-

JAMES EDWIN LINDSAY

James E. Lindsay

No amount of work seems able to wear out some men—to the contrary, their very activity seems to bring to them a hale, hearty old age as its especial reward. For fifty years James Edwin Lindsay, of Davenport, Iowa, has been actively engaged in the lumber business and now at the age of nearly four score years still retains active control of large interests. He was born at Schroon, Essex county, New York, April 12, 1826. His schooling terminated with one year's training in civil engineering at Norwich, Vermont. His father was a hotel keeper, farmer and lumber manufacturer combined.

Young Lindsay worked at measuring and hauling logs at his father's mill, a water power affair propelled by the old style flutter wheel. This saw mill was facetiously called the "thunder shower mill" on account of its utter inability to operate unless a copious rain would kindly fill the small creek dam from which it derived its power. Young Lindsay lived in an atmosphere that tended to make him a lumberman, and included among his neighbors Israel Johnson, the inventor of the much used "mulay" saw, and Philetus Sawyer, the long-time prominent lumberman who was for many years United States senator from Wisconsin.

Before his twenty-first birthday Mr. Lindsay had gained some experience in the logging business in partnership with his brother-in-law, John Tompkins. The firm was known as Lindsay & Tompkins and existed for four years. In the fall of 1856, the year he was thirty years old, Mr. Lindsay went west, and with his own savings and some money that had been entrusted to him, secured through land warrants about $7,000 worth of lands in the Black River Falls (Wisconsin) country.

In March, 1861, Mr. Lindsay located at Davenport, Iowa, and his Black river timber was logged and rafted to Davenport, where it was sawed into lumber at the mills at that place. He had formed a partnership with E. Harris, of Queensbury, New York, the understanding being that Mr. Lindsay was to go west, look about for business opportunities and take an interest in whatever seemed most favorable.

The absolute trust of his partner in Mr. Lindsay's judgment seems to have colored the latter's subsequent career. He had not only his own interests to further but also had absolutely in his keeping the interests of another. This tended to make him conservative, which characteristic he has never lost. This conservatism, however, should not be misjudged, for he has ever had an aggressive and enthusiastic confidence in the future values of timber lands.

Later in 1861 Mr. Lindsay secured a lease of the so called Renwick mill at Davenport, Iowa. Shortly afterward John B. Phelps bought Mr. Harris' interest and the firm became Lindsay & Phelps, and it has so continued—barring its incorporation as the Lindsay & Phelps Company in 1890—for forty-four years. In 1866 Lindsay & Phelps built a mill at Davenport. It started with a circular saw; a gang saw, at that time the only one in that section of the country, was added in 1867; and later, in 1880, a band mill was added, together with other machinery necessary to the equipment of a more modern plant. The mill at Davenport is still in operation and is classed among the old landmarks along the upper Mississippi. John B. Phelps, Mr. Lindsay's partner for so long a time, died in July, 1900.

Mr. Lindsay's confidence in pine timber was of the broadest kind, and as early as 1882 he personally supervised the location of the first holdings of the Lindsay Land & Lumber Company in Arkansas. Mr. Lindsay and C. R. Ainsworth might be named among the pioneer northern lumbermen in Arkansas, for certain it is that they were among the earliest to purchase timber lands in that section and they have continued to be prominently identified with lumber operations in that state.

The Richardson Land & Timber Company, of which J. E. Lindsay is a director, made purchases in Little River, Dallas, Sevier and Howard counties, Arkansas, and later extended its operations into Mississippi. At one time it held a large acreage in Arkansas. At the present time, however, it owns only 45,000 acres in Mississippi.

In 1884, when Messrs. Renwick, Shaw and Crossett went north to Cloquet, Minnesota, and organized the Cloquet Lumber Company, with George S. Shaw as manager, Mr. Lindsay and Mr. Phelps became members of that company, and after Mr. Phelps' death Mr. Lindsay succeeded him as a director.

The big trees of the Pacific Coast next attracted the attention of Lindsay & Phelps, and, associated with Weyerhaeuser & Denkmann and the Richardson interests, they organized the Sound Timber Company, December 23, 1899. This company owns over 50,000 acres of fir, cedar and spruce on the Skagit river, Skagit county; Stillaguamish river, Snohomish county, and Nooksack river, Whatcom county, all in Washington. These lands carry upwards of 1,500,000,000 feet of timber.

In 1901 Mr. Lindsay's attention was again directed to the South, and with Weyerhaeuser & Denkmann, the Laird, Norton Company, Dimock, Gould & Co. and the Richardson interests, on May 4 of that year he formed the Southland Lumber Company to engage in the purchase of timber lands in Louisiana. The present holdings of the company are in southwestern Louisiana and approximate 125,000 acres of longleaf yellow pine.

The Southern Lumber Company of Arkansas was organized January 28, 1902, by Weyerhaeuser & Denkmann, Dimock, Gould & Co., the Richardson interests and J. E. Lindsay, and has at the present time a saw mill in active operation at Warren, Arkansas, and 75,000 acres of shortleaf yellow pine.

Local interests have always received the strong support of

Lindsay & Phelps, Mr. Phelps being identified with many local organizations before his death and Mr. Lindsay still being connected with a large number of them.

Mr. Lindsay married in 1858 Mary Helen Phelps. He has three children—Ralph E. Lindsay, Mrs. Fred Wyman and George F. Lindsay.

Mr. Lindsay impresses one with his personal dignity, yet he is approachable at all times. He is a quiet, unassuming man, yet possesses those qualities that give strength and firmness to character. He may be compared to one of the giants of the forests with which he has been so long associated: Tall and sturdy, having borne the storms of years, yet towering as majestically as though not having withstood the vicissitudes of many seasons.

Primarily a coal man, Richard H. Keith, of Kansas City, Missouri, president of the Central Coal & Coke Company, has become a lumberman by the steady growth and development of his interests, which now include the ownership of hundreds of miles of magnificent timb[illegible] Southwest, the manufacture of which furnishes activity to a number of great mills.

Mr. Keith was born at Lexington, Lafayette county, Missouri, in 1842. His ancestors were among the first residents of Virginia and also belonged to one of the first families of that state. His parents moved to Missouri in 1839. Mr. Keith was educated at the old Masonic College at Lexington until his seventeenth year, when he became deputy clerk of the circuit and probate courts and recorder of deeds of the county. In 1861, when he had reached the age of eighteen, he enlisted in the Confederate service as a private in Colonel John Bowman's regiment of the Missouri State Guards. He saw active service in the battles of Lexington, Oak Hill and Pea Ridge. He then went to Memphis and enlisted in the Confederate service in the Landis battery of artillery. With that organization he went through the first and second battles of Corinth, Iuka, Hatchie River, Grand Gulf, Fort Gibson, Champion Hills, Black River and the siege of Vicksburg. Mr. Keith refused parole at Vicksburg and had a taste of Yankee prison life at Camp Morton, Indianapolis. At the conclusion of his army service, which terminated with his escape from prison, he went to California. He later spent two years trading between Leavenworth, Kansas, and New Mexico. For a year he was in the dry goods business at Leavenworth.

Mr. Keith went to Kansas City in 1871 His capital when he arrived there amounted to $40, with which he opened a

RICHARD H. KEITH

Richard H. Keith

Primarily a coal man, Richard H. Keith, of Kansas City, Missouri, president of the Central Coal & Coke Company, has become a lumberman by the steady growth and development of his interests, which now include the ownership of hundreds of miles of magnificent timber in the Southwest, the manufacture of which furnishes activity to a number of great mills.

Mr. Keith was born at Lexington, Lafayette county, Missouri, in 1842. His ancestors were among the first residents of Virginia and also belonged to one of the first families of that state. His parents moved to Missouri in 1839. Mr. Keith was educated at the old Masonic College at Lexington until his seventeenth year, when he became deputy clerk of the circuit and probate courts and recorder of deeds of the county. In 1861, when he had reached the age of eighteen, he enlisted in the Confederate service as a private in Colonel John Bowman's regiment of the Missouri State Guards. He saw active service in the battles of Lexington, Oak Hill and Pea Ridge. He then went to Memphis and enlisted in the Confederate service in the Landis battery of artillery. With that organization he went through the first and second battles of Corinth, Iuka, Hatchie River, Grand Gulf, Fort Gibson, Champion Hills, Black River and the siege of Vicksburg. Mr. Keith refused parole at Vicksburg and had a taste of Yankee prison life at Camp Morton, Indianapolis. At the conclusion of his army service, which terminated with his escape from prison, he went to California. He later spent two years trading between Leavenworth, Kansas, and New Mexico. For a year he was in the dry goods business at Leavenworth.

Mr. Keith went to Kansas City in 1871. His capital when he arrived there amounted to $40, with which he opened a small coal yard on Bluff street. At that time about thirty or forty cars of coal were handled daily in Kansas City. . The quantity is now three hundred and fifty to four hundred. He operated this retail business for several years, and now, through his connection with the Central Coal & Coke Company, he is one of the largest retail coal dealers in the country.

He opened his first mine at Godfrey, Bourbon county, Kansas, in 1873. In 1874-5 he opened other mines at Rich Hill and subsequently extensive mines in the Bonanza, Arkansas district. The Central Coal & Coke Company now owns enough mines to aggregate in production 4,000,000 tons of coal a year.

When Colonel Keith began business on Bluff street in Kansas City he employed only two or three men; the men now employed by the Central Coal & Coke Company number about 10,000. By way of comparison it may also be stated that the annual coal output of the Central Coal & Coke Company is now 120,000 cars, making a business of $7,000,000 annually. The company mines coal in Missouri, Kansas, Indian Territory, Arkansas and Wyoming. In connection with its coal business the company owns twenty-five stores which handle $3,000,000 worth of merchandise annually. The company is also interested in the retail coal business at Wichita, Kansas; St. Joseph, Missouri; Omaha, Nebraska, and Salt Lake City, Utah. It owns three retail yards in Kansas City. It distributes its products over Missouri, Kansas, Nebraska, Indian Territory, Arkansas, Louisiana, Texas, Utah, Wyoming, Montana, Nevada, California and Washington, and conducts the largest commercial coal business in the western states.

The Keith & Perry Coal Company was organized June 1, 1883, and reorganized as the Central Coal & Coke Company May 1, 1893. Before the reorganization of the company, it had been a dealer in lumber in a small way in connection with the coal business. The sale of lumber and coal frequently go hand in hand. But shortly after the Central Coal & Coke

Company was chartered the lumber department took on greater importance, and the company assumed a place among lumber manufacturers as well as lumber dealers. The property of the Bowie Lumber Company, of Texarkana, Texas, was purchased, including twenty-five acres within the city limits of Texarkana. Shortly afterward the circular saw mill was torn down and replaced by a gang and the fastest band mill that ever sawed yellow pine.

The actual lumber manufacturing operations of the Central Coal & Coke Company began in January, 1894, at which time the new plant, begun the previous August, was ready for business. This plant at Texarkana was operated until the summer of 1902, when it was torn down and removed to Carson, Louisiana, as the timber holdings at Texarkana had become exhausted. At Carson the company's band and gang circular mill cuts about 5,000,000 feet a month, or about 175,000 feet a day. The logs are brought in over a road practically owned by the Central Coal & Coke Company, known as the Missouri & Louisiana. It is fifty-one miles in length. The second saw mill plant erected by the Central Coal & Coke Company was at Keith, Louisiana, now known as Neame, two hundred miles south of Texarkana, on the Kansas City Southern. It manufactures 140,000 feet of logs into lumber every day.

Mr. Keith is also interested in 165,000 acres of pine lands in Houston county, Texas, lying between the Cotton Belt and the International & Great Northern railroads. The stumpage runs about 7,000 feet to the acre. This business is entirely separate from that of the Central Coal & Coke Company, having been incorporated under the name of the Louisiana & Texas Lumber Company. A mill plant was erected at Kennard, Texas, equipped with double bands and gang, with a capacity of 300,000 feet a day. This is the largest mill in the South. Mr. Keith is the president and Charles Campbell the secretary and treasurer of this company. The product of the

Louisiana & Texas Lumber Company's plant is handled by the Central Coal & Coke Company.

Mr. Keith has always had that love of detail which is often more effective in the building up of a great business than reach of plan or enthusiasm of purpose. He has always been one of those practical men who have pushed their thought to useful result. While he has been able to look along extended lines of action, yet he has had the ability to deal with the smallest matters essential to success with unerring judgment and with rapidity. His independent and confident nature, together with his determination of purpose, all of which spurred him on in his young manhood, doubtless were instrumental in a large measure in raising him to be the power that he now is in the lumber and coal industries.

LIBRARY
OF THE
UNIVERSITY
OF
CALIFORNIA

Some sage has declared that a man's education begins a hundred years before he is born. Taking this as a premise in the case of John Barber White, of Kansas City, Missouri, the training of the man in his particular calling should have placed him by this time in the highest class of lumbermen. And it has. As lumbermen, his Massachusetts ancestors two hundred years ago opened the way for the vast army of their ow operating in the United States. While America yet an untouched timber land these embryo lumbermen and soldiers, keen, quick witted, hardy, hacking pathways through the woods and felling trees for colonial needs, recognized and seized upon the wealth which nature dispensed so generously. One of these Whites, with practical wisdom which has borne rich fruit in his descendants, built in 1639 a saw mill at Salem, Massachusetts, which was the first ever erected in eastern New England.

While clearing the land these vigorous architects of the young civilization were fighting for their homes. John Barber White's great-great-grandfather, with the virile, peremptory disposition of his race to take the lead headed a regiment in the Colonial Wars and fought bravely in the battle of Lake George. With the next generation comparative peace reigned, and Josiah White, the colonel's son, suiting his occupation to the needs of the time returned to his family's other hereditary employment and built and operated a saw mill at Leominster, Massachusetts. Still standing at Leominster are a dam and a house that he erected in 1751. Josiah White's nine sturdy sons all fought in the Revolutionary War with that indomitable spirit and hardiness of purpose which characterized the colonial soldiers, and which wrenched the colonies from the British

JOHN BARBER WHITE

John B. White

Some sage has declared that a man's education begins a hundred years before he is born. Taking this as a premise in the case of John Barber White, of Kansas City, Missouri, the training of the man in his particular calling should have placed him by this time in the highest class of lumbermen. And it has. As lumbermen, his Massachusetts ancestors two hundred years ago opened the way for the vast army of their kind now operating in the United States. While America was as yet an untouched timber land these embryo lumbermen and soldiers, keen, quick witted, hardy, hacking pathways through the woods and felling trees for colonial needs, recognized and seized upon the wealth which nature dispensed so generously. One of these Whites, with practical wisdom which has borne rich fruit in his descendants, built in 1639 a saw mill at Salem, Massachusetts, which was the first ever erected in eastern New England.

While clearing the land these vigorous architects of the young civilization were fighting for their homes. John Barber White's great-great-grandfather, with the virile, peremptory disposition of his race to take the lead, headed a regiment in the Colonial Wars and fought bravely in the battle of Lake George. With the next generation comparative peace reigned, and Josiah White, the colonel's son, suiting his occupation to the needs of the time, returned to his family's other hereditary employment and built and operated a saw mill at Leominster, Massachusetts. Still standing at Leominster are a dam and a house that he erected in 1751. Josiah White's nine sturdy sons all fought in the Revolutionary War with that indomitable spirit and fixedness of purpose which characterized the colonial soldiers, and which wrenched the colonies from the British.

Among these sons was Luke White, who had a son named John. John White was a school teacher for several years, but the old, inherited tendency took possession of him and he also entered the saw mill business. He operated a mill in Ulster county, New York, and a saw and veneer works in Chautauqua county, the same state. Later he owned a saw mill near Union City, in Erie county, Pennsylvania. To him was born an only son, John Barber White.

John Barber White is the latest representative of the family to follow the inherited inclination. He was born in Chautauqua county, New York, December 8, 1847, and was but five years old at the time of his father's death. The boy was given a common school education, supplemented by a course at Jamestown Academy. Later he taught school during the winter and worked upon the farm in the summer.

In 1868-9, in partnership with two brothers named Jenner, he purchased a tract of about two hundred acres of pine land near Youngsville, Pennsylvania. They boarded themselves in the woods, cut their own logs and had them sawed at a neighboring mill. In 1870 Mr. White purchased the brothers' interests and became associated with R. A. Kinnear, of Youngsville, in the ownership of a lumber yard at Brady, a second yard being established at Petrolia, all in Pennsylvania. These interests were sold in 1874 and Mr. White moved to Tidioute, where he bought the "Arcade" mill, also opening a yard at Scrubgrass, Pennsylvania. Here he broke away from family traditions and assisted in establishing the Warren County News, a weekly paper at Tidioute which was independent in politics. He afterwards bought all of the stock and sold it to C. E. White, and then returned to his first love.

In 1876 Mr. White moved to Youngsville and bought a stave, heading and shingle mill at Irvineton. He had always been and is now a Republican, but in 1878 he was nominated by the Democratic and Greenback parties for the state legislature, and elected. During his six years' residence in Youngsville he was president of the Board of Education.

In 1880 he made a trip westward for the Grandins and others of Tidioute, purchasing more than 200,000 acres of pine timber land, organizing the Missouri Lumber & Mining Company and becoming a stockholder in and the manager of the company. E. B. and J. L. Grandin, Capt. H. H. Cumings and the late Jahu and L. L. Hunter were heavily interested in the concern. Mr. White has since been continuously its manager and a director, and for several years lately its president. This company has a capital and surplus of more than $1,000,000. It first started a planing mill at Mill Spring, Missouri, in 1881, and built the first saw mill at Grandin, Missouri, in 1887. Mr. White lived at the mills at Grandin and served as postmaster there for four years. At this point the company employs eight hundred men and produces 70,000,000 feet of lumber annually. It owns forty miles of logging railroad, with two hundred cars and six locomotives, and enough timber to keep the plant in operation for at least eight years.

Mr. White has been a leader in southern pine development. He was the organizer and first president of the Missouri & Arkansas Lumber Association, which was the first yellow pine organization in the country and one which owed its inception to the personal efforts of Mr. White. In 1890 he was elected president of the Southern Lumber Manufacturers' Association and was twice reelected. He is still a director. He is an officer in a large number of companies, being president of the Forest Lumber Company, of Kansas City, owning a line of retail yards; president of the Louisiana Central Lumber Company, of Clarks, Louisiana, which has a capital and surplus of $1,200,000; secretary and one of the directors of the Louisiana Long-Leaf Lumber Company, with a capital and surplus of over $1,000,000 and owning mills at Fisher and Victoria, Louisiana; secretary, treasurer and general manager of the Louisiana Lumber & Land Exchange Company, of Kansas City, which is the selling agency for the Missouri Lumber & Mining Company, the Ozark Land &

Lumber Company, of Winona, Missouri, the Cordz-Fisher Lumber Company, of Birch Tree, Missouri, the Louisiana Long-Leaf Lumber Company and the Louisiana Central Lumber Company, having a combined annual product of 250,000,000 feet of lumber, and president of the Reynolds Land Company, owning several thousand acres of hardwood timber in Butler county, Missouri. He is also president of the Bank of Poplar Bluff, at Poplar Bluff, Missouri, and a director in the New England Bank of Kansas City.

In the social and intellectual life of his state, and we might say of his country, Mr. White is no less prominent than he is in the business and financial world. He is deputy governor general of the general society for the state of Missouri of the Society of Colonial Wars, and is one of the Board of Managers of the Sons of the Revolution of the state of Missouri. He is a member of the Historical Society of the State of Virginia, and a member and one of the vice presidents of the Historical Society of the State of Ohio.

In appearance Mr. White is tall and imposing, with the military bearing resulting from a long line of soldierly ancestry. In this case the character fits the stature of the man, for Mr. White combines within himself mental and moral traits that are as big as they are admirable. The lessons of industry and hardihood learned in his boyhood have served as a basis upon which to rear a substantial after life. Although Mr. White has never seen military service, the impress left upon him by the Whites who have gone before is so indelibly stamped upon his nature that he seems to wear by right the title of "Captain," by which he is generally known. It fits him, also, because he is a born commander, though the strict discipline which he enforces is tempered by justice and by a native humor that relieves its asperity.

The character of an individu[illegible] than any particular opportunity he may [illegible] to prosperity. The success which John [illegible] Missouri, has won for himself in the [illegible] will be attributed by those who read the [illegible] more to the elements within the man than [illegible] circumstances. Circumstances that a less [illegible] sidered serious obstac[illegible] tools with which he must [illegible] acted upon the belief that man [illegible] of circumstances.

Mr. Berkshire was born in the [illegible] catine county, Iowa, July 27, 18[illegible] merchant tailor in Muscatine, gave [illegible] to acquire such education as the publ[illegible] afforded. The first work the boy [illegible] boy for a gang of men on the old [illegible] railway. At the age of thirteen he [illegible] Joseph Bennett in a flour mill at M[illegible] in the mill in various ways he [illegible] operation of the engine. He [illegible] Chaplin, the engineer of the [illegible] interest in the machinery, taught [illegible] engine that he was soon able to r[illegible] Having a liking for the river and the [illegible]ng thereon he soon secured a position as engine[illegible] started him on a career as a steamboat [illegible] which continued for several years.

In 1858 he became the [illegible] engineer on the packet Northerner which plied between St. Louis and St. Paul. His river experiences included positions as engineer on the Missis-

JOHN HENRY BERKSHIRE

John H. Berkshire

The character of an individual rather than any particular opportunity he may have, makes for his prosperity. The success which John Henry Berkshire, of Winona, Missouri, has won for himself in the West and Southwest will be attributed by those who read the story of his career more to the elements within the man than to any exterior influences. Circumstances that a less determined man would have considered serious obstacles were regarded by him as the very tools with which he must carve out success. He has always acted upon the belief that man is the maker, not the creature, of circumstances.

Mr. Berkshire was born in the town of Sweetland, Muscatine county, Iowa, July 27, 1841. The elder Berkshire, a merchant tailor in Muscatine, gave his son John opportunity to acquire such education as the public schools of the time afforded. The first work the boy engaged in was that of water boy for a gang of men on the old Mississippi & Missouri railway. At the age of thirteen he entered the employ of Joseph Bennett in a flour mill at Muscatine. While engaged in the mill in various ways he was much attracted by the operation of the engine. He sought the friendship of Charles Chaplin, the engineer of the mill, who, pleased at the boy's interest in the machinery, taught him so much about the engine that he was soon able to run it during the night shift. Having a liking for the river and the steam craft plying thereon he soon secured a position as engineer on a ferry boat. This started him on a career as a steamboat man which continued for several years.

In 1858 he became the assistant engineer on the packet Northerner which plied between St. Louis and St. Paul. His river experiences included positions as engineer on the Mississippi, Ohio and Missouri rivers. He was with Charles Chaplin as second engineer on a boat that did much service for the government during the Civil War. Young Berkshire forged ahead fast in his vocation for one so young. In fact, when twenty years old he was raised to the rank of chief engineer, an unusual promotion for a youth.

After he had reached that height of his youthful ambition and had seen much service he returned to Muscatine on a visit, and while there was offered by Benjamin Hershey the position of chief engineer in his mill at a salary of $2,000 a year and board. This temptation Mr. Berkshire could not resist and he accepted the offer. The relations thus begun with the Hershey interests have continued for many years, resulting in satisfaction and profit to all concerned. Mr. Berkshire became successively foreman, superintendent and manager of the Hershey Lumber Company's mills at Muscatine, retaining the management until 1894. During the time he was employed with the Hershey Lumber Company at Muscatine he had acquired stock in that corporation, thus becoming financially identified with it.

In 1891 Mr. Hershey sent Mr. Berkshire to Missouri to look over a plant in which he was largely interested, belonging to the Hershey Land & Lumber Company, which owned lands in Shannon, Texas, Oregon and Carter counties. Here Mr. Berkshire found that, owing to the location, it would be advisable, in order to get the best results from the timber holdings, to buy the Ozark Lumber Company's plant at Winona, Missouri.

In 1892 Mr. Hershey again sent Mr. Berkshire to Missouri with instructions to purchase the Ozark Lumber Company, which he did, taking an interest in it himself and being appointed to its vice presidency and management at that time. In May, 1895, the capital stock of the Ozark Lumber Company was increased to $200,000, and this company and the Hershey Land & Lumber Company, of Sargent, Missouri, were consolidated under the name of the Ozark Land &

Lumber Company, with a capital stock of $500,000, all paid in. Mira Hershey was made president and treasurer, J. H. Berkshire, vice president and manager, and A. B. Brown, of Muscatine, secretary. The mill capacity of the Ozark Land & Lumber Company is 140,000 feet daily, the annual output being over 36,000,000 feet.

The Ozark Land & Lumber Company is associated with a group of companies well known throughout the country as manufacturers of yellow pine in the Southwest, with mills at Grandin, Winona and Birch Tree, Missouri, and Victoria, Fisher and Clarks, Louisiana, the total annual cut of which mills reaches about 215,000,000 feet. This immense product is marketed through the Missouri Lumber & Land Exchange Company, with headquarters at Kansas City, of which Mr. Berkshire is president.

Mr. Berkshire's inventive mind wrought out several improvements in mill machinery which were extensively adopted in practice. At first several of these were put into use without protection by patent, but several others have been patented. Among his inventions are a feed water filter; a device to put on a steam pump to keep an even pressure on the water main; and the "Niagara" hydrant, now in general use.

Mr. Berkshire is prominent in several important corporations as well as being the head of the Ozark Land & Lumber Company. He is president of the Current River Lumber Company, of Kansas City; president of the Missouri Lumber & Land Exchange Company; vice president for Missouri of the Southern Lumber Manufacturers' Association; president of the Church Mercantile Company, of Winona; vice president of the J. J. C. Mining Company, of Boise, Idaho; vice president of the Barry Manufacturing Company, of Muscatine, Iowa; vice president of the Victoria, Fisher & Western Railroad Company; president of the Eminence Land & Mining Company, of Eminence, Missouri; vice president of the Slater Copper Mining Company, of Eminence; a stockholder and director in the Louisiana Long Leaf Lumber

Company, of Fisher, Louisiana, and the Louisiana Central Lumber Company, of Clarks, Louisiana.

Mr. Berkshire married Miss Georgia Abbott at Weston, Missouri, November 1, 1866. They have one daughter, Hattie Bell, and one son, Ben H. The daughter married Robert Cherry and resides at Mason City, Iowa. The son is the active manager of the Current River Lumber Company, at Southwest boulevard and Thirty-first street, Kansas City.

Mr. Berkshire is high in Masonic circles, being a member of Iowa Lodge No. 2, A. F. & A. M., Washington Chapter No. 4, R. A. M., De Molay Commandery No. 1, K. T., in Muscatine, and of Ararat Temple of the Ancient Arabic Order of Nobles of the Mystic Shrine, of Kansas City. He is also a member of the Ancient Order of United Workmen.

In his business ventures Mr. Berkshire has had for many years the advice and coöperation of his wife, who is a woman of great business ability. As an evidence of this it is stated that Mrs. Berkshire is really manager of the mercantile part of the extensive business of the Ozark Land & Lumber Company, at Winona, Missouri.

In the evolution of his company from the condition of an infant industry to the present corporation of large resources and extensive operations Mr. Berkshire has always been the principal factor. He has learned the lumber business as he did engineering—thoroughly. He familiarized himself with its peculiarities and its intricacies by experience, and made each new experience count.

It is a well recognized fact [illegible] J. White has done more for McComb City, [illegible] than any other of her citizens. For this reason [illegible] interest in Captain White's business [illegible] not only by the fact that he was a great lu[illegible] by the fact that he was a man who used his wealth [illegible] the benefit of his fellow men.

Captain White was born in [illegible] South Carolina, April 1, 18[illegible]. His father, [illegible] White, went to Charleston, South Carolina, in [illegible], where he had studied navigation with the idea [illegible] his life to the sea. When he arrived at Charleston [illegible] he became an apprentice in the carpentering [illegible] seven years in that capacity. In 1828 he [illegible] Elizabeth McMurtray, of South Carolina, who [illegible] parentage. Their son John J. White was the [illegible] children. In 1838 the family moved to Madison [illegible] Mississippi, where the elder White engaged in the [illegible] of lumber. His water power mill furnished lumber [illegible] the earliest houses erected in Canton. In [illegible] he gave up the lumber business, and operated a farm [illegible] up to the time of his death, which occurre[illegible]

John J. White was eight years [illegible] his parents moved to Mississippi. He received [illegible] the common schools, studying with such dilige[illegible] later became an assistant teacher, and in 1852 [illegible] twenty-two, he became a principal. As school teaching did not seem to be a healthful occupation for him, he gave it up and served a long apprenticeship as a carpenter.

In 1859, in partnership with his brother, Robert Emmett White, he engaged in the saw mill business near Summit,

JOHN J. WHITE

John J. White

It is a well recognized fact that Capt. John J. White has done more for McComb City, Mississippi, than has any other of her citizens. For this reason one feels an interest in Captain White's business career that is inspired not only by the fact that he was a great lumberman but also by the fact that he was a man who used his wealth for the benefit of his fellow men.

Captain White was born in Anderson county, South Carolina, April 1, 1830. His father, William Moore White, went to Charleston, South Carolina, in 1821, from Ireland, where he had studied navigation with the idea of devoting his life to the sea. When he arrived at Charleston, however, he became an apprentice in the carpentering trade and served seven years in that capacity. In 1828 he married Miss Elizabeth McMurtray, of South Carolina, who was of Scotch parentage. Their son John J. White was the first of seven children. In 1838 the family moved to Madison county, Mississippi, where the elder White engaged in the manufacture of lumber. His water power mill furnished lumber for many of the earliest houses erected in Canton. In later years he gave up the lumber business, and operated a farm near Camden up to the time of his death, which occurred in his eighty-ninth year.

John J. White was eight years old when his parents moved to Mississippi. He received his education in the common schools, studying with such diligence that he later became an assistant teacher, and in 1852, at the age of twenty-two, he became a principal. As school teaching did not seem to be a healthful occupation for him, he gave it up and served a long apprenticeship as a carpenter.

In 1859, in partnership with his brother, Robert Emmett White, he engaged in the saw mill business near Summit,

Pike county, Misssissippi. In 1861 came the great Rebellion and Mr. White found himself placed in a peculiar position. He was not in sympathy with secession, but he was loyal to his state; and when the rupture came he enlisted in the Confederate cause. His brother, Robert E., had already enlisted in the McNair Rifles and later died of brain fever at Murfreesboro, Tennessee. After his brother had gone to the war John J. White continued the business at Summit for a time. He furnished a considerable quantity of timber for the building of Confederate gunboats, but soon closed the mill and enlisted in the Wilson Guards, which were mustered in as Company H of the Thirty-ninth Mississippi regiment. He was a lieutenant in his company and participated in the second battle of Corinth and the fight at Port Hudson. At the latter place he was captured and taken as a prisoner to Johnson's island, near Sandusky, Ohio, where he remained until the end of the war. He then resumed his saw mill business at Summit, which prospered from the very beginning and grew from its first small proportions to be one of the leading lumber producing plants of the state.

When McComb City, now known simply as McComb, in Pike county, was located by the Mississippi Valley Company, and the Illinois Central Railroad Company moved its machine shops to that place, Mr. White, having a large tract of land just south of McComb City, moved his mill plant to that location and since that time has operated it in the same place—the site where Whitestown is now located—one mile from the station at McComb City.

Captain White built his first mill at McComb City in 1873. In the spring of 1882 he shipped to P. G. Dodge & Co. what was probably one of the first carloads of yellow pine sent to Chicago. His mill burned in 1881, and within thirty days after the fire he built a small mill with which he kept his customers' trade and manufactured sufficient lumber to build another mill. His present mill at McComb City is a circular one producing 75,000 feet of evenly manufactured lumber a day. His timber land holdings aggregate about 70,000 acres located in Pike, Amite, Marion, Perry, Pearl River and Franklin counties, Mississippi, and St. Helena parish, Louisiana. On Captain White's pay-rolls are the names of about four hundred men, which means that there are probably 1,500 inhabitants of Whitestown.

One historical fact in connection with Captain White's enterprise is that he was the first man to build a tram road in the state of Mississippi to be used for hauling logs to the saw mill by a steam locomotive. In connection with this fact it may be stated that the first locomotive used by him, a small H. K. Porter, is yet in service on his line of road, which is now about twenty-five miles long, of standard gage, and is called the Liberty-White railroad, running between Liberty, the seat of Amite county, and McComb City. The trains make two trips daily in connection with the Illinois Central railroad at the latter place. This road now has an equipment, in addition to the Porter engine, of two eighteen-ton and two thirty-five-ton engines. Captain White is the sole owner of this road.

Captain White was president of the old Alabama, Georgia & Florida Yellow Pine Lumber Association, and has been president of the Southern Lumber Manufacturers' Association and is now a director in that body.

In addition to lumbering, he is also active in other lines of business. He has for many years been president of the McComb City Female College. He is the principal stockholder in the McComb City Cotton Mill, built at a cost of $250,000 and equipped with 10,000 spindles and 370 looms, giving employment to a large number of people. Captain White is a heavy stockholder in the Pike County Bank and several other banking institutions in that section of the country. He owns an electric plant which furnishes light for McComb City and Summit, and has been a heavy investor in New Orleans real estate.

The biography of J. J. White is of exceptional interest as

a record of lifelong effort in the service
White is southern born and his life h
the promotion of the interests of the
mendable enterprise has had his appr
coöperation, even though it meant so
Surely the career of such a man should
nent record.

OF TH
UNIVERSITY
OF
CALIFORNIA

It is necessary to go somewhat into the history of yellow pine, particularly the longleaf variety in order to show what lumber pioneers such as John Nathan Gilbert, of Beaumont, Texas, had to overcome in order to achieve success. Nearly every yellow pine manufacturer—whether he operates in the longleaf districts of Georgia, Florida, Alabama, Mississippi, Louisiana and Texas, or in the shortleaf regions of Arkansas, Missouri and the northern belt of that timber—who reads this work knows that Mr. Gilbert's struggles were largely a duplicate of his own.

The Texas-Louisiana lumber district contains huge saw mills at Lake Charles and Westlake, Louisiana, and Orange and Beaumont, Texas, and at other isolated points in that general district, and in this area longleaf yellow pine is found in its highest forestal development. The valleys of the Calcasieu, the Sabine and the Neches rivers contain tracts of timber lands unequaled for stumpage results and unexcelled for timber of a superior quality; and it is these lands that Mr. Gilbert and other pioneers have ransacked for the supply of the great mills in that country.

The work began only a few years ago, comparatively. Twenty-five years ago the Southern Pacific railroad system was not the unit it is now, in 1905. Westward from New Orleans the road stopped before Orange was reached. Eastward from Houston, Texas, also, it was uncompleted. The lumber pioneers rode or toilfully walked through the valleys of the Sabine, the Neches and the Calcasieu rivers, up one bank and down the other, penetrating miles of unbroken forests. The size and quality of the timber amazed them. The question of logging was solved by the presence of the three rivers and their tributaries. Lands were purchased and mills were

John N. Gilbert

It is necessary to go somewhat into the history of yellow pine, particularly the longleaf variety, in order to show what lumber pioneers such as John Nathan Gilbert, of Beaumont, Texas, had to overcome in order to achieve success. Nearly every yellow pine manufacturer—whether he operates in the longleaf districts of Georgia, Florida, Alabama, Mississippi, Louisiana and Texas, or in the shortleaf regions of Arkansas, Missouri and the northern belt of that timber—who reads this work knows that Mr. Gilbert's struggles were largely a duplicate of his own.

The Texas-Louisiana lumber district contains huge saw mills at Lake Charles and Westlake, Louisiana, and Orange and Beaumont, Texas, and at other isolated points in that general district, and in this area longleaf yellow pine is found in its highest forestal development. The valleys of the Calcasieu, the Sabine and the Neches rivers contain tracts of timber lands unequaled for stumpage results and unexcelled for timber of a superior quality; and it is these lands that Mr. Gilbert and other pioneers have ransacked for the supply of the great mills in that country.

The work began only a few years ago, comparatively. Twenty-five years ago the Southern Pacific railroad system was not the unit it is now, in 1905. Westward from New Orleans the road stopped before Orange was reached. Eastward from Houston, Texas, also, it was uncompleted. The lumber pioneers rode or toilfully walked through the valleys of the Sabine, the Neches and the Calcasieu rivers, up one bank and down the other, penetrating miles of unbroken forests. The size and quality of the timber amazed them. The question of logging was solved by the presence of the three rivers and their tributaries. Lands were purchased and mills were erected at Lake Charles, Orange and Beaumont. Those of the mill companies that did not invest in lands purchased logs from the many tram companies which began operations simultaneously with the mills. To the farseeing lumberman the section was ideal for milling operations. It has proven so, as exemplified in the success of the fifteen or more great plants in the district.

Among the Beaumont, Texas, mill men John Nathan Gilbert is conspicuous as a lumberman. His father, a native of Connecticut, went to Texas, where his son, John N. Gilbert, was born in 1855 near Kosse, a small town, which, however, is one of the oldest in the state. It is on what is now the Houston & Texas Central railroad, in Limestone county. When John Gilbert was six years of age his father moved from that point, going to Sabine Pass, where he engaged in general merchandising. Beaumont, now a prosperous city of 15,000 people, then contained a population of only 300. When young Gilbert was about seventeen years of age he went to work in Beaumont as a clerk in the store of Long & Son, which firm built the first saw mill there. Having by nature a leaning toward the lumber industry, he decided to learn this business from the foundation, and began in the mill commissary. He gradually but thoroughly learned the intricate details of manufacturing lumber. Having been saving of his money, he invested it in the mill when it was rebuilt in 1877. The plant was then cutting about 40,000 feet daily and was the largest mill in Beaumont.

Soon afterward Long & Son went out of the saw mill business and started a shingle mill, the saw mill becoming the property of the Beaumont Lumber Company, which was a copartnership. The firm became a corporation in 1882, and was operated under a charter with the following officers: F. L. Carroll, of Waco, Texas, president; George W. Carroll, of Beaumont, vice president; John N. Gilbert, secretary, treasurer and general manager, and L. B. Pipkin, assistant secretary and treasurer. The capital stock, originally $100,000, was afterward increased to $300,000. An offshoot of the Beaumont Lumber Company was the Nona Mills Company, Limited, of Louisiana. Its location is at Leesville, Louisiana, on the Kansas City Southern railway. The two companies together owned about 200,000 acres of longleaf timber. This was the status of the Gilbert interests when in 1901 the Beaumont plant, with the timber tributary to it, was sold outright to the Kirby Lumber Company, which was organized in that year, for the round sum of $1,200,000. While, therefore, Mr. Gilbert's lumber and timber interests are less than they were, he is still at the date of this publication heavily interested in yellow pine and its products.

One of the most remarkable events in the commercial and industrial history of the country was the discovery of petroleum in enormous quantities at Beaumont, Texas, in 1900. Many of the lumbermen of that city being land owners, participated in the profits that accrued from that ownership or from the operations of oil properties. Among them was Mr. Gilbert. Furthermore, he had inherited from his father, in conjunction with other heirs, a large piece of landed property in the Sourlake district, which afterward developed into one of the most prolific oil fields in the United States and succeeded in the public attention the Beaumont field. A considerable portion of the property falling to the estate was sold at that time at a large profit, although enough was retained to serve as the basis for successful operating companies. In the various transactions resulting therefrom Mr. Gilbert and his associates realized large sums of money.

Returning to Mr. Gilbert's lumber career: When he became associated with the Beaumont Lumber Company its trade was confined to Texas. White pine was then a fierce competitor of the native product. Nevertheless, as long ago as 1882, prices for yellow pine railroad ties went as high as $14 a thousand feet. The mill sawed railroad stuff exclusively at that time. The other Beaumont operators were the Wiess brothers, Captain W. A. Fletcher, the Longs and the Keiths.

Timber lands were then selling at fifty to seventy-five cents an acre, and Mr. Gilbert and others were wise enough to anticipate the certain profit to be realized from investment at such prices. As stated previously, Mr. Gilbert's companies had acquired title to 200,000 acres of magnificent longleaf pine, and the combined capacity of the mills was about 230,000 feet a day. There remains still the Nona Mills Company, with a producing capacity of more than 100,000 feet a day, with a large timber acreage back of it.

Mr. Gilbert has been living at Beaumont continuously for twenty-five years. He owns a beautiful home in that city, where he is a respected and honored citizen. His family, consisting of three sons and a daughter, is his especial pride. He married a Texas girl—Miss Willbarger, of Bastrop. Mr. Gilbert stands high in Masonic circles. He is a stockholder and director in the First National Bank of Beaumont, and a director of the Texarkana & Fort Smith railroad. Among his brother manufacturers he is greatly esteemed for his business ability and for his social qualities.

material extent in these far-re
an element does vitalize the
indicates an unusual persona
pression beyond the thresh
Long. He, matching his
gence against men as able
at the same time retained
beyond mere moneyed succ
makes this felt not only among
but also in that broad, almost
world of business. There
up a great business beyond its

"Knowledge is an asset.
lumber history of America
Southern Lumber Manufac
1902. A Greek philosopher
long before and said, "Know
man of thought as well as
edge was the greatest asset

Robert Alexander Long
ber business in the great ... He was

ROBERT ALEXANDER LONG

Robert A. Long

A biography of Robert Alexander Long should mean more to the world at large than a general record of statistical facts pertaining to the life of the successful man of business.

The presumption that the life of the average "captain of industry" is ruled by the purely practical alone does not hold good in the case of Mr. Long. While standards of honor and probity may stand behind the architects of great industrial enterprises and the organizers of far-reaching corporations, and must do so if permanent success is to be assured, still it is the exception rather than the rule that idealism figures to any material extent in these far-reaching institutions. When such an element does vitalize the existence of a businessman it indicates an unusual personality, and must necessarily find expression beyond the threshold of his home. So it is with Mr. Long. He, matching his own clear, comprehensive intelligence against men as able as he, has won his spurs fairly and at the same time retained that great something over and beyond mere moneyed success—which we call the ideal. He makes this felt not only among his friends and acquaintances, but also in that broad, almost limitless territory known as the world of business. There is an ethical value in so building up a great business beyond its measure in dollars and cents.

"Knowledge is an asset." One of the great factors in the lumber history of America made this assertion before the Southern Lumber Manufacturers' Association in January, 1902. A Greek philosopher came to the same conclusion long before and said, "Knowledge is power." To the ancient man of thought as well as to the modern man of action knowledge was the greatest asset in the stock account.

Robert Alexander Long gained his knowledge of the lumber business in the great school of experience. He was born in Shelby county, Kentucky, in 1850. For seventeen years he lived on a farm and went to school. He then decided that farming was not to be his business in life, and for a year or two drifted about in an effort to find the right opening for his future career. For a short time he was a clerk in a country store, but he soon came to the conclusion that the opportunities presented by his home community to a young man of ambition and determination were not particularly inviting.

In 1873 Mr. Long went to Kansas City, where lived an uncle, C. J. White, who was at that time cashier in the National Bank of Commerce. Here Mr. Long bought a meat shop. However, the future successful businessman was not to be a butcher; fate had marked out for him something else.

Another business venture now claimed his attention. Upon the advice of his uncle, who thought that his boyhood farm experiences might be of value, Mr. Long entered into a partnership with Victor B. Bell in which he contracted to put up hay near Columbus, Kansas. The venture was not a success and the enterprise at the end of the season showed only much hard work and no money. Among the assets when the deal closed, however, was a carload of lumber from Kansas City, which had been shipped down to cover the hay. It was sold locally for as much as it had cost. This circumstance was an incentive to larger operations in lumber, and on April 30, 1875, the new firm of R. A. Long & Co. started in the retail lumber business at Columbus, Cherokee county, Kansas. The firm consisted of Robert A. Long, Victor B. Bell and Robert White. There was neither money nor experience back of the firm, but there were instead unlimited American pluck and the credit which capital is always ready to extend to the honest, persevering young man of brains.

Mr. Long became general manager of this retail yard. So little did he know of the practical, technical side of the lumber business that when the first invoice came to be checked the items "dimension" and "S1S&E"—familiar to the veriest tyro in the lumber business—were not understood by him. It was in this yard Mr. Long learned his lesson, "Knowledge is an asset," and so well did he learn it that thirty years afterward we find him addressing a representative body of lumbermen and giving what has been declared to be the most definite statistical information extant on the subject of yellow pine stumpage. Later another address before the National Wholesale Lumber Dealers' Association on monetary affairs placed him in the foremost rank of lumber financiers in the whole country.

At the end of the first year's business there was $800 to be distributed among the members of the firm. The next year evinced an increase in lumber knowledge on the part of the manager, for the books showed that $2,000 had been earned. Then it was determined to branch out and, although the first venture, at Empire, Kansas, was not a paying one, the firm of R. A. Long & Co. continued to expand, and in 1880, five years after its organization, six retail yards in six flourishing Kansas towns bore its sign. At the end of 1883 fourteen new yards in different places attested to the success of the firm, which in 1884 was incorporated as the Long-Bell Lumber Company, with $300,000 capital stock, and with Mr. Long still general manager. In 1891 the company became a manufacturer of lumber through the purchase of a lumber plant at Van Buren, Arkansas, and a year later it actively entered the wholesale trade. The following year it moved its headquarters from Columbus, Kansas, to Kansas City, Missouri.

In 1902 the retail yards of the Long-Bell Lumber Company numbered fifty, the working force of men had grown to 1,600 and the fine manufacturing plants were all furnished with modern equipment. Important branches established at St. Louis, Texarkana and Tacoma, Washington, and a capital stock of $1,250,000 attested the success of the man behind the executive desk.

Today Mr. Long is president of the Long-Bell Lumber Company, of Kansas City; the Rapides Lumber Company, Limited, of Woodworth, Louisiana; the King-Ryder Lumber

Company, of Bonami, Louisiana; the Hudson River Lumber Company, of De Ridder, Louisiana; the Globe Lumber Company, Limited, of Yellow Pine, Louisiana; the Minnetonka Lumber Company; the Fidelity Land & Improvement Company; the Fidelity Fuel Company and the Long-Bell railway system. Mr. Long is also a heavy stockholder in the Weed Lumber Company, of Weed, Siskiyou county, California.

America is said to be the land of the dollar and its people are often taunted with their fondness for reducing everything to figures; but certainly the facts that in 1903 the Long-Bell Lumber Company and affiliated interests made sales amounting to $7,199,237.25, paid freight amounting to $1,927,509.71, shipped 23,488 cars of material, had on its pay-roll 3,713 men and lost by bad accounts only $6,189.24, are impressive. To one who looks beyond the monetary value of these figures they are also impressive, as they show what can be done by a man who counts knowledge as an asset.

In this recapitulation is encouragement for the timid and instruction for the unknowing, and young men of every temperament and inclination must surely ponder on the moral taught by the life and achievements of the originator and guiding spirit of the Long-Bell Lumber Company—Robert Alexander Long.

The story of successful [illegible] pine lands contains no more interesting [illegible] career of William Wiess [illegible] his connection with the lumber industry [illegible] over a period of [illegible] a pioneer, as the lumber business [illegible] to look [illegible] days. At the [illegible] lumberman, [illegible] but the strong [illegible] the [illegible] of its value [illegible] sh[illegible] circumstances that were encountered [illegible] rapid development of this industry, and finally his faith was rewarded in an expansion fully equal in its rapidity and scope to his anticipations.

William Wiess is Southern born and bred. His father, Simon Wiess, and his mother, formerly Miss Margaret Sturrock, were married at Natchitoches, Louisiana, in 1835 and moved to Nacogdoches, Texas, the following year. Here his father was made collector of customs for the Republic of Texas under President Sam Houston. Later, about 1837 or 1838, he moved to Sabine Pass, Texas, and in 1839 to Grigsby's Bluff. In 1840 he went to Beaumont, where he engaged in a mercantile business until 1841. In that year he moved to Wiessbluff, which was at that date in the wilderness, on the bank of the Neches river in Jasper county, in the center of the longleaf yellow pine belt. In 1836 the eldest of the family was born at Nacogdoches. In 1839 a son, Napoleon, now deceased, was born at Griggsby's Bluff. In 1842 two sons, Mark and William (the subject of this biography), were born. In 1845 another son was born and in 1848 the sixth son was born. There was also a daughter, Pauline. The father gave all of

WILLIAM WIESS

William Wiess

The story of successful investment in southern pine lands contains no more interesting chapter than the career of William Wiess, of Beaumont, Texas. Although his connection with the lumber industry as a manufacturer covers a period of but twenty-two years, he may truthfully be called a pioneer, as the lumber business of eastern Texas does not have to look backward over many years to recall its pioneer days. At the commencement of William Wiess' career as a lumberman, yellow pine occupied a very humble position; but the strong faith which he had in the ultimate recognition of its value never wavered through all the discouraging experiences that were encountered. He eagerly watched the development of this industry, and finally his faith was rewarded in an expansion fully equal in its rapidity and scope to his anticipations.

William Wiess is southern born and bred. His father, Simon Wiess, and his mother, formerly Miss Margaret Sturrock, were married at Natchitoches, Louisiana, in 1835 and moved to Nacogdoches, Texas, the following year. Here his father was made collector of customs for the Republic of Texas under President Sam Houston. Later, about 1837 or 1838, he moved to Sabine Pass, Texas, and in 1839 to Griggsby's Bluff. In 1840 he went to Beaumont, where he engaged in a mercantile business until 1841. In that year he moved to Wiessbluff, which was at that date in the wilderness, on the bank of the Neches river in Jasper county, in the center of the longleaf yellow pine belt. In 1836 the eldest of the family was born at Nacogdoches. In 1839 a son, Napoleon, now deceased, was born at Griggsby's Bluff. In 1842 two sons, Mark and William (the subject of this biography), were born. In 1845 another son was born and in 1848 the sixth son was born. There was also a daughter, Pauline. The father gave all of his children the best educational advantages that it was possible for him to provide.

Early in the '50's the elder Wiess erected on the bank of the Neches river one of the old fashioned "Peck" saw mills, which was run by a wheel extended into the current of the river. His principal business enterprise at Wiessbluff was a store, which was continued during his lifetime and managed by himself and his sons. Wiessbluff was at the head of tide-water and was an important shipping port. William Wiess, alone, received and discharged freight from three steamboats in one day.

In July, 1861, William Wiess, then eighteen years of age, with all his brothers, enlisted in the Confederate army and served until the close of the war in 1865. Returning home without even a dollar, the father gave each of the sons a small amount of money with which to make his start in the business world. William secured a position with a New York commission house which was buying cotton and remained with it five months, being able to save some money during that time.

In December, 1865, he embarked in the mercantile business at Beaumont, where he still resides. He continued in this line, having also some small interest in the lumber business, until March, 1880, when his active connection with the lumber industry began. He disposed of his entire mercantile interests and invested in the Reliance Lumber Company, taking charge of this concern as business manager. It was during his twenty-two years' management of this company that he won for himself a conspicuous place in the history of the American lumber trade.

When he took charge of the affairs of this concern it was practically bankrupt, being in such financial straits that it had to borrow every dollar with which it did business. Owing to the excellent business ability of Captain Wiess and the strict attention which he gave to the affairs of this company, it was soon not only out of debt but also taking its place among the largest and most important yellow pine manufacturing institutions, and it was only a short time until it was well known throughout the country.

Captain Wiess conducted the business of the Reliance Lumber Company until January 1, 1901, when he accepted a proposition from John H. Kirby, of the Kirby Lumber Company, of Houston, Texas, for the sale of its timber holdings, which by this time aggregated about 80,000 acres, and the manufacturing plant. This sale was for cash.

With the sale of this business, Captain Wiess retired from active lumbering and proceeded to enjoy the benefits of his hard earned and well deserved success. When he first took up his residence in Beaumont, that now beautiful and prosperous little city was but an insignificant village; but his firm belief in its future prosperity—like his faith in the permanent success of the yellow pine industry—was rewarded by realization. He was not only a witness to this prosperity but took an active part in bringing it about, always being a public spirited citizen and working ceaselessly for the good of the community in which he lived. That he should receive a share of the prosperity that came to his town was but appropriate and just, and not one of his townsmen has ever shown any envy at his success.

William Wiess was married January 11, 1866, and of this marriage were born two sons, Eugene C. and Perry M., and one daughter, Nena. He had the misfortune to loss his first wife, and married again in March, 1880. Speaking to a friend in reference to the much debated question of marriage being a failure, he once said: "I stand ready to prove that marriage is not a failure, as I know that I married two of the best women in the world."

Captain Wiess is a man of genial, courteous manner, possessing enough dignity to make the combination a pleasing one. His private office at the Reliance Lumber Company's place of business was for years the scene of many a pleasant conference, as this much engaged man was never too busy to welcome any who wished to see him. Rich and poor were

greeted alike, the courtesy so character
extended impartially. He was always t
paper fraternity, and his cordiality to
appreciated by its representatives. N
of Texas is more respected and es
William Wiess.

LIBRARY
OF THE
UNIVERSITY
OF
CALIFORNIA

suddenly terminated by death at Morgan City, Louisiana, February 6, 18[illegible].

William Cameron was born in Perthshire, Scotland, January 11, 1834. He received a common school education such as is given the children of the common people of Scotland, and at the age of fourteen was apprenticed to [illegible] Edinburgh. In 1852, at the age of eighteen, he came to the United States, landing in New York with barely enough money to carry him from that port to Illinois, where he had relatives. He worked on a farm for a time and then engaged with a relative who was in the grain business [illegible] state. Later he went to Missouri and became a [illegible] on the Missouri Pacific railway at the time it was being extended west from St. Louis.

When the war broke out he was at Sedalia, Missouri, helped in organizing the "home guards" of that [illegible] was captured at the battle of Springfield, carried to [illegible] and paroled. When he was captured he had $150 and a watch, which he turned over to a locomotive engineer [illegible] Missouri Pacific to be sent to his sweetheart in [illegible] death during the war. This lady subsequently be[illegible] wife.

After being paroled he returned to St. Louis and engaged in supplying hay and feed of various kinds to the [illegible] About the same time he entered the lumber [illegible] small way. His contracts with the government were profitable and a short time afterward he opened a lumber business at Warrensburg and also at Sedalia, Missouri. From Sedalia he extended his operations south, following the extension of the

WILLIAM CAMERÓN

William Cameron

The career of William Cameron, one of the great lumber manufacturers and lumber merchants of the Southwest, was suddenly terminated by death at Morgan City, Louisiana, February 6, 1899.

William Cameron was born in Perthshire, Scotland, January 11, 1834. He received a common school education such as is given the children of the common people of Scotland, and at the age of fourteen was apprenticed to an attorney in Edinburgh. In 1852, at the age of eighteen, he came to the United States, landing in New York with barely enough money to carry him from that port to Illinois, where he had relatives. He worked on a farm for a time and then engaged himself with a relative who was in the grain business in that state. Later he went to Missouri and became a section boss on the Missouri Pacific railway at the time it was being extended west from St. Louis.

When the war broke out he was at Sedalia, Missouri, and helped in organizing the "home guards" of that town. He was captured at the battle of Springfield, carried to St. Louis and paroled. When he was captured he had $150 and a silver watch, which he turned over to a locomotive engineer of the Missouri Pacific to be sent to his sweetheart in case of his death during the war. This lady subsequently became his wife.

After being paroled he returned to St. Louis and engaged in supplying hay and feed of various kinds to the government. About the same time he entered the lumber business in a small way. His contracts with the government were profitable and a short time afterward he opened a lumber business at Warrensburg and also at Sedalia, Missouri. From Sedalia he extended his operations south, following the extension of the

Missouri, Kansas & Texas railway, establishing yards at Clinton, Nevada, and other small towns in Missouri, and also at Fort Scott, Kansas. He started a pork packing establishment at Clinton, Missouri, but as it did not prove very successful he closed it out after a few years. He followed the Missouri, Kansas & Texas railway into Texas and opened yards at Denison, Sherman and Dallas. His identity with the lumber interests of Texas extended over a quarter of a century.

William Cameron & Co.'s north and south divisions were formed in 1882, but were consolidated four years later, with headquarters at Waco, Texas, which town was Mr. Cameron's place of residence. The firm's retail yards were at Waco, Lott, Rosebud, Gatesville, San Antonio, McKinney, Brownwood, San Angelo, Dublin, Stephenville, Granbury, Weatherford, Paradise, Bridgeport, Chico, Decatur, Wichita Falls, Vernon and Quanah, Texas; Terral, Ryan, Comanche, Duncan, Marlow, Rush Springs, Chickasha and Minco, Indian Territory, and Elreno, Okarche, Kingfisher, Enid, Waukomis and Hennessey, Oklahoma Territory.

The wholesale business of William Cameron dated from 1884. In 1886 he acquired with a partner a saw mill business at Saron, Texas, of which he became later the sole owner. Among other interests of which he was part or sole proprietor were the Texas Lumber Company, a timber land concern; the Whitecastle Lumber & Shingle Company, at Whitecastle, Louisiana; the Cameron Lumber Mills Company, at Carmona, Texas; the William Cameron cypress manufacturing plant at Bowie, Louisiana, and the Tyler Car & Lumber Company, at Michelli, Texas. This plant was operated under the style of William Cameron & Co. and the name of the place was changed to Angelina. In addition to these numerous interests, William Cameron & Co. controlled the cut of a number of large manufacturing concerns, and the firm was among the heaviest owners of timber land in the South and Southwest.

Mr. Cameron was also an owner of flouring mill property

in Texas, and at one time was considered one of the largest dealers in grain and one of the heaviest flour mill operators in that state. He was at the time of his death chief proprietor of the Cameron Mill & Elevator Company, of Fort Worth. His interests and investments were not confined, however, to the lumber and grain industries, for he was a heavy stockholder in the Slayden-Kirksey Woolen Mills, at Waco. In addition to his manufacturing and commercial interests, he was heavily interested in banks, being a prominent stockholder of the First National Bank, of Waco, the Hibernia Bank & Trust Company, of New Orleans, and the Southern National Bank, of New York.

Mr. Cameron had secured control of the Jeanerette Lumber & Shingle Company, Limited, of Jeanerette, Louisiana, at which place he was putting in a fine new saw mill when death terminated his activities. He had also more recently acquired the saw milling property at Rockland, Texas, formerly owned by W. H. Aldridge, and at the time of his death was erecting at that point one of the finest saw mill plants in the South.

The will of William Cameron was probated February 11, 1899, and the inventory showed an appraised valuation of about $4,000,000.

The man who accumulates so great wealth from nothing may sometimes be spoken of with more or less contempt by the abstract thinker, who forgets that it is money—or rather the lack of it—which makes workers of men. Most of the results of ingenuity, skill and intellect are due to its unremitting pursuit. The very labor a man has to perform and the self-denial he has to cultivate in acquiring money are an education in themselves. They compel him to put forth energy, vigilance and intelligent effort, and bring out many of the stronger qualities of his nature.

Let no one, then, underrate the character of a man like William Cameron. Certainly no other man in the Southwest has so thoroughly impressed his personality upon its lumber business and commercial interests generally as he did. Energetic and forceful, enterprising to a high degree, nothing in the way of investments in timber or manufacture was too formidable for him. Hence it was that in the yellow pine and cypress manufacturing industry he was always a leader. As a wholesaler and retailer his interests were of greater volume than those of any other individual or corporation in Texas or Louisiana.

Mr. Cameron was twice married, his first wife having died after they were married about eight years, leaving two daughters, one of whom is now Mrs. Sadie McDonald, wife of F. A. McDonald, of Fort Worth, Texas—and the other is now Mrs. Anna Downman, wife of Robert Henry Downman, of Waco, Texas. Mr. Cameron was survived by his second wife and three children by his second marriage—Flora, now Mrs. Frank B. Baird, William W. and Margaret.

The remains of William Cameron were taken to Waco, Texas, the day of his death and buried February 8, 1899, with honors by the Grand Army of the Republic, the Confederate Veterans and various civic societies of which he had been a member.

UNIVERSITY
OF
CALIFORNIA

Texas, is probably ... Texas having ... overwhelming his ... and wholesale and ... executive i

judgment in the conduct of the great [illegible] retail lumber interests in which he is [illegible] considered excellent by those who know [illegible]

William Waldo Cameron was born Aug[illegible] Waco, Texas. He was educated at the Agri[illegible] Mechanical College, at College Station, Texas, [illegible] the Lone Star State. [illegible] pletion of [illegible] there he took a [illegible] at San Albans University, at Radford, Vir[illegible] returned to Waco and spent a year with the [illegible] Woolen Mills. He spent the six following [illegible] lumber business in the office of William Cam[illegible]

Immediately upon the death of his father [illegible] ron, which occurred February 6, 18[illegible] called upon to act as president of William [illegible] pany, Incorporated. The corporation [illegible] suant to his father's expressed desire [illegible] tinued by the Cameron family. He [illegible] of his father's Texas properties and [illegible] yellow pine mill department, the [illegible] the wholesale lumber business and the [illegible] corporation with a capital of $2,400,000. His [illegible] business are his mother, Mrs. Flora B. Cam[illegible] ters, Mrs. Flora M. Baird and Miss Marg[illegible] The original Cameron fortune, before the [illegible] estate, exceeded $5,000,000 and was equally divided [illegible] the four here named and two other married [illegible] Cameron.

The yellow pine mills owned [illegible] operated by

WILLIAM WALDO CAMERON

William Waldo Cameron

While William Waldo Cameron, of Waco, Texas, is probably the youngest lumberman in the United States having so large a capital invested in his business, nevertheless his judgment in the conduct of the great mills and wholesale and retail lumber interests in which he is the chief executive is considered excellent by those who know him well.

William Waldo Cameron was born August 1, 1878, at Waco, Texas. He was educated at the Agricultural and Mechanical College, at College Station, Texas, one of the leading educational institutions of the Lone Star State. Upon the completion of his course there he took a postgraduate course at San Albans University, at Radford, Virginia. He then returned to Waco and spent a year with the Slayden-Kirksey Woolen Mills. He spent the six following years learning the lumber business in the office of William Cameron & Co.

Immediately upon the death of his father, William Cameron, which occurred February 6, 1899, the young man was called upon to act as president of William Cameron & Company, Incorporated. The corporation had been formed pursuant to his father's expressed desire that the business be continued by the Cameron family. He assumed the management of his father's Texas properties and compactly organized the yellow pine mill department, the pine timber holdings, the wholesale lumber business and the line yards into one corporation with a capital of $2,400,000. His direct associates in the business are his mother, Mrs. Flora B. Cameron, and his sisters, Mrs. Flora M. Baird and Miss Margaret Cameron. The original Cameron fortune, before the division of the estate, exceeded $5,000,000 and was equally divided among the four here named and two other married sisters of Mr. Cameron.

The yellow pine mills owned outright and operated by

this company are at Saron, Rockland, Angelina, Carmona and Haysland, all in the east Texas region. The yellow pine mills are owned absolutely by the Waco company, as are the retail yards and wholesale business. The retail yards are at San Angelo, Brownwood, Waco, Marlin, Fort Worth, Wichita Falls, Vernon, Quanah and Childress, Texas; Ryan, Marlow, Rush Springs, Chickasha and Comanche, Indian Territory, and Hobart, Anadarko, Mountain View and Mangum, Oklahoma Territory. The yards are in the hands of capable managers and are conducted on the same general lines as are the other departments of the company. The wholesale department is entirely distinct from the mills or the line of retail yards, and caters to the railroad and general consuming trade, including an extensive business in the western states as well as in Texas and Mexico.

Mr. Cameron, in addition to being so largely identified with these lumber interests, is a director in the Slayden-Kirksey Woolen Mills, in the New Auditorium Company, both at Waco, and in the Country Club. He is president of the Texas Lumber Company, an Illinois corporation owning large tracts of yellow pine land in Texas; of the Cameron Lumber Mills Company, at Carmona, Texas, and of the Whitecastle Lumber & Shingle Company, at Whitecastle, Louisiana. He is secretary of the Swinden Pecan Orchard Company and an active and prominent member of the Texas Lumbermen's Association. He takes a personal interest in the progress of his native city and is always active and foremost in every movement having for its object the welfare of Waco, subscribing liberally to the upbuilding of that city and setting aside a considerable sum annually for charity.

In January, 1901, he was united in marriage to Miss Faith Darling Baird, of Buffalo, New York, whose brother, Frank Baird, had married Mr. Cameron's sister three or four months previous. Mr. and Mrs. Cameron reside on Austin avenue, Waco, in the old home of the Cameron family. One child has been born to them.

Since he has assumed charge of the lumber and other properties left by his father, William Waldo Cameron has materially augmented the family fortune. The great increase in the lumber business of the company is due largely to his personal supervision and to the able work of his lieutenants, and the future of William Cameron & Company, Incorporated, is full of promise. The large timber holdings and the excellent mills owned by the company have greatly enhanced in value during the last few years, and within the same time the wholesale business and the retail yard department have grown steadily and added their share to the increased gains. It is safe to say that the company has made splendid profits in all its departments and that, under young Mr. Cameron's executive control, the $2,400,000 has been nearly doubled. Certainly William Waldo Cameron has demonstrated that mental discipline may be obtained from money-getting as real as that which is gained from mathematics. "The soul is trained by the ledger as much as by the calculus and can get exercise in the account of sales as much as in account of stars."

Although the possessor of so large wealth, William Waldo Cameron displays none of the arrogance and pride that so often accompany the ownership of riches. He is plain and unassuming, and in his relations with people of less fortunate circumstances there is no indication of any feeling of condescension. This admirable trait of character has endeared him to his friends and associates, as has also his other predominating trait—his unbounded confidence in his intimate friends. He has no secrets apart from them, conversing without the least reserve concerning his own business and personal affairs. Among those who know him best—in his own town and state—he is most popular and is invariably spoken of in the highest terms.

His vast interests are conducted by clean business methods and with that good judgment and keen discernment that characterized his father's operations. He seems to have inherited from his father those business traits that were potential factors in William Cameron's success in building up the mam business which is now so creditably continued by the Mr. Cameron has often made the statement to friends th has no desire to heap up more riches for himself, as he not care for money beyond what is necessary to suppl comforts of life to his family; but he devotes his life to c ing on and increasing the business bequeathed to himsel mother and his sisters because he considers it a sacred left to his keeping by his father, and because by its pr conduct he may be of genuine service to the community.

It cannot be denied that there is quite often an element of chance in the most successful working out of human affairs. However, while it may be true that circumstances may bring to a man success in a certain line of business, it is almost a foregone conclusion that he would have been quite as successful in any other line if he had devoted to it the same sound

in organizing and tact in managing

the one which fate seems to have flung

man, of New Orleans, Louisiana, made

as a druggist, but Cupid, who is always

a lumberman and cypress specialist.

born near Warrenton, Fauquier county, Virginia, and was educated at the Virginia Agricultural and Mechanical College at Blacksburg. He was one of a family of nine children. He entered the employ of a hardware and lumber concern at Warrenton and continued there until he was twenty years of age, when he moved to Texas, entering the retail drug business at Bryan. In 1880 he moved to Waco, in the same state, where he at first clerked in a drug store and later embarked in the retail drug business for himself. He sold this business in the summer of 1882 and entered the office of J. W. Castles & Co., wholesale druggists at Waco. In 1883 the company was absorbed by Cameron, Castles & Story, Mr. Downman becoming manager of the drug department. In 1886 this department was sold to Behrens & Castles, but Mr. Downman continued to represent Mr. Castles' interests in the firm until 1889.

On June 6, 1886, he married Miss Anna S. Cameron, the second daughter of the late William Cameron, at the family home at Waco, and in February, 1889, he transferred his busi-

ROBERT HENRY DOWNMAN

Robert H. Downman

It cannot be denied that there is quite often an element of chance in the most successful working out of human affairs. However, while it may be true that circumstances may bring to a man success in a certain line of business, it is almost a foregone conclusion that he would have been quite as successful in any other line if he had devoted to it the same sound judgment, energy, skill in organizing and tact in managing men that he devoted to the one which fate seems to have flung into his lap.

Robert Henry Downman, of New Orleans, Louisiana, made his start in business life as a druggist, but Cupid, who is always playing pranks, made him a lumberman and cypress specialist.

Mr. Downman was born near Warrenton, Fauquier county, Virginia, and was educated at the Virginia Agricultural and Mechanical College, at Blacksburg. He was one of a family of nine children. He entered the employ of a hardware and lumber concern at Warrenton and continued there until he was twenty years of age, when he moved to Texas, entering the retail drug business at Bryan. In 1880 he moved to Waco, in the same state, where he at first clerked in a drug store and later embarked in the retail drug business for himself. He sold this business in the summer of 1882 and entered the office of J. W. Castles & Co., wholesale druggists at Waco. In 1883 the company was absorbed by Cameron, Castles & Story, Mr. Downman becoming manager of the drug department. In 1886 this department was sold to Behrens & Castles, but Mr. Downman continued to represent Mr. Castles' interests in the firm until 1889.

On June 6, 1888, he married Miss Anna S. Cameron, the second daughter of the late William Cameron, at the family home at Waco, and in February, 1889, he transferred his business activities to the wholesale and retail lumber business of William Cameron & Co., becoming a junior partner. In 1897 William Cameron & Co. was dissolved and Mr. Downman had full charge of the business until William Cameron's death in February, 1899. From that time until December, 1900, he was the managing executor of the William Cameron estate for the heirs.

In the fall of 1900 it was decided to divide the estate among the widow, the four daughters and the son. This was accordingly done, and in this division the yellow pine and cypress interests were separated completely, Mr. Downman acquiring in his wife's right the entire cypress business of the deceased with the exception of a block of stock in the Whitecastle, Louisiana, property, which was held by the Camerons at Waco until their entire interest in this property was acquired by Mr. Downman and his associates in June, 1902. The cypress properties falling to Mr. Downman were the great saw milling plant and timber lands located at Bowie, Louisiana, the Cameron holdings in the Jeanerette Lumber & Shingle Company, at Jeanerette, Louisiana, and a proportionate division of the stock in the Whitecastle Lumber & Shingle Company, at Whitecastle.

A notable event incident to this great consolidation was the almost immediate incorporation of the Bowie Lumber Company, Limited, with a capital of $1,000,000, Mr. Downman becoming president of the new corporation. This was quickly followed by the purchase of the Des Allemands property, which was acquired in November, 1900, for the purpose of securing additional timber lands for the benefit of the Bowie plant. This purchase was made from Francis Martin and included the saw milling plant, which was subsequently incorporated under the name of the Des Allemands Lumber Company, Limited. The purchase of the P. L. Renoudet Cypress Lumber Company plant at New Iberia was made by Mr. Downman in December of the same year. It included from 250,000,000 to 300,000,000 feet of standing timber and was soon afterward incorporated under the name of the Iberia Cypress Company, Limited. Mr. Downman is president of all these companies.

The line of action as a cypress operator mapped out by Mr. Downman was upon a large scale, and he has carried it out with remarkable success since its inception. It means cypress timber holdings in Louisiana aggregating 800,000,000 feet of stumpage, with an annual manufacturing output of 90,000,000 feet of red cypress lumber, 180,000,000 shingles and 22,500,000 lath, all of which Mr. Downman directly controls. It also means the development of the cypress business in the hands of one man on a scale undreamed of a decade ago, and it places this great consolidated interest in the foremost rank of cypress manufacture.

The cypress interests of the late William Cameron fell into good hands when Mr. Downman received them. Already the great milling and timber interests of the deceased Scotchman have multiplied by 50 percent under Mr. Downman's aggressive management, and the end is not yet. His plans are for still further enlargement of his properties and for still further establishment of wholesale distributing offices throughout the territory where cypress lumber is used or will be used. He has surrounded himself with able managers—men who have had long experience in the manufacture of cypress lumber as well as men who thoroughly understand how to market it. He is at present, in 1905, adding new machinery to his mills and widening the scope of his operations in various other ways.

Mr. Downman's personal headquarters are at New Orleans, Louisiana, where he maintains his offices and from whence he directs his managers. The offices are modest and unpretentious for a lumberman controlling such large milling plants. The legend on the doors of the rooms, which are located in the Liverpool, London & Globe building, is simply "R. H. Downman." One who is uninitiated in lumber affairs would never dream that they are the general headquarters where orders and instructions are issued to five great cypress mills.

But the facts are typical of the man. He makes no pretension of power but simply goes ahead, working on the plans he has drawn, without the blare of a trumpet or other ostentatious methods not strictly necessary.

The milling plants absolutely controlled by Mr. Downman are the Cypress King mill, at Bowie, Louisiana, under the name of the Bowie Lumber Company, Limited; the Jeanerette Lumber & Shingle Company, Limited, at Jeanerette, Louisiana; the Des Allemands Lumber Company, Limited, at Des Allemands, Louisiana; the Iberia Cypress Company, Limited, at New Iberia, Louisiana, and the Whitecastle Lumber & Shingle Company, Limited, at Whitecastle, Louisiana.

himself in the history of that locality. Such a [illegible] Savage Crossett, of Davenport, Iowa, who for a half century has played a conspicuous part in the lumber business of the Mississippi valley. Mr. Crossett was born in West Plattsburg, Clinton county, New York, February 4, 1828, near the scene of the battle of Plattsburg, in which his father, [illegible] Savage Crossett, participated actively as a soldier in the American army in the War of 1812.

Mr. Crossett received his education in the public [illegible] and in an academy. His first employment was in the [illegible] office of Bardwell & Kneeland, at Troy; this work, however, he abandoned on account of failing health and secured [illegible] tion as clerk in a shoe store at a salary of $2.50 a [illegible] board.

In 1846, when eighteen years of age, he went to [illegible] Lake, New York, as clerk in a village store and [illegible] later he and his brother purchased the establishment [illegible] place he first became interested in the lumber business [illegible] ling pine and spruce lumber in small quantities [illegible] some logging.

At the age of twenty-two Mr. Crossett turned [illegible] over to his brother and went west. From [illegible] journeyed by steamer to St. Louis, and in the spring of [illegible] St. Paul. From there he went to La Crosse, Wisconsin, where he remained a year and six months. In the meantime his brother had sold the property in the East at a loss, leaving young Crossett handicapped with debts; but with the restive-

Edward S. Crossett

A man who has spent the fifty most active years of his life in a single industry in one section of the country with ultimately fortunate results to himself, certainly must have assisted in the development of that industry and have won a place for himself in the history of that locality. Such a man is Edward Savage Crossett, of Davenport, Iowa, who for a half century has played a conspicuous part in the lumber business of the Mississippi valley. Mr. Crossett was born in West Plattsburg, Clinton county, New York, February 4, 1828, near the scene of the battle of Plattsburg, in which his father, John Savage Crossett, participated actively as a soldier in the American army in the War of 1812.

Mr. Crossett received his education in the public schools and in an academy. His first employment was in the printing office of Bardwell & Kneeland, at Troy; this work, however, he abandoned on account of failing health and secured a position as clerk in a shoe store at a salary of $2.50 a month and board.

In 1846, when eighteen years of age, he went to Schroon Lake, New York, as clerk in a village store and two years later he and his brother purchased the establishment. In this place he first became interested in the lumber business, handling pine and spruce lumber in small quantities and doing some logging.

At the age of twenty-two Mr. Crossett turned the business over to his brother and went west. From Cincinnati he journeyed by steamer to St. Louis, and in the spring of 1852 to St. Paul. From there he went to La Crosse, Wisconsin, where he remained a year and six months. In the meantime his brother had sold the property in the East at a loss, leaving young Crossett handicapped with debts; but with the restiveness of an honest nature under the weight of debt, Edward shouldered the obligations and eventually paid them off to the last dollar.

In the fall of 1853 Mr. Crossett went to Black River Falls, Wisconsin, where he took charge of a supply store for lumbermen. He was in entire command of this enterprise, from the making of contracts for supplies to the sale of the goods. His experience as a merchant in the Adirondack mountains was of good service to him in this situation, and so satisfactory was his work that his employers united their four stores into one and gave the management of it to Mr. Crossett.

From 1854 until 1856 he was postmaster of Black River Falls, and in the latter year associated himself with W. T. Price in a supply store business of their own.

In the year 1857 he resumed work for his former employers. Then came a period of reverses in which Mr. Crossett suffered heavy losses. The freshet of the following year swept the company's logs down the river and out of reach. As a consequence the company itself was forced to suspend operations and to go into bankruptcy. A portion of Mr. Crossett's capital and two years' salary were sunk in the general collapse.

In 1859 he started a supply store of his own, but was burned out shortly thereafter with a complete loss of stock and building. Still undaunted, Mr. Crossett gathered up the threads of his ravelled business and attempted to weave them together again. Succeeding in obtaining the equivalent of some bills due him in the shape of lumber and hewn timber, he rafted it down the river in 1861 and sold it where he could; but was obliged to take in exchange "stump tail currency," which depreciated to 10 percent before he could dispose of it. Thus Mr. Crossett's first eight years in the West brought him little more than valuable experience.

In this same year Mr. Crossett was employed to assist J. E. Lindsay, who was shortly thereafter joined in partnership by J. B. Phelps. Subsequently Mr. Crossett was connected with other concerns until 1870. For several years he ran the yards of Isaac Spaulding in East St. Louis, spending his winters in picking up stock on Black river.

From 1870 to 1875 he engaged in the scaling of logs and estimating of timber, buying parcels of timber land whenever such were available and seemed valuable.

In 1873 Mr. Crossett was united in marriage to Miss Harmony E. Clark, of Pittsfield, Massachusetts, and from that auspicious day he declares his real prosperity dates. The two made their home in Nielsville, Wisconsin, until February, 1875, when they moved to Davenport, Iowa, where Mr. Crossett became a member of the firm of Renwick, Shaw & Crossett. Their son, Edward Clark Crossett, was born at Davenport, August 7, 1882. The same year marks Mr. Crossett's first investment in yellow pine, at which time he was one of the organizers of the Lindsay Land & Lumber Company.

In 1884 Renwick, Shaw & Crossett bought a saw mill and pine lands at Cloquet, Minnesota. Two years later Mr. Crossett sold his interest to Mr. Shaw, taking in part payment 10,000 acres of Arkansas lands covered with yellow pine. In the opinion of Mr. Crossett's friends he had made a great mistake in acquiring Arkansas property, but subsequent events proved the soundness of his judgment.

Convinced by further personal inspection that the possibilities in yellow pine were great, he became extensively interested in other companies operating in the South. Already a heavy stockholder in the Eagle Lumber Company, of Eagle Mills, Arkansas, and the Gates Lumber Company of Wilmar, Arkansas, he, in company with C. W. Gates and J. W. Watzek, purchased the Fordyce Lumber Company, of Fordyce, Arkansas, in 1892.

Coöperation has always been Mr. Crossett's hobby. Like William Morris, its modern apostle, he believed that the profits accruing from an enterprise should in some equitable way be divided among those responsible for them. In 1899, the Crossett Lumber Company, of Crossett, Arkansas, was organized on a coöperative basis—not as the result of any dreaming of a modern Utopia, but as a business proposition, and partly, no doubt, because of his own long bout with the "slings and arrows of outrageous fortune." In this coöperative organization, Messrs. Crossett, Watzek and Gates held three-fourths of the stock and certain employees the other one-fourth. In recognition of Mr. Crossett's generosity, fine sense of justice in this decidedly self-centered age, and of his kindly advice always freely given, his associates conferred on the company and its town the name of Crossett.

More recently Mr. Crossett has further extended his holdings and, as an influential member of the Jackson Lumber Company, of Lockhart, Alabama, invested with his associates, in 150,000 acres of virgin timber in Alabama and Florida. Together with Messrs. Watzek and Gates, the two remaining members, he built a large saw mill plant at Lockhart, Alabama, and otherwise developed the property.

Brains and concentration of purpose, bulwarked by patience and self-reliance, constitute the master key which unlocks the difficulties of life—or at least the difficulties of the financial world. If a man hold this sort of magical implement within his hand he is as near independence as it is given a man to be. So when thus equipped, Albert Hawkins Gates, of Wilmar, Arkansas, began his first purposeful movements in the world of business while not possessing wealth itself, he held within his hand the next best thing—the certainty of acquiring it.

The power of concentrating energy and of driving forward continuously toward a definite end which has enabled Mr. Gates to do so much in life, never once wavered through the twenty years in which he tried his key untiringly on the door of lumber opportunity. In the end he found the right lock and the door was opened. Twenty of the best years of Mr. Gates' life were spent in this fruitful effort. But what [illegible] decade or two decades when an end is accomplished?

A pioneer in southwestern yellow pine, Mr. Gates made a study of this particular kind of timber, in every stage [illegible] growth, production and distribution. For years it made [illegible] progress toward the popularity he felt must eventually [illegible] it. However, full of faith and confidence, and not regarding the difficulties which beset the promoter of any new enterprise, Mr. Gates stood determinedly by the timber selection and by 1899 had the satisfaction of seeing that his convictions were well founded and his predictions at last realized. The value of the timber and milling properties belonging to the Gates Lumber Company at Wilmar, Arkansas, was assured, and the company stands on a level with other powerful and firmly established lumber organizations.

Albert Gates is the eldest of a family including five

Albert H. Gates

Brains and concentration of purpose, bulwarked by patience and self-reliance, constitute the master key which unlocks the difficulties of life—or at least the difficulties of the financial world. If a man hold this sort of magical implement within his hand he is as near independence as it is given a man to be. So, when thus equipped, Albert Hawkins Gates, of Wilmar, Arkansas, began his first purposeful movements in the world of business; while not possessing wealth itself, he held within his hand the next best thing—the certainty of acquiring it.

The power of concentrating energy and of driving forward continuously toward a definite end which has enabled Mr. Gates to do so much in life, never once wavered through the twenty years in which he tried his key untiringly on the door of lumber opportunity. In the end he found the right lock and the door was opened. Twenty of the best years of Mr. Gates' life were spent in this fruitful effort. But what is a decade or two decades when an end is accomplished?

A pioneer in southwestern yellow pine, Mr. Gates made a study of this particular kind of timber, in every stage of growth, production and distribution. For years it made slow progress toward the popularity he felt must eventually come to it. However, full of faith and confidence, and not regarding the difficulties which beset the promoter of any new enterprise, Mr. Gates stood determinedly by the timber of his selection and by 1899 had the satisfaction of seeing that his convictions were well founded and his predictions at last realized. The value of the timber and milling properties belonging to the Gates Lumber Company at Wilmar, Arkansas, was assured, and the company stands on a level with other powerful and firmly established lumber organizations.

Albert Gates is the eldest of a family including five

brothers, all of whom are heavily interested in yellow pine operations. He went to Arkansas in 1882 to undertake the management of a saw mill. Previous to that time he had been manager of a general mining store at Rapids City, Illinois, for H. M. Gilchrist, then a large coal miner. Mr. Gilchrist was interested with Messrs. E. B. Hayward, G. W. Cable and E. S. Crossett, of Davenport, Iowa, in Arkansas timber lands, owning a considerable tract of shortleaf yellow pine tributary to the Ouchita river. They wished to develop their timber and chose Mr. Gates as the man to superintend these operations. Accordingly he selected Camden, Arkansas, on the St. Louis, Iron Mountain & Southern and the St. Louis Southwestern railway systems as a desirable location for manufacture and erected mills at that place.

The company owning the property was a limited partnership and was called the Camden Lumber Company in which Messrs. Gates, Hayward, Cable and Gilchrist were the principals. Their enterprise was at first but moderately profitable, as the market proved as yet unripe for the new lumber product. However, in spite of discouragements, experience proved that where conditions were favorable the promise in yellow pine possibilities was of the richest. So Mr. Gates again reconnoitered with an eye to a new point of attack and found the desired field at Thornton, Arkansas, about twenty-five miles to the north, on the line of the St. Louis Southwestern railway. Here he erected a saw and planing mill plant which he conducted with success. Four years at Thornton sufficed to clean up the timber in that locality and Mr. Gates then moved to Wilmar, on the Valley branch of the St. Louis, Iron Mountain & Southern railway, where the Gates Lumber Company has been operating on a large scale ever since.

Finding the timber in that part of Arkansas of excellent quality, Mr. Gates utilized to advantage the valuable experience gained at Camden and Thornton in the production of lumber at Wilmar. He erected a first class saw and planing mill, equipped with gang and circular saws and modern wood working machines in the planer, built up-to-date dry kilns and went into the milling business with the determination to make money. The plant had an abundance of good timber behind it, which was added to each year until the company now owns ample acreage to run for many years. The timber lies chiefly in Drew county, Arkansas, and is strictly Arkansas shortleaf pine.

Albert H. Gates is a typical Arkansas lumber pioneer. He has made a handsome competence in the business and is safely removed from want for the remainder of his life. He therefore decided to retire from the active management of the mill at Wilmar, and accordingly moved to St. Louis, Missouri, with his family, where he could enjoy the pleasures of city life and be able to educate his children. He left the control of the business in the competent hands of his son, Charles C. Gates, who was chosen vice president to succeed his father, and of H. C. Rules, who has been for years the successful secretary and manager of the company. These two young men are continuing to push with energy and ability the work of A. H. Gates along the lines mapped out by him for the future conduct of the business. Mr. Gates, senior, visits the mill frequently for consultation with the young officers, but the details of the actual work have been dismissed from his mind and he is now enjoying the fruits of twenty years of labor in the Arkansas woods.

Mr. Gates is interested as a stockholder in the Grant Lumber Company, an incorporated concern of Louisiana. This company purchased a large body of longleaf yellow pine timber lands in Grant parish, that state, on the Alexandria branch of the St. Louis, Iron Mountain & Southern railway. His associates were T. H. Garrett, F. E. Sheldon and O. R. Pearson, all of St. Louis, and all prominently identified with yellow pine operations, and also his brother, Peter G. Gates. He is a stockholder in the stave company at Wilmar, a similar company at Hamburg, Arkansas, the output of which is very large, and also in the Jackson Lumber Company, at Lockhart,

Alabama. The yellow pine timber in which Mr. Gates, with various associates, is interested, aggregates 479,000 acres, located in Arkansas, Louisiana, Alabama and Florida.

During his career as a yellow pine manufacturer Mr. Gates has been an active and consistent association man. He has always been a member of the Southern Lumber Manufacturers' Association and was for many years a director of that organization from Arkansas. He has attended every annual meeting for years and his counsel has been frequently sought by the association on matters relating to the betterment of the manufacturing business. He is a conservative by nature and training and his work on the various committees has always been of a high order. He was also identified with various other yellow pine associations, such as the Arkansas & Missouri Yellow Pine Company and the association of Arkansas manufacturers, both now defunct, but once powerful organizations.

Mr. Gates has done a great deal toward building up the town of Wilmar. Mainly through his instrumentality the many attractions of the pretty little town, such as excellent water, churches and schools, beautiful homes and well shaded streets, have been doubly enhanced by the addition thereto of collegiate advantages. Through the personal efforts of Mr. Gates, Beauvoir College, now registering from two hundred to three hundred students, was located at Wilmar.

Born in Castleton, Vermont, February 3, 1854, A. H. Gates has carved out a splendid success in the southern lumber field. He married October 23, 1878, Mary A. Parsons, at Big Rock, Iowa. Three sons were born to them, the eldest now being vice president of the Gates Lumber Company. The other two are receiving their education at St. Louis.

Mr. Gates was born at Big Rock, ... He had
practical experience in lumbering before ... in Arkansas
... His father was engaged in general
... four years previous to the year mentioned young Peter G.
Gates held a position in Colorado as superintendent
ing company, which, owing to ill health, he was
resign. While in Colorado an accident befell ...
which came very near resulting fatally. ...
mountains one day he was caught by a ...
down at terrific speed for a distance of ...
this awful experience being a sheer drop
depth of one hundred and twenty feet. He
dead, but recovered from the accident ...
proved fatal in ninety-nine cases out of a hundred.
... Mr. Gates turned his attention
began his career as a lumberman as secretary ...
Lumber Company. A short time later Mr. ... and his associates decided to erect mill plants elsewhere ...
location at Eagle Mills, Arkansas, a few ...
den, on the St. Louis Southwestern railway ...
the Eagle Lumber Company has since been operating.
At the same time Albert H. Gates, his elder brother ...
northward to Thornton, also in Arkansas and on the St. ...
Southwestern road, and formed the Thornton Lumber Company, in which P. G. Gates was a partner, thus ...
two brothers' interests into two milling plants
ton mill was run for four years, when the timber

Peter G. Gates

If Peter G. Gates, one of Arkansas' best known yellow pine manufacturers, were asked the secret of success he would probably say, in his usual crisp and concise way: "Mixing brains with business."

Mr. Gates was born at Big Rock, Iowa, 1855. He had no practical experience in lumbering before going to Arkansas in 1885. His father was engaged in general merchandising, and for four years previous to the year mentioned young Peter G. Gates held a position in Colorado as superintendent of a mining company, which, owing to ill health, he was compelled to resign. While in Colorado an accident befell Mr. Gates which came very near resulting fatally. While exploring the mountains one day he was caught by an avalanche and swept down at terrific speed for a distance of 1,700 feet, a part of this awful experience being a sheer drop over a precipice to a depth of one hundred and twenty feet. He was picked up for dead, but recovered from the accident, which would have proved fatal in ninety-nine cases out of a hundred.

In 1885 Mr. Gates turned his attention to Arkansas and began his career as a lumberman as secretary of the Camden Lumber Company. A short time later Mr. Gates and associates decided to erect mill plants elsewhere, and the present location at Eagle Mills, Arkansas, a few miles north of Camden, on the St. Louis Southwestern railway, was chosen and the Eagle Lumber Company has since been operating there. At the same time Albert H. Gates, his elder brother, went northward to Thornton, also in Arkansas and on the St. Louis Southwestern road, and formed the Thornton Lumber Company, in which P. G. Gates was a partner, thus extending the two brothers' interests into two milling plants. The Thornton mill was run for four years, when the timber was cleaned up and A. H. Gates moved to Wilmar, Arkansas, on the Valley branch of the Iron Mountain railway, organizing the Gates Lumber Company, where he has operated as a shortleaf pine manufacturer ever since. Peter G. Gates retained his interest with his brother in the Gates Lumber Company, and still has his stock interest in that enterprise. E. S. Crossett, of Davenport, Iowa, also invested in this concern's stock.

It was before the formation of the two companies mentioned that Peter G. Gates began to investigate the shortleaf timber lands in the vicinity of Eagle Mills and gained the knowledge of that timber which afterward proved so profitable to him and to the Eagle Lumber Company.

Mr. Gates was well aware that mere industry and economy were not the only requisites in building up the yellow pine or any other sort of business; that he must possess himself of all possible information about the business in hand and use the information with intelligence and originality. To this end he spent many weeks in the woods, much of the time on foot, and eventually became one of the most expert woodsmen and estimators in the Southwest.

With the knowledge gained in this close-to-nature study, he began quietly to buy all the lands he could get, and secured them at low average prices. He interested others from his native state, who joined him in heavy purchases of lands, the Eagle Lumber Company acquiring thousands of acres of virgin shortleaf yellow pine. The holdings of the company at this date amount to timber enough, at the present capacity of the Eagle Mills plant, to run it for twenty years; in fact the timber is growing as fast as it is cut and, in consequence, is practically inexhaustible.

As an estimator of timber Mr. Gates is probably without a superior. In this line of work his services have been in considerable demand for state appraisements, and also by railroad companies in estimating the tonnage of forest products for certain localities and, on occasion, he has inspected and estimated large tracts. A few years ago he was invited to do this by the State of Idaho, and spent several months on that state's timber holdings. He estimated a large tract at the special request of the governor, for which work he was handsomely compensated. It was more an expert examination, however, than an estimate, his report showing how the state could best handle its lands and get the greatest returns. In Arkansas Mr. Gates personally went over every acre of land controlled by his company, and his reputation as a judge in such matters is high.

While the five Gates brothers are interested in six different milling plants in Arkansas, Louisiana and Alabama, and their milling connections are not identical, their timber land holdings are not wholly separated and it may therefore be stated statistically that these six companies own 479,000 acres of yellow pine lands, as follows: The Eagle Lumber Company, of Eagle Mills, Arkansas, 50,000; the Gates Lumber Company, of Wilmar, Arkansas, 42,000; the Fordyce Lumber Company, of Fordyce, Arkansas, 60,000; the Crossett Lumber Company, of Crossett, Arkansas, 130,000; the Grant Lumber Company, of Selma, Louisiana, 53,000, and the Jackson Lumber Company, of Lockhart, Alabama, 144,000. This large total makes the holdings of the Gates brothers and their allied interests the largest in southern pine. It is supposed that the present value of the combined mill and timber interests of the allied companies will aggregate between $8,000,000 and $8,500,000. The several interests are now manufacturing at the combined rate of 870,000 feet a day.

The original incorporators of the Eagle Lumber Company were H. M. Gilchrist, E. B. Hayward, P. G. Gates and G. W. Cable. Mr. Gilchrist was president until his death, when Mr. Hayward assumed that office. Mr. Gates was general manager at the incorporation and for many years afterward, but has now retired from that office. He still continues as vice president. D. S. Gates is manager and O. F. Wyman is secretary. Messrs. Hayward and Cable were also interested in the Camden Lumber Company.

The original capitalization of the Eagle Lumber Company was modest, but it has been increased from year to year as the uniform and steady growth of the business warranted.

Mr. Gates has always been an ardent and consistent association man. He is high in the counsels of the Southern Lumber Manufacturers' Association and was a member of the Missouri & Arkansas Yellow Pine Company, a combination of mill men in existence some years ago but since disbanded. He has been a familiar figure at yellow pine manufacturers' meetings for the past fifteen years, and even since his retirement from active management has attended many of these gatherings, although he has recently made his home in South Pasadena, California.

The success of Peter G. Gates shows that although this world is a hard world, in the long run it is essentially a just one. Actuated sometimes by the best motives and sometimes by the most selfish, it is always groping about for men of ability and integrity to fill its places of responsibility. Once these men are found, however, the world is quick to recognize and reward them.

To make a success in any business a man must not only believe in himself and have a wholesome respect for his own capabilities, but must also have confidence in the commercial value of the commodity he makes or handles.

One of the number of southern pine manufacturers who have always possessed faith in that product is Charles Warner Gates, of Fordyce, Arkansas. The Gates brothers are as well known in Arkansas lumber manufacturing operations as is Andrew Carnegie in Pennsylvania steel making, and they have won the distinction in a comparatively few years. No one of them is a better exemplar of their fitness for this particular calling than Charles Warner Gates. From the position of a bookkeeper to that of the presiding genius of plants producing 100,000,000 feet of lumber annually is no small step. It is an achievement that few men can accomplish in a lifetime, to say nothing of a dozen years, yet that is the progress Mr. Gates has made in the brief space mentioned.

Charles Warner Gates was born near Detroit, Michigan, July [illegible]. He is one of the family of eleven children of Don C. and Cornelia Gates. Soon after his birth his parents moved to Iowa, where Mr. Gates passed his boyhood. After he finished the grammar school course he attended the Iowa State Agricultural College, located at Ames, until he decided to abandon his college life and embark on a business career. He went to the great Southwest, where he accepted a position at Waco, Texas, as bookkeeper and cashier for the wholesale grocery firm of Cameron, Castles & Story, the senior member of which was the late William Cameron. Here young Gates learned the rudiments of business and applied himself so vigorously to his vocation that he soon won the esteem and confidence of his employers. He lived for a number of years

Charles W. Gates

To make a success in any business a man must not only believe in himself and have a wholesome respect for his own capabilities, but must also have confidence in the commercial value of the commodity he makes or handles.

One of the number of southern pine manufacturers who have always possessed faith in that product is Charles Warner Gates, of Fordyce, Arkansas. The Gates brothers are as well known in Arkansas lumber manufacturing operations as is Andrew Carnegie in Pennsylvania steel making, and they have won the distinction in a comparatively few years. No one of them is a better exemplar of their fitness for this particular calling than Charles Warner Gates. From the position of a bookkeeper to that of the presiding genius of plants producing 100,000,000 feet of lumber annually is no small step. It is an achievement that few men can accomplish in a lifetime, to say nothing of a dozen years, yet that is the progress Mr. Gates has made in the brief space mentioned.

Charles Warner Gates was born near Detroit, Michigan, July 11, 1860. He is one of the family of eleven children of Don C. and Cornelia Gates. Soon after his birth his parents moved to Iowa, where Mr. Gates passed his boyhood. After he finished the grammar school course he attended the Iowa State Agricultural College, located at Ames, until he decided to abandon his college life and embark on a business career. He went to the great Southwest, where he accepted a position at Waco, Texas, as bookkeeper and cashier for the wholesale grocery firm of Cameron, Castles & Story, the senior member of which was the late William Cameron. Here young Gates learned the rudiments of business and applied himself so vigorously to his vocation that he soon won the esteem and confidence of his employers. He lived for a number of years at Waco, and it was there that he first embarked in the lumber business, owning and operating a yard for himself. This first venture in lumber by young Gates proved a success and was the foundation for his subsequent career and rapid rise to his position as one of the largest manufacturers in the Southwest.

After conducting the retail yard a few years he became one of a party which purchased the Fordyce Lumber Company, at Fordyce, Arkansas, and immediately took up the duties of vice president and general manager. The mill then seemed to take on new life and soon made itself known as a shipper of splendid grades of carefully manufactured yellow pine lumber. This was early in the '90's.

As the development of shortleaf pine in Arkansas continued, and the companies in that state began to expand, the Fordyce Lumber Company was the first to tear down and rebuild on modern lines, and in 1895 a new mill was erected which was one of the model Arkansas saw mills of the time. This plant, constructed under Mr. Gates' earlier regime as mill manager, reflects great credit upon his judgment—fully as much as does the great plant of the Crossett Lumber Company, also erected under his supervision.

Mr. Gates went to Fordyce knowing nothing about manufacturing, but his natural aptitude for grappling with business problems, and a certain mechanical bent, served him well, and it was but a short time before he had the plant running like clockwork and in the neatest possible order—which condition he insists shall characterize all his plants.

He possesses to a high degree the faculty for organization, and applies with the most striking advantage the universally acknowledged business principle, that in acquiring wealth a man must utilize both the brain and brawn of others better than those others can do it for themselves. The able lieutenants in charge of the various departments of the mills and the results they achieve prove that Mr. Gates is one of the men who can do this. Among his other qualifications as a manager of men, Mr. Gates has fine judgment of human nature and a happy knack of retaining in his employ those best suited to his purposes. Master of these requisites of a leader, it is not surprising that Mr. Gates has achieved so much in the operation of his lumber mills.

The Fordyce Lumber Company, of which C. W. Gates is vice president and general manager, is located at Fordyce, Arkansas, below Pine Bluff, on the St. Louis Southwestern (Cotton Belt) railway. It is a band and gang mill in equipment. The lands owned by this company lie in Dallas and Cleveland counties, Arkansas, and are regarded as being above the average in quality. The mill manufactures 30,000,000 feet of excellent shortleaf yellow pine lumber annually and enjoys a high reputation in the general market. E. S. Crossett is president, C. W. Gates vice president and general manager, Dr. J. W. Watzek treasurer and C. V. Edgar secretary and manager.

The Crossett Lumber Company was organized in May, 1899, and Mr. Gates was made its president and general manager. Its timber, consisting of about 130,000 acres, lies in Ashley county, Arkansas, in the southeastern part of the state, bordering on the Louisiana line. The mill is at Crossett, Arkansas, on a branch of the St. Louis, Iron Mountain & Southern railway. It produces between 60,000,000 and 70,000,000 feet of shortleaf yellow pine lumber every year. The officers of this company consist of C. W. Gates, president and general manager; E. S. Crossett, vice president; Dr. J. W. Watzek, treasurer, and E. W. Gates secretary and manager.

Before beginning the construction of this great plant, and even before accepting any plans from mill builders, Mr. Gates, accompanied by others interested in this company, made a tour of every large yellow pine saw mill in the entire South in order to get ideas and suggestions. The tour included Louisiana, Mississippi, Alabama, Florida, Georgia and the Carolinas, and several weeks were spent in investigating the advantages of other great plants. Then the party returned home and Mr. Gates called for plans in accordance with his ideas of what a modern saw mill ought to be. The town of Crossett is owned by the company and is a model village.

One of the late transactions by Mr. Gates and his associates, E. S. Crossett and Dr. J. W. Watzek, of Davenport, Iowa, was their acquirement by purchase of a two-thirds interest in 144,000 acres of timber lands in Covington county, Alabama, and Walton county, Florida, up to that time controlled by the Jackson Lumber Company, of Washington, District of Columbia, and also of Riderville, Alabama, of which former Governor E. E. Jackson, of Maryland, was president. The timber is of the finest quality of longleaf yellow pine. A plant with a capacity of 60,000,000 feet has been constructed on this tract.

There is an output of 160,000,000 feet annually from the Fordyce, Crossett and Jackson plants.

Mr. Gates has investments in other of the allied companies which are so closely connected. One of the most pleasant of his business affiliations came through the formation of the firm of Crossett, Watzek & Gates, in 1893, as a natural result of their many years of uniformly satisfactory business association. This partnership was entered into for the purpose of handling the mutual interests of E. S. Crossett, J. W. Watzek and C. W. Gates.

Mr. Gates has his home and office in St. Louis and keeps in touch with the mills from that city and through frequent trips to the South. He has ever been an ardent association man, having served during several terms as vice president for Arkansas of the Southern Lumber Manufacturers' Association. He was also prominent in the sometime Missouri & Arkansas Yellow Pine Company and the Arkansas association of manufacturers. He has been an association mainstay ever since he has been a mill man.

J. W. Watzek

When the lumberman of experience and the man of capital enter into partnership, the investor should bring to the business something more than his capital; he should also bring to it and give fully of the same thought, effort and care that made him successful in other walks of life. If he does not a satisfactory result is by no means certain. This is the secret of the success of men like Dr. J. W. Watzek, of the Crossett-Gates interests. Doctor Watzek's training was that of a physician and his personal success has been achieved in that profession. He was thirty-five years of age before he made his first investment in timber, but in less than two decades he has made for himself a reputation as a lumberman that exceeds in range his distinction as a physician. He brought to the lumber business the same thought and application he exercised in his study and practice of medicine.

Dr. J. W. Watzek is a native of Austria, where he was born in 1856. His father's death left him dependent upon his own resources, and, hearing that opportunities for advancement were better in America than in his own country, he took his boyhood savings to buy a "ticket for Amerika," and emigrated to the land of his adoption at the age of fourteen.

Believing that an education is the best kind of a foundation that a young man can lay, no matter what his calling in after life may be, every dollar that he was able to earn at anything that he could find to do, he spent in acquiring mental equipment. The night schools—those friends of many a poor but aspiring young man—gave him his education in the language; and, after an academic training received at Wyoming Seminary, at Kingston, Pennsylvania, he decided to study medicine. Moving westward in search of better opportunity to complete his education and to find a promising place in which to practice his profession, he graduated in 1881 from the State University of Iowa as a Doctor of Medicine.

He first located at Sigourney, Iowa, and four years later moved to Davenport, Iowa, where he enjoyed a large and lucrative practice, and, through his professional work, became intimately acquainted with many of the prominent lumbermen of that city. His success as a physician is not excelled by any practitioner in the state and his reputation is more than local. That he went into the lumber business with the same painstaking care which made him a great physician was an earnest of success in the lumber field.

Doctor Watzek's first investment in southern pine was made in 1891 when, with J. A. Freeman and M. C. Smith, he formed the Freeman Lumber Company, of Millville, Arkansas. He was made vice president of that company, but later disposed of his holdings. In the same year he became interested with E. S. Crossett and C. W. Gates in the Fordyce Lumber Company, of Fordyce, Arkansas, and this was the beginning of the pleasant and uniformly successful business relationship which finally culminated in their copartnership under the firm name of Crossett, Watzek & Gates for the more convenient management of their various and extensive interests in the South. Doctor Watzek at once proceeded to familiarize himself with the business in which he had made his investments, with Mr. Crossett as his able tutor, by making frequent visits to the woods and mills in the South for practical study of the timber and the processes of its manufacture. He has acquired a knowledge of the lumber industry which causes his associates to respect his opinions in the settlement of questions of business policy. Becoming a firm believer in the advancement of values in yellow pine, he has been unceasing in his efforts for the acquirement of standing timber and its development, taking especial pleasure in the solving of the financial problems necessarily connected with these operations.

When, in 1891, he joined Mr. Crossett and C. W. Gates in

the formation of the Fordyce Lumber Company he was elected one of its directors and later its treasurer. During the next year or two this company severely felt the general business depression of the time. Money was scarce and the rate of interest was high, while the price of lumber hardly equaled the cost of production. The company, however, weathered the storms, and when the tide turned it was ready for expansion, the capital was enlarged, a modern saw mill plant built and the timber holdings so increased that in 1905, after a steady run of fourteen years of manufacturing an average of 30,000,000 feet of lumber a year, the company owns 60,000 acres of standing timber and a stumpage of 500,000,000 feet and points with pride to the fact that it is entirely out of debt.

In 1899 Doctor Watzek, E. S. Crossett, C. W. Gates and E. W. Gates purchased from Hovey & McCracken, of Muskegon, Michigan, 50,000 acres of selected pine lands in Ashley county, Arkansas, and Morehouse parish, Louisiana, and organized the Crossett Lumber Company. Doctor Watzek was elected a director and made treasurer of the company. This nucleus of 50,000 acres was added to until the company now owns 135,000 acres of the best shortleaf pine. In 1900 the town of Crossett was started in the midst of the timber of Ashley county, Arkansas, and two modern saw mill plants were erected to manufacture lumber for at least twenty years to come.

In 1902 the opportunity and desire to own more timber led Messrs. Crossett, Watzek and Gates to buy two-thirds of the stock of the Jackson Lumber Company, of Lockhart, Alabama, ex-Governor E. E. Jackson, of Baltimore, retaining the other third. This company owns 144,500 acres of longleaf pine with a stumpage of 1,200,000,000 feet.

Doctor Watzek was elected president, and the financing of the deal was left largely in his hands. It is his particular pride that he has been able so to convince capital of the value of this property as to enable him to secure the bonding of it for

$1,000,000 at 5 percent, with the bonds at par. Development was proceeded with immediately, and under the able local management of W. S. Harlan, a brother-in-law of Doctor Watzek, the town of Lockhart was laid out and a saw mill plant, having a capacity of 60,000,000 feet, erected and ready for operation in less than ten months. At the same time the naval stores industry, until then new to Doctor Watzek and his associates, was also developed.

Doctor Watzek is a close student of conservative forestry methods in lumbering, and the large tract of timber owned by the Jackson Lumber Company is being treated with a view to one recut at least, all trees under a diameter of thirteen inches being left standing. Besides the foregoing companies, Doctor Watzek is also interested in the Gates Lumber Company, of Wilmar, Arkansas, and the Grant Lumber Company, of Selma, Louisiana.

These five companies, with which Doctor Watzek is identified and of which he is a conspicuous member, own an amount of timber and conduct operations that are monumental. Their land possessions embrace 420,000 acres, with 3,350,000,000 feet of standing pine and 400,000,000 feet of standing hardwoods; the daily cut of their saw mills produced by six bands, four circulars and five gangs is 800,000 feet; their planing mills have a capacity of 720,000 feet per day; their better grades of lumber are dried by thirty-four steam kilns; they own one hundred and sixty miles of logging railroads, with sixteen locomotives and two hundred and twenty-six cars; they employ over two thousand people, and the value of their annual output is between $2,500,000 and $3,000,000.

The story of Doctor Watzek's life is a remarkable one, a fact readily recognized when comparison is made of the young immigrant of three decades ago and the extensive lumber operator of today.